'*No Bullshit Therapy: How To Engage People Who Don't Want to Work with You* is excellent. Enjoyable to read, full of good ideas and compelling examples, it is a book our profession and clients need. It will help you to connect and be effective with a range of clients, especially those who are often described as 'resistant' and difficult to work with. Highly recommended!'

Michael F. Hoyt, *PhD (USA), author of* Brief Therapy and Beyond: Stories, Language, Love, Hope, and Time and Brief Therapy Conversations: Exploring Efficient Intervention in Psychotherapy (*with Flavio Cannistrà*).

'This book is not just for therapists trying to work with clients who hate the idea of therapy. It is for all of us who have ever avoided that difficult conversation we know we should have. Jeff Young guides us through the philosophy and practice of NBT, with detailed client transcripts, all exuding his own particular combination of warmth and honesty.'

Pam Rycroft, *MPsych, (Australia), co-editor of* Single-Session Thinking and Practice in Global, Cultural, and Familial Contexts: Expanding Applications.

'Jeff Young's work on 'No Bullshit Therapy' is, in my view, one of the most important developments in the field of therapy since Single-Session Therapy came onto the scene towards the end of the last century. In fact, the combination of these developments increases the potency of both. Mandatory reading if you have to work with mandated clients...and if you don't.'

Windy Dryden, *Ph.D (UK), Emeritus Professor of Psychotherapeutic Studies, Goldsmiths University of London.*

T0384834

No Bullshit Therapy

Do you have clients who do not want to be helped? Clients who don't trust you, your profession, or your service? Clients who don't want to change despite your best efforts?

Then No Bullshit Therapy (NBT) is for you! Most simply, NBT is about being authentic.

Many people are cajoled, pressured, or mandated to see therapists, counsellors, and other helpers. Hence, they are reluctant, suspicious, and resistant to being helped. This puts professionals in the difficult position of trying to help someone who does not want to be helped. To make things worse, there are few practice models designed to engage people who don't want to be engaged.

NBT creates a context for mutual honesty and directness in working relationships. Creating a context for mutual honesty and directness can be refreshingly effective, especially with people who are suspicious of counselling or distrustful of the counsellor. When combined with warmth and care, honesty and directness can enhance co-operation, connection, and trust, especially if the practitioner avoids jargon and acknowledges constraints to the work. NBT is ideal for working with people who:

- Don't like therapy or the idea of therapy (even if they've never had it)
- Don't trust warm fuzzy "do-gooders" or "psychologisers"
- Are suspicious of services because they have experienced trauma and have had abusive institutional experiences or unsatisfactory treatment in the past
- Don't see themselves as a client, don't agree with the referrer's description of them or their problems, and appear to not want to change

Practical and engaging, this book is an essential guide for therapists, counsellors, and other allied-health professionals who are looking for a more effective way to connect with reluctant clients and ensure they get the support they need. It may also help you create more robust relationships at work and at home.

Jeff Young, PhD, is Emeritus Professor of Family Therapy and Systemic Practice at La Trobe University, Melbourne, Australia. He was Director of The Bouverie Centre, the world's largest family therapy agency (2009–2022). His awards include the ANZJFT Special Award for Distinguished Contributions to Family Therapy (2017) and the THEMHS Exceptional Contributions to Mental Health (2022).

No Bullshit Therapy

How to Engage People Who Don't
Want to Work with You

Jeff Young

Routledge
Taylor & Francis Group

LONDON AND NEW YORK

Cover image: Jeff Young

First published 2024
by Routledge
4 Park Square, Milton Park, Abingdon, Oxon OX14 4RN

and by Routledge
605 Third Avenue, New York, NY 10158

Routledge is an imprint of the Taylor & Francis Group, an informa business

British Library Cataloguing-in-Publication Data
A catalogue record for this book is available from the British Library

ISBN: 9781032408392 (hbk)
ISBN: 9781032408385 (pbk)
ISBN: 9781003354925 (ebk)

DOI: 10.4324/9781003354925

Typeset in Times New Roman
by codeMantra

I dedicate this book to my family (Tric, Sweeney, and Billie) for putting up with yet another of my obsessions, for their occasional no bullshit feedback, and for their love, no matter what.

I want to acknowledge the Wurundjeri People of the Greater Kulin Nation, the Traditional Custodians of the unceded land on which I live, and pay my respects to Elders, past, present, and emerging. I am inspired by our First Nations' cultural heritage, traditional wisdom of interconnectivity, and relationship to the land, rivers, and sea.

Contents

Figures

Acknowledgements

There are many people to thank.

I owe a debt to the clients who initially didn't want to work with me, helped me understand the cut-through power of radical authenticity in vexed situations, and taught me so much about engaging people who are suspicious and untrusting of professionals.

This book is also informed by my many colleagues, practitioners on the ground, and academics who have contributed to making therapy more accessible to people who may benefit from talking to a professional but for whom mainstream approaches and services are not immediately appealing.

Colleagues who combined directness with warmth – Amaryll Perlesz, Colin Riess, Pam Rycroft, Jenny Dwyer, and Robyn Miller, amongst others – helped me find my early No Bullshit Therapy (NBT) voice. Colleagues who co-trained with me have contributed to the development of NBT: Karen Holl, Shane Weir, Pam Rycroft, Karen Smith, Sally Ryan, Jacqui Sundbery, Kerrin Basil, Sarah Jones, Nick Barrington, Angie Nyland, and Greg U'ren. I'm indebted to Robyne Latham, Alison Elliott, Banu Moloney, and Clarisse Slater, who encouraged me to present NBT workshops to the Graduate Certificate in Family Therapy: First Nations students and for the students' enthusiastic feedback about its cultural application. Colleagues who helped me explore the theoretical ideas around hidden power in therapy and in the attraction of obfuscation to hide less than pure ethical motives are Mark Furlong, the late Tom Paterson, and Ron Findlay, to name a few. I've also been inspired by the writings of George Orwell, Max Black, Harry Frankfurt, and Robert Dessaix. Michael Hoyt encouraged and pushed me to publication, for which I am in his debt. Flavio Cannistrà provided support from Italy, and Windy Dryden provided wise counsel to help my proposal get up. Windy incorporated NBT ideas into his feedback on my work, which made it more powerful and easier to accept.

A big thank you to George Zimmer from Routledge US, whom I met in 2014. He encouraged me to publish with Routledge as did Sarah Gore, Vilija Stephens, and Georgia Oman from Routledge UK. They were a great team and provided wonderful support in getting this work to print.

Ken Wolfe courageously allowed me to describe his personal experiences of being a client suspicious of counselling and how it influenced his approach to counselling fellow inmates in jail, and generously allowed me to use an interview I did with him about his experience in a Bouverie self-paced online NBT course, and in this book. Colleagues Nick Barrington, Liz George, Robyn Elliott, Angie Nyland, Allie Bailey, Jenn McIntosh, and the Bouverie production crew helped me to create the online course which deepened my understanding of NBT.

Similarly, the participants in the NBT workshops I've conducted over the decades, many of whom work in the toughest and most important and challenging human services, such as prisons, on the streets, and in other contexts where they are required to engage disenfranchised clients respectfully, have contributed to the development of NBT.

I love my Bouverie Centre colleagues who enact the principles of NBT with elegance, commitment, and strenuous compassion. La Trobe University's senior librarian, Bernadette Gargan provided literature review expertise, which saved me time and frustration. Sandra Nobes and Geoff Kelly generously provided professional figures at the last minute, which *saved my bacon*, and W.H. Chong provided creative advice on the book cover. And finally, Sarah Jones gave feedback on a very early draft; Tric O'Heare, my wife and rock, Andrew Jarnicki, my neighbour and friend, and my old writing buddies, Pam Rycroft and Michael Hoyt, all provided invaluable, generous, and detailed editorial advice, which made *No Bullshit Therapy* a better book.

1 Introduction to No Bullshit Therapy

Hi, I'm Jeff Young and I practice what I call No Bullshit Therapy.

Client: What's that?

That's when I don't bullshit you and I hope you won't bullshit me.

This is how I introduced myself to Gary, a man in his late 30s who was angry – angry that he had to spend $70,000 on legal fees trying unsuccessfully to have greater contact with his two boys, Toby (6) and Will (8); angry that his in-laws had joined forces and conspired against him. Gary's ex-partner had initiated family therapy without his knowledge, and now as a result, he was expected to attend an individual session with me. Furious, he felt manipulated, lied to, and ganged up on.

At this briefest of introductions, Gary's shoulders relaxed, and he responded, "That's exactly the way I like to operate." I spoke honestly and directly to Gary with small and judicious moments of warmth and care. I was upfront about the difficult circumstances which had brought us together. Clearly, unambiguously, and unilaterally, I explained how I saw the purpose of the meeting and how I imagined it would unfold. I pointed out I was keen to help him but would understand if he walked away. In essence, I broke all the rules I had learnt in my therapeutic training about how to engage clients.

Later in my work with Gary I needed to raise an extremely sensitive topic with him. Toby and Will had claimed that their dad did not feed them enough during visits. I expected Gary to be hurt and shamed when I raised the boys' concerns with him and feared he would come out fighting. I stumbled over my words. Gary interrupted my tentative *umms* and *errs* and reminded me, "Jeff, remember, No Bullshit!"

That was 2002 and the first time I used the term No Bullshit Therapy (NBT) directly with a client. At difficult points during my work with Gary, I was relieved that by stating *I practise No Bullshit Therapy* early in our relationship, I had created a context for mutual honesty and directness. Gary's acceptance of this way of working provided an agreement that I could return to whenever I needed to ask the tough questions required to help him and to ensure he got what he ultimately wanted.

I love therapy. I chose to make it my career, and I want to make it available to everyone. It took me several decades of working – first as an individual psychodynamic psychotherapist and then as a family therapist – to realise that many people

DOI: 10.4324/9781003354925-1

don't share this love. I have come to accept that people, like Gary, who don't like therapy often don't care much for us helping professionals either. As David Wexler, a clinical psychologist from San Diego who specialises in high conflict relationships, points out, relying on traditional models of therapeutic practice or trying to massage people like Gary into being more like clients who are accepting of therapy and its benefits does not work (Wexler, 2013). Rather than doubting my own professional ability or worse still labelling these clients as defensive, resistant, or lacking emotional intelligence, I have found that accepting that some clients just don't like therapy is more likely to lead to effective, creative, and sustainable ways of working with *difficult to engage* populations. NBT is a therapeutic approach developed in an Australian cultural context that has grown out of my desire and the desire of my colleagues from The Bouverie Centre, La Trobe University, Melbourne, to work effectively and respectfully with people like Gary who are cynical and suspicious about therapy and therapists. Of course, all Aussies don't hate therapy, and all therapy-haters aren't Aussies.

People who appreciate therapy expect the therapist to create a safe and supportive environment and that the process of talking to a trained and empathic professional is likely to lead to an improved quality of life. People who don't embrace therapy commonly view therapists as manipulative, indirect, touchy-feely types who stick their noses in where they don't belong or as wishy-washy do-gooders who have no idea about the *real world* and who, given half a chance, love nothing better than making regular folk look like idiots, or weak by psychologising everything they say. I realised over time that rightly or wrongly, many people who are marginalised by traditional therapeutic approaches fear therapists like me will use their educational training, skills, techniques, and professional status to intimidate, manipulate, and shame. Throughout this book, I will refer to people who hold extreme negative views about therapy as *therapy-haters*, which is meant to be a light-hearted but confronting term to acknowledge that not everyone likes therapy. I do not blame therapy-haters for this stance; there are many contexts that lead to therapy hating, such as when a person is mandated or pressured to attend counselling by family, friends, or practitioners. I also respect that hating therapy is not an unreasonable stance in itself – it is simply different from my own view of therapy.

Whilst the name *therapy-hater* is meant to be a light-hearted term, it is designed to help us take on a serious task – to have the debate I feel we need to have about making therapy accessible to all who could benefit from it. It is a term that has encouraged me to further explore the contexts that lead to therapy hating. It is a term that has helped me to develop personally and professionally so that I can engage a broader range of people other than therapy-lovers. The term *therapy-hater* and its counterpart *therapy-lover* represent extreme points on a continuum of how clients approach therapy and therapists. Focusing on these extreme positions helps differentiate how NBT is used differently and at different points in the therapeutic process dependent on context and individual client.

Therapy-lovers afford professional counsellors the luxury of time. If something is unclear about the context of the encounter, the description of the work, or the therapist's approach, the therapy-lover will often interpret this uncertainty in the best possible light or at least in a neutral way that will allow the therapeutic process to evolve over time. The therapy-lover is usually open to co-constructing a mutually satisfying therapeutic agenda, even if the work itself may be difficult. Therapy-lovers approach therapy in good faith, allowing the practitioner time to clarify and to re-orient the work if needed. For example, a therapy-lover is likely to interpret my questions about their family-of-origin as, *I guess Jeff is asking about my family background, even though I'm here to talk about why my daughter is refusing to go to school, because he wants to understand my background so he can help me address my daughter's truancy, eventually.* The therapy-lover may ask a facilitative question to help get me back on track or to link my inquiry with their main concerns, in this case why their daughter is refusing to go to school. The therapy-hater, on the other hand, typically approaches therapy with understandable bad faith and is likely to interpret any ambiguity in the worst possibly light. For example, *Jeff is asking about my family background because he obviously thinks it's my fault that my daughter isn't going to school and he's trying to rake up some muck so he can pinpoint exactly where he thinks I screwed up!*

The use of NBT with therapy-lovers is a much more subtle process than with therapy-haters like Gary. Therapy-lovers Lyn and Wayan were keen to work with me from the start. No one had forced them to attend therapy. Although a little nervous, they warmed to me quickly. They expected me to help and were open to my input. Unable to have contact with their grandson, Lyn and Wayan felt bereft. Lyn, a social worker, and her husband Wayan, a retired manager of a large building company, were both in their 50s. They sought help to find ways to re-connect with their son and daughter-in-law from whom they were estranged, hoping this re-engagement would lead to time with their grandson Jimmy. Lyn described Jimmy as cute, cheeky, and three years of age. I got on well with Lyn and Wayan from the start. Lyn was energetic, warm, and maternal. Wayan was sophisticated, gentle, and charming. Lyn and Wayan had regularly minded Jimmy during his early years as Jimmy's parents Alice and Benjamin struggled with mental health issues. Things changed when Alice became suspicious that Lyn and Wayan had made a notification to protective services with concerns about Jimmy's safety. Alice and Benjamin broke off all contact with Jimmy's grandparents. When Lyn and Wayan told me that they were not able to see their grandson, I could feel their pain, but I also began to see how Lyn's maternal warmth, hyper-responsibility, and her desperation to be in Jimmy's life were probably inadvertently making her daughter-in-law furious and, as a result, were driving away her son as well. For example, Lyn continued to buy clothes and toys for her grandson without consulting Jimmy's parents which, according to Wayan, annoyed Alice.

I felt caught between being honest and direct about what Lyn should do differently and maintaining the warm, close, and empathic therapeutic alliance I had quickly built with her. To address my dilemma, I asked Lyn and Wayan if I could be open and honest and share my thoughts directly with them. I pointed out that I could feel their pain and wanted to be direct because I thought it would help. Both said they would appreciate me being honest. The simple act of asking if I could be direct, in a warm and caring way, created a marker that we were going to change the tenor of our conversation from a polite and relaxed tone to a more challenging one. This was the first time I used an NBT approach with a couple and with a woman who not only embraced therapy but was a therapist herself – although I didn't use this term immediately like I did with Gary. Having an implicit agreement to share my thoughts honestly allowed me to be upfront in suggesting that Lyn should respect her daughter-in-law's maternal role and ask Alice what clothes and toys her son Jimmy needed rather than just buying what she thought he needed. It helped.

In a subsequent session, I coached Lyn to take a No Bullshit approach to communicating with her daughter-in-law. I asked Lyn and Wayan to role-play the usual conversational style they used to try and engage Alice around seeing Jimmy. I role-played Alice, Jimmy's mother. Lyn's approach towards me as Alice was soft, tentative, apologetic, and counsellor-like. As Alice, I found myself increasingly suspicious of her motives – was she angling to take over the parenting of my son, Jimmy? I shared this insight and introduced Lyn to the principles of NBT to which Lyn responded, "You mean don't pussy foot around!" We re-ran the role-play in the session with Lyn more direct and dispassionate, and in the role of Alice I experienced her as more trustworthy.

During the following session, Lyn reported that she had contacted Benjamin and told him she'd called protective services, as Alice had suspected. She reported that Benjamin had thanked her for her honesty and that both she and Benjamin had found the revelation therapeutic, although he had appeared angry the following week. She also mentioned that Wayan had invited Benjamin and Jimmy for lunch and for the first time in many months Benjamin accepted, and Alice permitted Jimmy to go. Over time Lyn and Wayan resumed regular contact with Jimmy and their son Benjamin.

Following the conclusion of our work together, a colleague, Kate Ingram, recorded an interview with Lyn and Wayan, as part of a clinical wisdom project, about their experience of the therapy including the NBT component, which, while only a small element of the 13 sessions we had together, sped up the work. Using the principles of NBT certainly allowed me to matter-of-factly provide feedback I felt would assist Lyn to engage Alice more effectively.

Earlier in the interview, Kate discovered that Lyn and Wayan felt the focus on honesty in the therapy had helped them grieve for major losses including the death of Lyn's mother, Benjamin's mental illness, and the estrangement of their son's family. Wayan confided that therapy had helped him climb out of what he said felt like chronic depression caused by his and Lyn's ongoing tensions with Benjamin and Alice. Lyn reflected that she and Wayan had fallen into treating their 35-year-old son Benjamin like an 18-year-old which had led him to feel resentful towards them. The following transcript begins with Kate asking about Benjamin's resentment. It illustrates the use of NBT with therapy-lovers.

Lyn: I was caught in a trap where I was thinking that I had to be more empathic all the time – I tended to put on my therapist hat because I'm a social worker and counsellor and I thought that was the best approach to use to try and build up some rapport with Benjamin and Alice. And some things we learnt in therapy and Jeff terms it the no bullshit approach (laughter).

Wayan: And for me it is a business-like approach ... to be objective and you don't need to get too emotionally overwhelmed by it and treat it like a business issue rather than an emotional issue.

Lyn: And by being that sort of much more direct rather than sort of wishy-washy you know, it tended to, well Benjamin knew where he stood with us, and I think it made it clearer for him and he knew how to respond to us, and it seemed to take the anger out of his response. And it improved our communication, basically.

Kate: Was it hard to change from an empathic approach to the NBT approach?

Lyn: Extremely hard for me if I was to be really honest.

Kate: We want to know how hard it was and how you helped yourself to do it.

Lyn: Each time I went to say anything I'd have to count to 10 and ask how should I be putting this, rather than launching into a natural response which was to be empathic.

Kate: What was it about how Jeff presented this idea that appealed to you? How was it that the NBT was more appealing than an empathic approach because it seems counter-intuitive almost?

Lyn: Well Jeff has this knack of sort of relaxing you. First of all, it was quite a shock because I thought, "Hang on, he is a counsellor talking to me as a counsellor and this is not the way I've learnt." And also, it was contrary to me because my mother was a very caring nurturing sort of person, and I took on a lot of her role. But I could see that once I tried it, it worked better. Um, also what Jeff was suggesting because our daughter-in-law and she says in her own words that she is a bit of a control freak and Jeff was suggesting that to be upfront with Benjamin and get Alice's permission before I did anything and that very direct sort of direct verbal communication helped tremendously. Because then Alice didn't feel so threatened.

As these examples show, NBT is used differently with therapy-lovers and therapy-haters. The approach can also be used to help clients have the difficult conversations they need to have with other family members. In Chapter 9, I will introduce tools designed to help clients have these difficult conversations, as well as tools designed to help supervisors have direct conversations with their supervisees.

Although NBT is used very differently with therapy-lovers and therapy-haters, the clinical guidelines, which are summarised below, are the same.

NBT clinical guidelines: At a glance

The clinical guidelines of NBT are simple and can be used quite quickly, but they are not simplistic, and can take time to be put consistently, creatively, and effortlessly into practice. Explained in detail in Chapter 5 and Chapter 6, the guidelines are summarised here to orient the reader.

The four simple but not simplistic guidelines are designed to create contexts for mutual honesty and directness in working relationships. They are:

1 Establish a mandate[1]
2 Marry[2] honesty and directness with warmth and care
3 Be upfront about constraints
4 Avoid jargon

Many readers, especially those working regularly with therapy-haters, will recognise their own work in these guidelines and may simply use NBT to legitimise their own intuitive approach to this work. For example, Fiona, a participant in an NBT workshop I conducted, confided in me that she had instinctively developed a very upfront and direct way of working with her clients in a prison setting and although she had found it was effective, she felt guilty that she was not acting professionally. Another participant in an early NBT workshop evaluation wrote: "This NBT fits well with my work as an outreach worker. This gives me more confidence to be myself in my professional role." I suspect there are many closet No Bullshit Therapists who work in low-status areas and don't get the recognition they deserve.

Acting professionally is of extreme importance but that does not mean being captured by professional stereotypes. I remember a salutary lesson I gained as a 24-year-old working for the first time as a clinical psychologist at Mont Part Psychiatric Hospital, a large mental health facility, in Victoria, Australia. Not having grown up in a professional family and somewhat anxious about my authority, I had constructed the view early in my career that a professional psychologist should always know what to say, always be articulate, and know what to do – and unfortunately, I tried to conduct my first family session with two parents and three adolescent girls in this way. As I sat stiffly in a newly acquired suit jacket neatly coiffured, attempting to sound authoritative, the three adolescent sisters giggled, whispered, and looked disdainfully at me – I crumbled. I had unwittingly and unintentionally created a strong sibling coalition at my own expense. Luckily, I viewed a video from the Master Therapist Series of a family therapy session conducted by one of the world's most prominent family therapists at the time, the experiential American Psychiatrist, Carl Whitaker. I'm not sure whether I was more surprised or relieved to see Carl warmly interact with the family's small children; handing out lolly pops as he engaged with the parents whilst the kids bounced off his lap. I realised instantly that I could be warm, friendly, and professional, at the same time. I began the following family session more relaxed, slightly slumped in my chair, and freer to explore the difficulties and dilemmas facing the family. Thirty years later, after having headed up Australia's largest family therapy service, I am proud that *friendly professionalism* remains one of the organisation's underlying values.

Whilst *No Bullshit Therapy* is the title of this book and a useful term to counter community cynicism about the motives of professional therapists and the purpose of therapy, there is nothing sacrosanct about the name. Over the years my clients, including Lyn and Wayan, colleagues, and trainees, have come up with a range of terms to convey the broad intention of striving towards honesty and directness and ultimately authenticity, including: *not beating round the bush, taking a business-like approach, being upfront, calling a spade a spade, talking straight, keeping it real, being on the level, being honest and direct, not pussy-footing around, not walking on eggshells, speaking from the heart, cutting to the chase, sharing what I'm thinking, telling it like it is,* or *taking a risk. No Bull Therapy, Nobull Therapy,* or even *Noble Therapy,* work too.

The "unprofessional" sounding title *No Bullshit Therapy* was very helpful to counter the expectations of obfuscation that Gary brought to therapy and helped me to be bold in my work with him. I'm sure my work with Gary would have struggled without using the *No Bullshit* concept and title to provide a context for me to raise sensitive and difficult topics with him, in ways he could hear. Maybe it helped because, according to Mohr (2013), swear words are generated in the primitive part of the brain, in the basal ganglia and amygdala of the limbic system, an area broadly responsible for emotion, and that most swear words carry an emotional charge that exceeds the referent social taboo. Hence, the use of the term *bullshit* may provide an emotionally powerful way of expressing things we normally don't talk about with clients. The term *bullshit* certainly resonates with therapy-haters, and we will explore the links to the traumatised brain in Chapter 11. The NBT approach, if not the term itself, helped me combine honesty and directness with warmth and care in my work with Lyn and Wayan and provided a rationale for how Lyn could approach her son and daughter-in-law in a more direct way. I suspect it also created a subtle culture of honesty and directness which allowed Lyn to admit to Benjamin that she had called protective services when concerned about her grandson's safety, especially given we had talked about respecting the constraints to her and her son having such a conversation. It helped Lyn and Wayan add honesty and directness to their natural capacity for warmth and care.

NBT simply strives to create constructive contexts for mutual honesty and directness in working relationships. Levels of honesty and directness can be collaboratively negotiated with therapy-lovers but may have to be presented unilaterally, as your favoured way of working, at least initially, with therapy-haters. Either way, I have found creating contexts for mutual honesty and directness, sometimes just by stating that is how I like to work, to be liberating and productive. If combined with warmth and care, honesty and directness can enhance intimacy, connection, and trust. Trust is further enhanced by addressing the complications and unspoken constraints to the work in a non-defensive, clear, straightforward, and direct way. NBT strives to engender the elements that make all therapeutic work effective (trust, safety, and confidence) with a wider range of clients including therapy-haters. The practice of NBT is consistent with the general trend towards greater transparency between therapists and their clients about how to approach the work, how the work is progressing, and whether the goals are being met. Direct discussions about what's working and what is not have been shown to improve outcomes by researchers exploring the common factors underlying therapeutic success (e.g., Duncan et al., 2004). Most tasks, but especially sensitive tasks such as those that make up therapy and other work in the human services, are typically facilitated when everyone knows the purpose of the encounter, the goals of each participant, the process in which the goals of all parties will be addressed and the rules that will govern the work. People starting therapy who don't know the rules of the *therapeutic game* are at such a disadvantage that they, not surprisingly, are likely to respond by politely disengaging from therapy or trying to actively, sometimes aggressively, disrupt it.

In times of increasing media hype and ever more blatant political spin and false news, the general population appears to have grown cautious of political leaders and suspicious of professionals, including therapists. An NBT approach can help break through prevailing stereotypes of therapists as being warm and fuzzy as well as indirect and ineffective or subtlety manipulative. NBT counters these negative perceptions, where they exist, by offering a refreshingly direct approach where mutual honesty and directness are negotiated overtly so that the purpose of the work and the rules that govern it are known, explicit, and transparent. I suspect all of us endeavour to be clear and direct in our work; however, the more vexed, complex, or potentially conflictual the work, the more attractive indirectness seems, even though this type of work typically and paradoxically requires greater levels of honesty and directness.

Therapists who successfully engage clients marginalised by traditional therapeutic approaches such as (some) men, First Nation peoples, working class people, rural people, and adolescents, to name only a few, commonly emphasise the importance, if not centrality, of authenticity, if therapeutic work is to have any chance of being successful. Authenticity of the therapeutic process and of the therapist is the driving value underlying NBT and an outcome of implementing all the clinical guidelines of NBT effectively.

The German American psychologist Kurt Lewin, often called the father of modern social psychology, stated many times, *nothing is as practical as a good theory* (e.g., Lewin, 1943). I have found that creating a theoretical framework around the practical techniques of NBT has helped expand my clinical repertoire and provided a helpful guide and way forward when complexity, my own fear of conflict or even worse, a client's disengaged politeness, has paralysed my effectiveness. Exploring the theoretical aspects of NBT has enriched my clinical work, helped me understand, and thus be less afraid of therapy-haters, while being more effective and efficient in my work with therapy-lovers. Exploring what works and what doesn't clinically, especially with therapy-haters, has led to rich theoretical debates with myself and with colleagues about concepts at the centre of NBT such as mandate, rationale, authenticity, power, responsibility, and trust.

NBT does not promote honesty as the only policy or even as always, the best policy – instead it encourages counsellors to negotiate overtly with clients the degree of honesty and directness that is required in the working relationship to get the job done. When a client approaches therapy with bad faith as most therapy-haters understandably do, honesty and directness do more to create trust than warmth, forced friendliness, formal professionalism, university credentials, or stated expertise. Honesty on the part of the therapist, for example, about what the therapist can and can't do or to clarify the purpose of the encounter and whether it is voluntary, mandated, or partially voluntary, promotes trust. When there is bad faith, a business-like directness (without blame or judgement) and upfront honesty do more to create trust than well-intentioned but misguided social attempts to build friendly relations. A straight-up acknowledgement of sensitive issues usually does more to create safety than trying to build a relationship capable of tolerating hard topics or avoiding sensitive topics altogether, especially when combined with an acknowledgement of things that may constrain the work and the working relationship.

I have found that people who attend NBT workshops show a range of attitudes and comfort with the different elements of the model. Hence, adopting an NBT approach requires professional development which in turn requires openness to personal, as well as professional, growth. For example, some participants are comfortable being direct, whilst others are more comfortable being warm and caring. The power of NBT is derived from combining all clinical guidelines in an integrated way driven by genuineness, authenticity, and wanting the best for others. NBT does not embrace honesty at all costs. NBT does not set out to be confrontational, or to outsmart "difficult" clients. It is not about strategically confronting tensions to engage reluctant clients, although this may work. NBT is about combining honesty and directness with warmth and care, making overt the complications and constraints to the work in a straightforward way using language that is backed up by authenticity and consistent non-verbals. In this way, NBT has elements in common with the early work of Virginia Satir (1972), a pioneer in the field of marriage and family therapy who was known for her capacity to engage warmly with an extraordinary range of clients. Satir found avoiding jargon backed up by non-verbals which were consistent and congruent with what she was communicating, a concept she called *levelling,* contributed to her success. Satir described levelling as *saying what you really want to say and keeping what you think, mean, and feel congruent and on the same level.* Satir's work has had an enduring impact in other areas, including on management practices. Nearly fifty years later, Ron Carucci extended Satir's advice to business. Having conducted 3,200 interviews exploring what creates honesty at work, he summed it up his findings as, "say the right thing (truth), do the right thing (justice), and say and do the right thing for the right reason (purpose)" (Carucci, 2021, p. 10). NBT is essentially about being authentic and on the level, for the greater good.

Aim of this book

Many readers will recognise their own work in this book and may already be natural No Bullshit Therapists. If you are one of these therapists, I hope you will find the articulation of the approach reassuring and the theory and clinical guidelines a useful framework in which to locate your own NBT work, like it did for the following workshop participant:

> I have realised that I practice no bullshit therapy in my daily work with homeless people. It now has a name and values the work practice. I will take the information back to our team and I am sure it will validate the positiveness of our work practice.
>
> — (NBT workshop participant, Melbourne)

Possibly this book will vindicate your current approach, but I also hope it will help expand your work. My experience of conducting many NBT workshops suggests that some participants come to the workshops with a strong capacity for honesty and directness but benefit from exploring ways to integrate warmth and care more effectively into their work, whilst others find exploring greater honesty and directness adds to their natural capacity for warmth and compassion.

The primary aim of this book is to contribute to client outcomes by helping you the reader increase the number of authentic, mutually respectful, and transformative encounters you have with clients, whether they be therapy-lovers or haters. My hope is that NBT will add to the existing good work that helps us engage people who are suspicious of therapy and I hope it also makes a small contribution to the existing strategies that help make therapy efficient, effective, and satisfying.

It is clear from my work, the work of many others, and the material presented in the following chapters that people may start out as therapy-haters and move towards accepting or even loving therapy. It is reassuring to see evidence that the roughest, toughest, therapy hating cynic can find some relief from the *talking cure* if the constraints to the work are made overt and adequately addressed. Whilst NBT can be used as a pragmatic approach to working with therapy-haters, I encourage you, the reader, to embrace the philosophy and values underlying the approach. The ideas that make up NBT are simple, but if embraced and explored over time, can be profound. Implementing them can lead to beautiful moments of authenticity and intimacy between people who may not be like us, who may not like us, and who may not want to work with us. When this occurs, something akin to a spiritual feeling can be evoked; an authentic connection between two humans who have turned mutual suspicion and potential conflict into a respectful and productive interaction. For me, the strength of these beautiful moments is increased by the potential threat of the encounter, and the struggle to enter a world different from my own. I find the rewards of finding common ground and common values in these apparently different worlds very satisfying. NBT has helped me to look forward to working with therapy-haters rather than fearing them or the work with them. Through this process, they have forced me to challenge my own therapeutic practice and the values and theories upon which my practice was based. They have forced me to consider the political and organisational context in which I work, the style in which I communicate, and the clinical techniques I employ.

Therapy-lovers generously provide many beautiful moments in therapy; a significant phrase or gesture, a telling insight, a dramatic change, an intense working relationship or an amazing story freely told. Beautiful moments can also occur when you take a risk and find a way to provide critical feedback – the risk pays off – and the person transforms, and so do you.

A secondary aim, or maybe it is a hope, is that some readers will find ways to expand the clinical guidelines of NBT into new areas not addressed in this book and that this is communicated to me in some way. In the chapters that follow, colleagues have kindly allowed me to describe their NBT-esque clinical work in tough frontline services, complex service systems, or in response to sensitive issues such as abuse. Although not the focus of this book, I hope the ideas also find their way usefully into the wide range of relationships that make up your day-to-day life or in the organisations in which you work. In whatever sphere you apply the NBT ideas, I simply hope you will find them useful, like the following workshop participant:

> This session was very helpful to overcome the constraints of the 'helping model' in counselling. I really liked the upfront techniques and the communication strategies for clients. I feel I can relax a little in therapy sessions by being true and honest rather than always being in 'role'. Please write a small book on these techniques!
>
> — (NBT workshop participant, Melbourne)

I did!

Notes on language

As mentioned earlier, there is nothing sacrosanct about the title *No Bullshit Therapy*. To paraphrase Moshe Lang, a Melbourne-based family therapist, NBT is a useful term if you accept that it is not always about No Bullshit and not always about therapy. NBT workshop participants often have their own way to describe the approach, for example:

> It's called 'no-bullshit' therapy but it's more about directness – how to use it in a respectful way. It's also about transparency and clarity in the therapy relationship.
>
> — (NBT workshop participant, Melbourne)

> Using a straight up approach was always what I actually wanted to do but felt like I was short-changing the client. Being given permission to be more business-like (not the fluffy rapport building stuff) has proven to actually be more rapport-building than I had expected. As a result, the parents are also more on board now. I love the NBT approach, it really works!
>
> — (Workshop participant feedback, Bendigo)

Whilst I have used the term *therapist* throughout this book, I see it as a shorthand term for anyone in the caring or health area or anyone performing a counselling-like role in another type of job. Likewise, the term *therapy* is a shorthand term to cover any counselling or therapeutic type work, or counselling-type work performed as part of another role. In summary, I have found the ideas in this book are relevant to an extraordinary range of professional and non-professional workers, and to many areas of work outside the therapy room. The term *therapy* is used to remain consistent with the title of this book. I also like the juxtaposition of the terms *therapy* and *bullshit*, because *therapy* provides formality and prestige and a connection with mainstream services and *bullshit* oozes common touch and connects therapy to communities often side-lined by mainstream services.

It would be fanciful, however, to think of NBT as a complete model of therapy. At best, it is a set of simple and useful guidelines to create greater authenticity and integrity, especially when the work gets tough.

Notes on clinical examples

A range of examples and interviews are used throughout this book to demonstrate how the elements of NBT might look in practice. The interviews and some of the examples are verbatim accounts of real sessions that have been de-identified by making changes in personal details, some are descriptions of real sessions para-phrased from memory, some examples are from role-plays and verbatim transcripts of realistic simulations, and some are short examples made up to illustrate specific theoretical points. Each have their own advantage. It is not easy to get agreement from therapy-haters to record sessions, especially early sessions, as initially they are not interested in engaging in any work or co-operating in any way. The realistic simulations, from which the verbatim transcripts have been taken, can be viewed in their entirety, along with many other simulated sessions, by purchasing the NBT self-paced online learning suite, available at www.bouverie.org.au/nbt

How this book is organised

This book is made up of 13 chapters. A theoretical account of bullshit in Chapter 2 provides a basis for understanding the need for NBT. The history and context that led to the development of NBT is presented in Chapter 3. This chapter situates the author and outlines what has informed the clinical guidelines and the overall approach. In Chapter 4, the therapy-lover–therapy-hater continuum is outlined in detail, which provides the basis for practice notes and clinical examples in Chapters 5 (therapy-haters) and 6 (therapy-lovers) detailing how the NBT guidelines are implemented differently when working with therapy-lovers and therapy-haters. Chapter 7 provides a verbatim example of engaging a therapy-hater in the early stages of a first session, along with commentary. Chapter 8 provides safety strategies to manage the fine line between challenge and hurt and suggests ways to respond when clients get upset. Together, Chapters 1 to 8 will prepare the reader to apply the NBT model.

Chapter 9 describes NBT clinical tools and how to use them. Chapter 10 takes a critical look at power within therapeutic relationships and addresses the myth that NBT is a *boys-only* approach. Chapter 11 presents a verbatim first session with therapy-hater Jamie, along with commentaries about how the therapist manages the impact of trauma, and addresses blame, shame, and protective behaviours that can get in the way of change. Chapter 12 outlines how the NBT principles can be implemented when working with couples and families. This chapter also provides the reader with ideas about how NBT could be used to increase honesty in the workplace. Chapter 13 concludes this book.

No Bullshit Therapy is a conceptual and practical book, rather than an evidence-based treatise. This is because, firstly, there is little direct research evidence. For example, Christian Miller (2021) claims to have written the only book to discuss the virtue of honesty in detail since Sissela Bok's 1978 book, *Lying: Moral Choice in Public and Private Life*. Bok, at the time of writing her book, made a similar claim. Secondly, much of the limited psychological research on lying, cheating, misleading, and breaking promises involves evidence extracted from coin tosses, dice-throwing, and narrowly focussed self-report studies, rather than the complicated and nuanced interaction between therapists desperate to help clients who are reluctant to be helped. Hence, the book in hand is largely informed by practitioners and clients. Apart from accounts of therapeutic work, the literature I have drawn on comes mostly from philosophy, cultural studies, and the social sciences, read over the past two decades, the time I have been working on this book.

The writing style of *No Bullshit Therapy* is that of an easy-to-read *popular book for professionals* without extensive secondary references. I have written in this style to make it accessible to a wider range of workers. Although I have endeavoured to strip back the veneer of jargon, the task of explaining new concepts without it was not always possible. Hopefully, this book communicates an important message; although there is only one way for each of us to be authentic, there are many ways to convey this authenticity to others.

Notes

1 Alumni of the graduate certificate in family therapy: First Nations (La Trobe University), informed me that *mandate* has colonial connotations and should be replaced with *Establish a clear agreement*, when working with First Nations people in Australia (see Chapter 9).
2 Alumni of the graduate certificate in family therapy: First Nations (La Trobe University), informed me that few Aboriginal Torres Strait Islander formally marry and hence the term *marry* should be replaced with *marry up* when working with First Nations people in Australia (see Chapter 9).

References

Bok, S. (1978). *Lying: Moral choice in public and private life*. Pantheon.

Carucci, R.A. (2021). *To be honest: Lead with the power of truth, justice and purpose*. Kogan Page.

Duncan, B.L., Miller, S.D., & Sparks, J.A. (2004). *The heroic client: A revolutionary way to improve effectiveness through client-directed, outcome-informed therapy*. Wiley.

Lewin, K. (1943). Psychology and the process of group living. *Journal of Social Psychology*, *17*, 113–131.

Miller, C. (2021). *Honesty: The philosophical and psychology of a neglected virtue*. Oxford University Press.

Mohr, M. (2013). *Holy sh*t: A brief history of swearing*. Oxford University Press.

Satir, V. (1972). *Peoplemaking*. Science and Behavior Books.

Wexler, D. (2013). Shame-o-phobia: Why men fear therapy. *Psychotherapy in Australia*, *20*(1), 18–23.

2   The theory of bullshit

I can't stand them (politicians). They can't give a straight answer!

— Talk back caller to John Faine's Morning Show, *ABC radio, Melbourne*, (4/2/2015)

... the war for truthful information that barrages us on a daily basis has many of us soul-weary and disgusted. The suffocating skepticism we are fed by the media, political leaders at every level, and experts we once trusted has spread like a bad rash. Most of us are sick of feeling manipulated and lied to, and long to feel like someone is shooting straight with us.

— Ron A. Carucci, author, To Be Honest: Lead with the power of truth, justice, and purpose, (2021, p.7)

In this chapter, I present the history of bullshit most relevant to the helping professions, in particular the enterprise of psychotherapy. I have three goals: To define the relevance of bullshit for aspiring No Bullshit Therapy (NBT) practitioners; to argue that the loss of faith in our institutions, from government to church, has for many also led to a growing cynicism towards health professionals; and to clarity that NBT promotes being truthful rather than seeking the "truth."

Bullshit: History and definitions

Most of us know when we encounter bullshit; even if we feel helpless to do much about it. We all rate ourselves highly in the detection of bullshit. In fact, most of us pride ourselves in having a finely tuned *internal bullshit meter*, or what Carucci (2021, p. 22) calls a "factory-installed honesty barometer," even if we might struggle to understand or define what we are detecting or reacting to. The moral philosopher Harry Frankfurt, in his bestselling treatise *On Bullshit*, argues that it is this very confidence in our ability to recognise and not be taken in by bullshit that ironically has meant there is little deliberate exploration of bullshit, despite its negative connotation and ubiquity (Frankfurt, 2005). He claims there was no theory

DOI: 10.4324/9781003354925-2

of bullshit until his philosophical exploration of the topic. This is not quite true. Max Black in his book, *The Prevalence of Humbug and Other Essays*, devotes a compelling chapter to Humbug, a more polite but similar concept to bullshit, as described by Frankfurt. Black defines *humbug* as, "deceptive misrepresentation, short of lying, especially by pretentious word or deed, of somebody's own thoughts, feelings or attitudes" (Black, 1983, p. 143). Sissela Bok in her book *Lying* points out that it is commonly assumed that the term *humbug* emerged in the nineteenth century because Victorians were especially prone to hypocrisy, but in fact it started as student slang in 1751 (Bok, 1978).

The writer Robert Dessaix in a more recent book entitled *On Humbug*, no doubt inspired by Frankfurt's successful *On Bullshit,* warns commentators against gaily confusing *humbug, bullshit,* and (with apologies) *mindfucking.* Dessaix defines *humbug* as, "a kind of bluster, with a casual disregard for whether something is strictly true or not" (Dessaix, 2020, p. 10). He argues that humbug does not intend to mislead or to deceive with false information and is more akin to a flippant exaggeration or *gilding the lily* than a serious hoax. In Dessaix's definition, an example of humbug in the helping professions may be the simple promotion and one-dimensional representation of therapists as always competent and always compassionate. A further example is the unreflective promotion of a particular approach – for example, the suggestion that family therapy is always effective in all situations for all people. *Bullshit* he sees as more sinister, and his definition is helpful to understand why clients who detect bullshit respond so strongly to it. Dessaix argues that when someone bullshits, there is some intended concealment of an ulterior motive, which is not talked about openly. Put another way, the bullshitter actively, if not entirely consciously, conceals the true nature of their enterprise or intention. In the helping professions this might look like, for example, a protective worker attempting to be friendly to a female client when actually conducting a covert assessment of her parenting ability and risk to her children. The crudely named *mindfucking* is described by Dessaix as an "enduring mind changing manipulation" (p. 55), not necessarily good or bad. Professional training, the cultural discourse of an organisation or workgroup, the indoctrination or acculturation to a particular religion or socio-political movement or even the experience of being in love are examples Dessaix uses to explain the gradual process of promoting a way of understanding the world. Dessaix uses *brainwashing* as a synonym. A less biased phrase in keeping with his definition would be *the acculturating of a person to a particular world view.* According to this definition, most professional counsellors will have been acculturated to a particular world view as part of our core training and as a result we accept a particular set of values which underlies our profession or discipline – in my case a systemic view of the world promoted by family therapy. What is important to the exploration of bullshit here is that *humbug* can merge into *bullshit* and *bullshit* can merge into acculturation of a person into a particular world view. Whilst too simplistic for direct translation into the helping professions, Dessaix's advice is to respond to humbug with laughter, presumably to make overt the bullshitter's hidden agenda, and to simply be aware we each have a different world view. Without the position and power or even clarity to enact them, however, responses like those suggested by Dessaix may be difficult. Furthermore, managing bullshit, as a client or therapist, will be more difficult if the client or therapist has been acculturated into an overarching or underlying world view that promotes therapy as always warm and caring or one that tolerates covert agendas. For Australians, *bullshit* is part of the national idiom. I suspect that for the average Australian its use spans Dessaix's definition of *humbug* and *bullshit* at the same time as being embedded in a cultural world view that is suspicious of authority emanating from a history of both convict settlers and colonisation.

Frankfurt's (2005) argument is that the term *bullshit* is a vast and amorphous concept often employed loosely and generically and which defies crisp definition. Alison MacKenzie and Ibrar Bhatt from Queen's University in Belfast, in an online 2020 article agree, pointing out that the difference between a lie, bullshit, and a fake news story, is complex, often context dependent, and defies simple definitions. Philosopher, Adrian Briciu (2021) from Romania, disagrees with Frankfurt's definition of bullshit as *a total disregard for the truth*, instead proposing that bullshit is best viewed as a form of misleading speech rather than as a form of deception (Briciu, 2021).

Luckily, the NBT practitioner does not require a precise definition. More helpful clinically, is to be curious about what would constitute bullshit in the eye of both client and practitioner.

A common thread to the definitions I've presented, however, is that bullshitting is *short of lying* and hence, when combined with our confidence in detecting it, is seen as less harmful and less immoral than deliberate acts of lying – hence our semi-acceptance of it, a point made strongly by Frankfurt. There are, however, significant consequences of letting bullshit slide by in our relationships and in our work. We only need to reflect on the effect of our detecting bullshit in a relationship with a friend, colleague, or professional. Unless we have the maturity, skills, and will, to assertively confront the bullshitting as Dessaix suggests, we tend to either get angry or, less visibly, back off and politely distance ourselves emotionally. In short, we dismiss the person and commence a polite but distant *bullshit relationship*. Hence the effect of bullshitting in working relationships, such as between health practitioner and client, can be angry rejection or equally polite inauthenticity, such as the client saying what they think the therapist wants to hear – neither are conducive contexts for addressing complex emotional issues. On the other hand, addressing a potential client's perception of bullshit in a non-blaming, non-shaming but confident way, can lead to a real understanding of the client and promote authenticity, even intimacy, especially in complex and conflictual situations.

An understanding of some broad social developments that I believe have contributed to many clients' being reluctant to engage open-heartedly with professionals can be helpful when directly acknowledging the constraints to engaging a reluctant client. One might say there has been a gradual loss of faith in political leaders, institutions and by association, therapists.

Loss of faith in political leaders in the world of spin, fake news, and post-truth

Although it has become more blatant, we would be ill-advised to consider that the art of obfuscation is a new phenomenon. In 1949 the author Eric Blair, better known as George Orwell, described doublethink in his classic novel *1984* as the willingness to forget any fact that has become inconvenient. Orwell also described the process of obfuscation in a 1946 essay entitled *Politics and the English Language.* He argued that when the facts do "not square with the professed aims of political parties the political language has to consist largely of euphemism, question-begging and sheer, cloudy vagueness" (p. 136). When I read Orwell's words, it resonated with how tempting psychology and family therapy jargon is when my aims for a session do not square with the aims of a "difficult" client.

Whilst spin has always been a necessary tool of empire builders and politicians, our era seems to have elevated it to an acceptable art form that is played out before our eyes. Norman Solomon, the outspoken media critic and founding CEO of the Institute for Public Accuracy, a US nationwide consortium of policy researchers, argues that the process of spin doctoring is "more flagrant and extreme than ever" (1999, p. 136). In this book *The Habits of Highly Deceptive Media: Decoding Spin and Lies in Mainstream News* which won the George Orwell Award for Distinguished Contribution to Honesty and Clarity in Public Language, Solomon gives powerful examples to support his contention, although I suspect the reader may not require too much convincing. He points out that when President Clinton was facing impeachment for workplace sexual inappropriateness with intern Monica Lewinsky, he was openly coached by reporters and political commentators, about how to respond – in the full glare of the media.[1] Solomon writes, "In effect, journalists openly advised Clinton on the smoothest way to manipulate them" (p. 136).

Howard Kurtz, who wrote *Inside the Clinton Propaganda Machine: Spin Cycle,* gives an insight into the techniques of spin – describing how Clinton spinmeister, Mike McCurry, would deflect difficult questions with practiced ease, sugar-coat ugly messes, mislead journalists, refer the press to in-house damage controlling lawyers, stonewall, run down the clock to avoid potentially damaging topics, or attack the accuracy of individual reporter's stories or the individual reporter themselves (Kurtz, 1998). All this delivered with quick wit and charm to keep the gaggle of press onside. Kurtz gives plenty of examples of how other US presidential administrations avoided major contentious topics through these methods. For example, in 1980 Jimmy Carter's press secretary, Jody Powell, told the Los Angeles Times that a rescue mission to free American hostages in Iran would make no sense. Two days later a mission to free the hostages was carried out and ended in disaster. Likewise, in 1983 Larry Speakes, Ronald Reagan's spokesperson, declared that an American invasion of Grenada would be preposterous; it happened the next day.

There are equally as many audacious examples of spinmeistering in Australia, but maybe the clearest indication of the general acceptance of spin is captured by the popular segment running until recently on the Australian Broadcast Commission (ABC) radio called the *Spin Doctors* which blatantly discussed media spin winners and losers of the week. It seems media manipulation and hence manipulation of the community is not only condoned but seen as a required and expected, if not respected, skill of people in public life. Even a heartfelt apology can no longer be trusted. For example, during the Oil-for-Food scandal, a leaked report showed that the Australian Wheat Board was advised by their spin doctors to *over apologise* to the Australian community for their involvement in paying commissions to Saddam Hussein's regime to sell Australian Wheat to Iraq, in contravention of the United Nations Oil-for-Food programme (Cole Report, 2006). You would think that the blatancy of spin doctoring would make us openly outraged, but as Solomon points out when referring to the American Government's spin doctoring, "No matter how many times they've lied in the past, US officials are credible in the present" (p. 54).

It could be argued that the more recent explosion of fake news and post-truth, confined largely to the fringes before 2016, further increases the average person's distrust of politicians and by inference the institutions they direct. In a large-scale investigation on how true and false news spreads online, Soroush Vosoughi, Deb Roy, and Sinan Aral analysed a data set of 126,000 rumour cascades spread by 3 million people on 4.5 million occasions on Twitter between 2006 and 2017. They found that:

> Contrary to conventional wisdom, robots accelerated the spread of true and false news at the same rate, implying that false news spreads farther, faster, deeper, and more broadly than the truth because humans, not robots, are more likely to spread it (Vosoughi et al., 2018, p. 1146).

The disturbing impact of the explosion of fake news is not that it is false – we have always had to determine the veracity of information – but that prominent politicians such as Trump are becoming bolder in describing any information that does not accord with their view as fake news, and that this fake news is likely to spread more effectively than factual news, thus further corrupting the public's confidence in our political leaders. This is not just a proposition. Vosoughi and his colleagues showed a clear increase in the total number of false political rumours during the 2012–2016 U.S. presidential elections. James Ball (2017), author of *Post-Truth: How Bullshit Conquered the World*, points out that the American political fact-checker, PolitiFact,[2] a Pulitzer Prize-winning site established by the Tampa Bay Times, even had to add a special category to their true-false continuum, of *pants on fire*, to report *ridiculous claims* in the election campaign (p. 238). As of February 26, 2017, PolitiFact had fact-checked 373 claims made by Trump and found just 15 (4%) were rated true, 123 (33%) rated false, and 63 (17%) rated pants on fire. Trump's pants on fire claims included allegations of voter fraud, which he would later develop into an ongoing campaign. Fake news is not confined to the conservatives. PolitiFact fact-checked 293 of Hilary Clinton's claims and found 72 (25%) were rated true 29 (10%) rated false, and seven (2%) rated as pants on fire. In his book, Ball argues that "fake news is only the most visible part of a much broader problem which includes false context, misleading rather than outright false facts, or drawing false connections between items" (p. 252). Surely this must create public doubt and mistrust in our politicians.

A recent Australian report would suggest this is the case. Between 1987 and 2022, the Australian Election Study (AES), the most reputable source of evidence collected on political attitudes and behaviour, found a "long-term trend of low levels of trust in politicians for both the major parties" (Cameron & McAllister, 2022, p. 101). When the AES asked a representative sample, "In general, do you feel that the people in government are too often interested in looking after themselves, or do you feel that they can be trusted to do the right thing nearly all the time?" voter responses showed that political trust had reached an all-time low in 2019 of 25%, and whilst there has been a slight improvement in 2022 (30%), seven in ten Australians believed at this time that politicians are more interested in looking after themselves (Cameron et al., 2022, p. 28).

Politicians, although always under scrutiny, now have fake news to either bolster, obscure, or protect their position. With this closer scrutiny and growing mistrust of politicians and, as I argue below, the failure of many helping institutions to live up to their lofty ideals, we therapists are also likely to be scrutinised rather than automatically trusted.

Many illustrious institutions considered historically beyond reproach no longer hold this unassailable moral authority. Institutions that professed to be safe and caring have proven to be fallible and, in some cases, as documented during the recent Royal Commission into Institutional Abuse in Australia, downright predatorial. A significant number of Christian priests, whose role is to provide safety, trust, and support, have been found to be morally corrupt rather than moral guardians.

Institutions, including helping institutions, need to prove that they are enacting their charter and stated agenda, and that they need to live their values to earn trust (Ball, 2021). Progressives may champion the liberation of this change, conservatives may lament the loss of stability, but no matter what, individual practitioners can no longer assume that their role or their status will ensure their clients' trust.

The loss of faith in health professionals

In addition to all professionals being tainted by the public's growing distrust of politics, politicians, and institutions, the status of health professionals as all-knowing has been challenged by the feminist critique of power and of the expert, democratised by the ubiquitous accessibility of information on the internet, balanced by the growing sophistication of consumers of health services, and damaged by the growing publicised cases of client abuse. A rigorous study of 2503 randomly generated people, representative of the German population, found that 56 (4.5%) of female and 17 (1.4%) of male participants reported being subject to professional sexual misconduct. Physicians were the highest culprits, followed by psychotherapists, then nursing staff, physiotherapists, and alternative practitioners (Clemens et al., 2021). Anonymous surveys of physicians estimate that 3.3–14% of physicians have committed sexual misconduct (Sansone & Sansone, 2009). I remember being horrified when psychiatrist, family therapist, and independent researcher Carolyn

Quadrio reported to an Australian and New Zealand Family Therapy Conference more than two decades ago the frequency of, and profound damaging impact on, clients who experienced professional sexual misconduct from my own profession (Quadrio, 1996). Quadrio reported that the majority of the 40 female clients she assessed, who had experienced professional sexual misconduct, believed their relationship with the therapist was special and had some expectations of marriage. What's more, 22 of the 36 offending professionals were high-status charismatic psychotherapy leaders and teachers.

In his 2022 book, *Trust, Distrust, and History*, Brian Levack points to a general decline in interpersonal trust over the past few decades: "We have, it seems, become a much less trusting society than in the past. The loss of trust has also affected public institutions, most notably national governments, but also law courts, banks, corporations, churches, the media, and educational institutions" (Levack, 2022, p. 6). If we accept that there is a growing cynicism about our political leaders, people in positions of privilege and authority in general, and in our institutions, then the helping professions are not likely to be immune from it. Finding effective ways to address absence of trust could therefore be considered an increasingly essential part of the range of skills health professionals require in the modern world.

To find our work as clinicians helpful, most clients have three basic prerequisites: Safety, trust in the practitioner, and confidence in the approach being used. Different approaches will be required for different clients to feel safe and to begin trusting their practitioner. Clients (therapy-lovers) who have confidence in us and who embrace our methods will show greater tolerance of our inadvertent spin doctoring, exaggerated claims (humbug), and avoidant or vague language (obfuscation) when we get into troubled waters or simply lose our way. On the other hand, clients (therapy-haters) who don't share this confidence will not be so tolerant and will have readily available examples of avoidant politicians, institutions that can't be trusted to deliver their mission, and professionals who abuse clients, to justify their bad faith.

NBT is an approach developed to engage clients who don't have confidence in traditional methods, do not trust us, and don't feel safe with professional health care workers. Addressing these potential constraints directly (Chapter 5) is a surprisingly effective way to begin to create safety and trust, which over time can lead to confidence that our work may be helpful for the most resistant client.

It may require personal reflection and courage to begin addressing these potential constraints directly, because it is not easy. I have found it helpful to understand the methods of spin doctoring and the attraction of slipping into language that is vague, woolly, or obfuscating, so that I'm aware when I am tempted by these "self-protective" strategies (usually when the going gets tough). I will give you a warning now – once you start describing yourself as a *no bullshit therapist*, you become immediately more aware of when you are bullshitting, spin doctoring, humbugging, obfuscating, or simply avoiding difficult topics.

Simply saying you practise *No Bullshit Therapy* can immediately create a context which invites honesty and directness. Of course, there is a lot more to the approach than this, and the next few chapters will begin to unpack it.

However, if NBT is seen simply as a collection of techniques or as a strategy to engage clients who are suspicious, cynical, cautious, rather than as authenticity enacted by striving towards honesty and directness, then the approach will be in danger of falling victim to the same loss of faith as any other professional tool for dealing with "difficult" clients. Stating one's intention of being honest or upfront too often rather than just enacting this intention, consistently, predictably, and in the face of the most challenging circumstance, will also be in danger of eroding, rather than growing, safety, trust, and confidence.

More than ever, our task as helpers, especially when engaging clients who are cynical, cautious, and anxious about professionals, is to avoid hiding behind professional persona, jargon, and institutional power – especially when being truthful becomes inconvenient. But is it *truthfulness or truth* that an NBT practitioner seeks?

Loss of consensual reality: Truthfulness versus the truth

There is no longer an unquestioning acceptance of truth, reality, science, and authority. The cover of *Time* magazine on April 3, 2017, asked, "Is Truth Dead?" Whilst these disruptions have led to many liberating practices, it could also be argued that they have led to a sharp rise in fragmentation and public disbelief, especially in a context in which the solidness of our political leaders and institutions have been questioned, as addressed earlier in this chapter.

A key purpose of *On Truth,* Frankfurt's sequel to *On Bullshit,* is to point out the value and importance of truth. His simplest point may also be his most profound, "that truth often possesses very considerable practical utility" (2005, p. 15). In his 2005 book *Winning,* the former CEO of General Electrics, Jack Welsh writes: "lack of candor permeates almost every aspect of business, including, bureaucracy, layers, politicking, and false politeness" (Welsh, 2005, p. 26). In the international corporate training sessions he conducted soon after retiring as CEO of General Electric, Welsh found that only between 10% and 20% of his audiences responded in the affirmative to the question *How many of you have received an honest, straight-between-the-eyes feedback session in the last year, where you came out knowing exactly what you have to do to improve and where you stand in the organisation?* The numbers don't improve when the audience was asked if they have given candid feedback to their staff. Welsh argues that in business, "if you've got candor – and you'll never completely get it, mind you – everything just operates faster and better" (2005, p. 25). He goes on to argue that the consequences of people in the workplace not opening up and sharing their true thoughts and criticisms, "blocks smart ideas, fast action, and good people contributing all the stuff they've got" (p. 25); "simply, candor works because it unclutters" (p. 35).

We have all experienced both personally and professionally the liberation of speaking openly and the value of straight talk when navigating a complex and confusing path. Straight talking in the right context is liberating and often gets results! In the subjective world of therapy and in the human services more generally, truth is not easily defined, especially for a family therapist who has learnt to value the multiple perspectives of various family members. Whilst I agree with Frankfurt's general thrust that truth is important, I do not blame the post-modernists like he does (maybe because I count myself as one) for reducing the importance of truth through its subjectification and contextualisation. I don't see that the beliefs of therapists who appreciate the power of context and validate individual client perspectives, even if they clash with their own, are incompatible with valuing truth. *Valuing truth* rather than trying to *elicit the truth* has a very different ring to it. Fighting over what's true and what's not brings a lot of clients to our door, but we are unlikely to engage or work successfully with these clients if we simply mirror this search for one truth.

Another way of exploring how to counter bullshit is to look at its opposite. Is it honesty, directness, or truth? Of these, truth is the most problematic. Being truthful or honest about our motives, our values, our role, our position, and what we think tends to be more helpful when attempting to engage clients, than a search for a universal truth. Nietzsche once described truth as a mobile army of metaphors (Hinman, 1982). Being truthful about one's position, view, or recommendation is different from thinking one has a monopoly on the "truth." Seeking authenticity rather than universal truth is a more relevant concept to NBT, starting with being authentic about the enterprise one is involved in, and then through honesty and directness, striving towards authenticity about the therapist's view of the client, the client's behaviour, and what might need to happen for the client to effectively address their problems. Honesty and directness are part of the clinical guidelines of NBT rather than truth because honesty and directness can co-exist with the acknowledgement of multiple perspectives – which I believe, as part of my world view, is an essential component of dealing successfully with complex emotional and relationship issues.

The following chapter describes the development of NBT. This chapter provides useful depth and context to the approach (including a transcript of an interview I conducted with Gary, who you met at the very start of the book). However, if you are keen to move quickly to the description of practice, please feel free to skip to Chapter 4.

Notes

1 Clinton made this infamous denial at a White House press conference held on January 26, 1998.
2 http:/www.politifact.com

References

Ball, J. (2017). *Post-truth: How bullshit conquered the world*. Biteback publishing.
Black, M. (1983). *The prevalence of humbug and other essays*. Cornell University Press.
Bok, S. (1978). *Lying: Moral choice in private and public life*. Pantheon.
Briciu, A. (2021). Bullshit, trust, and evidence. *Intercultural Pragmatics*, 18(5), 633–656. http://doi.org/10.1515/ip-2021-5003

Cameron, S., & McAllister, I. (2022). *Trends in Australian political opinion: Results from the Australian election study 1987–2022.* Australian National University.

Cameron, S., McAllister, I., Jackman, S., & Sheppard, J. (2022). *The 2022 Australian federal election: Results from the Australian election study.* Australian National University.

Carucci, R.A. (2021). *To be honest: Lead with the power of truth, justice and purpose.* Kogan Page.

Clemens, V., Brähler, E., & Fegert, J.M. (2021). #patientstoo – Professional sexual misconduct by healthcare professionals towards patients: A representative study. *Epidemiology and Psychiatric Sciences 30*, e50, 1–8. http://doi.org/10.1017/ S2045796021000378.

Cole, T.R.H. (2006). *Report of the inquiry into certain Australian companies in relation to the UN Oil-for-Food Programme, Volume 1, Summary, recommendations and background.* Attorney General's Department, Australia.

Dessaix, R. (2020). *On humbug.* Hachette Australia.

Frankfurt, H.G. (2005). *On bullshit.* Princeton University Press.

Hinman, L.M. (1982). Nietzsche, metaphor, and truth. *Philosophy and Phenomenological Research, 43*(2), 179–199.

Kurtz, H. (1998). *Inside the Clinton propaganda machine: Spin cycle.* Simon & Schuster.

Levack, B.P. (2022). *Distrust of institutions in early modern Britain and America.* Oxford University Press.

MacKenzie, A., & Bhatt, I. (2020). Lies, bullshit and fake news: Some epistemological concerns. *Postdigital Science and Education, 2,* 9–13 http://doi.org/10.1007/ s42438-018-0025-4 (Accessed, 5/4/2023).

Orwell, G. (1946). Politics and the English language. In S. Orwell & I. Angos (Eds.), *The collected essays, journalism and letters of George Orwell.* 4(1), (pp. 127–140). Harcourt, Brace, Jovanovich.

Quadrio, C. (1996). Sexual abuse in therapy: Gender issues. *Australian & New Zealand Journal of Psychiatry, 30*(1), 124–131.

Sansone, R.A., & Sansone, L.A. (2009). Crossing the line: Sexual boundary violations by physicians. *Psychiatry (Edgmont), 6*(6), 45.

Solomon, N. (1999). *The habits of highly deceptive media: Decoding spin and lies in mainstream news.* Common Courage Press.

Time Magazine. (2017, April 3). Is Truth Dead? Title Page, 189(12), U.S.

Vosoughi, S., Roy D., & Sinan Aral, S. (2018). The spread of true and false news online. *Science, 359*(6380), 1146–1151.

Welsh, J. (2005). *Winning* (with S. Welch) New York: HarperBusiness.

3   The development of No Bullshit Therapy

Therapy is too important for it not to be part of popular culture

— (Adaptation of Professor Brian Cox, Celebrity Physicist talking about science)

In 2003, I was asked to deliver a workshop on Single Session Therapy (SST) for the Australian National Conference of Centrelink telephone counsellors. The conference was held in Canberra, the capital of Australia. Centrelink is the national government agency that, amongst other social supports, manages unemployment benefits, providing assessment and support for people struggling with the consequences of unemployment. SST, based on research showing that the most common number of sessions clients have with counsellors across the world and across most service contexts and diagnoses, is one, encourages therapists to treat each session *as if* it might be the last. Therefore, SST practitioners attempt to make the most of every encounter. This was relevant to the telephone counsellors who frequently only have a single phone call with clients. SST will be explored later in this chapter as one of the models of practice that informs No Bullshit Therapy (NBT), especially with therapy-lovers. The Centrelink telephone counsellors were very experienced social workers dealing day-in-day-out with traumatised clients who not uncommonly respond with high levels of anger, frustration, and desperation when the Government support payments upon which they rely are interrupted. The desperation of this situation creates a context for Centrelink staff that is often vexed, conflictual, and highly stressful. Whilst the audience was interested in the SST ideas, they were even more interested in hearing my thoughts about NBT – which gave me the confidence to develop these ideas into a one-day workshop which I delivered with colleague Karen Holl the following year.

The first NBT workshop was held on July 29, 2004 as part of the professional development program at The Bouverie Centre, La Trobe University, where I worked and later became its director. The workshop was oversubscribed within four weeks, three months prior to the event, which was unusual for a new workshop. The advertising blurb read:

No Bullshit Therapy is an approach that is ideal for men and people who don't like therapy, have had traumatic experiences and are reluctant to trust

DOI: 10.4324/9781003354925-3

do-gooders, see counselling and therapy as a middle-class wank, don't like being psychologised, are suspicious of the worker's agenda or motives, have had a lot of unsatisfactory treatment, counselling or therapy and are hard-to-engage.

The learning outcomes were:

- To be introduced to the ideas guiding NBT
- Striving towards honesty with yourself and others
- Striving towards being genuine
- Being transparent, open, and direct
- Avoiding wasting time: yours and others
- Holding whilst pushing
- Striving to like clients who are doing unlikeable things

In the winter morning of the workshop, I was nervously preparing when a colleague, Greg U'Ren, sidled up to me and said, *Jeff, you won't be able to bullshit all day*, the idea of which was both terrifying and true. Once you state that you're a no bullshit therapist, it is disingenuous to obfuscate; there is a moral imperative to stay true to the values upon which NBT is based, especially honesty and directness. One of the fears I had prior to the workshop was that the participants working in front-line services would have far greater credibility as NBT practitioners than I could muster in my role as a therapist in a comfortable specialist state-wide family therapy agency. My anxiety was heightened by looking at the participant list and noting that the workshop was drawing a different audience than our usual mainstream therapeutic oriented offerings: people working with prisoners, outreach staff working on the streets, counsellors supporting workers in the building trade, child protection workers, support workers for the police, housing support workers, people working in the law-courts, and professionals working in rural areas. I decided to be upfront about my fears. I was surprised at what a relief it was to do so.

In this first workshop, Karen and I ran out of useful material soon after lunch. However, an extraordinary sense of connection had developed within the group of participants. I interpreted this as everyone joining around a mutual frustration that mainstream therapeutic approaches inadvertently struggle to engage people who don't understand, do not relate to, or are frightened by, traditional therapy.

In subsequent workshops, I always ask participants to reflect on the path that has led them to attending a workshop with such an unprofessional title. Their responses typically reflect two broad contexts:

1 People working largely with therapy-haters who are interested in an approach that speaks to their clientele and validates their experience of working with these clients

2 Workers who want to expand their therapeutic style to be more effective with the occasional therapy-hater with whom they come into contact

Five key personal and professional experiences led to the title *No Bullshit Therapy* and informed the development of the clinical guidelines:

1   Growing up on wheat and sheep farms in rural Victoria, I was acculturated to a practical approach to life from an early age. Driving a tractor alone at the age of 12, whilst my father took a load of harvested wheat to the silo, was just the done thing. The older I get, the more I appreciate that being involved in challenging or even dangerous activities created a sense of confidence to tackle new things or to tackle old things in a new way. This confidence helped counteract the feeling that, not having had a strong professional pedigree, (my parents were not professionals), I was an academic fake. On the one hand, I was proud that I did not take my profession of psychology too seriously, and on the other, I struggled at times to take myself seriously as a professional. Over time, I have resolved this dilemma by realising that I am very serious about the work of my profession, if not about the status of the profession itself. Growing up in a rural culture helped me to develop the ability to engage with a wide range of people and to be as comfortable with professional people (eventually) as I am with people without professional qualifications.

My experience of the rural culture is that directness is valued and professionals who do not sugar-coat difficulties gain greater respect. The unprofessional title of No Bullshit Therapy may have originated in my rural roots. I completed my PhD in 2012 (Young, 2012). Its subject matter looked at, amongst other things, how NBT may be useful in rural communities affected by drought. A key success of my study was that NBT tapped into the cynicism of therapy in rural communities and provided a culturally sensitive alternative which drought counsellors found useful. In fact, my research showed some evidence to suggest that rural people may not be as anti-therapy as we think. For example, The Birchip Cropping Group, a rural broad acre farming industry body in Victoria, Australia, commissioned the RMCG consulting group to conduct research into the emotional effects of drought on farmers. The resulting two-part comprehensive report (Rickards, 2007; 2008) found that 13% of 60 randomly chosen farmers had experienced counselling in the past and 100% had found it useful, 66% reported that they did not need counselling but felt that it should be available for those who wanted it and only 21%, a minority, thought that counselling was a waste of time. Despite this positive result, the report still concluded that rural people are anti-counselling. In keeping with my PhD findings, Rickards' reports suggest that the majority of rural people who sought drought counselling found it helpful, so long as it was culturally appropriate to them. Whilst not conclusive, these reports invite caution when accepting the prevailing views about different groups' cynicism about the benefits of counselling. The cynicism may be more about how therapy is presented rather than the actual value of the *talking cure* itself.

2   In 1994, along with my Bouverie Centre colleagues Pat Boyhan, Colin Riess, and Pam Rycroft, I began conducting family therapy sessions in ways guided by

a model of service delivery called *SST*. Made popular by the release of Moshe Talmon's book, *Single Session Therapy: Maximising the First and Often only Session*, in 1990, SST is best seen as a service delivery model which accepts the following three research findings:

I The most common number of therapy sessions attended by clients is one (the mode – not the average)
II The majority of therapy clients who attend for only one session are satisfied with the outcome from that one session
III It is difficult to predict which clients will attend one session and who will attend multiple sessions

Accepting these findings generates therapeutic approaches that seek to make the most of every session, especially the first, as the therapist cannot know if the session will be the first of many or the first and last. The SST framework encourages workers to actively find a focus for the work based on what the client wants, to cut to the chase, to check in from time to time to ensure the conversation and work is on track and to share thoughts or ideas about what might be helpful directly with the client/family (Young & Rycroft, 1997; SST core elements, with example questions, are presented in Chapter 6). The approach encourages therapists to allow for the possibility that one session may be enough whilst not putting any constraints in the way of clients deciding that they want further help. The *cutting to the chase* element of SST has been one of several influences on the development of NBT, providing a working context that supports practitioners to be more direct and upfront with clients. Having to conduct a session *as if* it may be the last provides a supportive frame in which clients and therapists can assertively address the most essential issues in a straight up or business-like way. SST helped me to see the value of *business engagement* as an additional tool to the training I had received in using *social engagement* to build rapport and therapeutic relationships. I have found that a business engagement approach (*Let's get down to business! What is it that you're here for? Let's not waste each other's time. How can I be helpful? Let's roll up our sleeves and get straight into it!*) is a more effective way of working with clients towards the hater end of the therapy-hater-lover continuum than exclusively using social engagement strategies. Therapy-haters want to get on with the work, they don't necessarily want to build a relationship with the therapist, not initially. Many years ago, I did not understand this and would simply re-double my efforts to win over reluctant clients, including asking non-threating questions to which I already knew the answers. Single session techniques provide valuable ways to gently clarify the purpose of therapeutic encounter, cutting to the chase and checking in during work with therapy-lovers, for example: *What would you like to walk away with by the end of the session? Is this what we should be talking about right now? Is this what you hoped for? Is there anything else I need to ask before I share my thoughts with you?* SST and NBT have a lot in common when working with therapy-lovers but are quite different when working with therapy-haters, as discussed in Chapters 4, 5 and 6.

3 Earlier in my career, although angry men only comprised about 5% of my clinical workload, they caused 95% of my worries. *Will they get into a fight between sessions and knock someone senseless? Will they have an accident driving erratically in their unregistered car? Will they walk in today and demand that I see them immediately and blame me for their latest set-back? How will they respond to me questioning their behaviour and how will I raise any of these and many other sensitive issues with them?* My struggles trying to work therapeutically with angry men led to strategic utterances like, I like to practice what I call No Bullshit Therapy to which these men typically responded with interest and curiosity. For me, it was initially a strategic way of engaging these clients and a clever way, I thought, to survive the first session. It was a way of getting some traction given these men did not want to be in therapy or to work with me. They had usually been forced to attend by their partners in order to see their children or to save the relationship. Or having to go through the motions of therapy to obtain a practical benefit like financial support or to mitigate legal action, which made trying to be therapeutic a struggle. Since these early days I have shifted from thinking about *angry men* to thinking about *therapy-haters* and begun to focus on what approaches are more palatable to therapy-haters. I have moved away from thinking how to engage therapy-haters strategically to thinking how to engage them genuinely and ethically. By this I mean, I've changed to focussing on how to adjust my models of practice to suit therapy-haters, and the contexts that lead to therapy hating, rather than trying to trick them into engaging with my standard ways of working.

4 It was only after I began running workshops on NBT with Karen Holl that I began to link participant workers' attitudes towards honesty and directness, and warmth and care, to their family-of-origin experiences. Human service workers have different relationships to honesty and directness, and to warmth and care depending in part, on their experiences of these qualities, growing up. We conducted exercises in which workshop participants were invited to recall how honesty and directness were viewed by the family in which they grew up in, how comfortable they were with these dimensions, and the subsequent impact of these family-of-origin experiences on their relationship to honesty and directness in their professional work. We conducted a similar exercise looking at warmth and care and then a final exercise exploring who in their family or social network was able to combine honesty and directness with warmth and care. We invited workshop participants to consider using the person they identified as having this integrative skill to be an imaginative role model for marrying honesty and directness with warmth and care, a clinical guideline of NBT. I have recreated this exercise for the reader in Chapter 5. Whilst watching Karen conduct one of these early sessions, I realised that whilst my own family-of-origin was honest and direct about criticism, they were not open or direct about warmth and care. I realised that I had a personal commitment to helping workers combine these seemingly opposing characteristics or styles. In many ways, the heart and certainly the art of NBT is the capacity to smoothly integrate honesty and directness with warmth and care in the most intricate, intimate, and nuanced ways.

5   Several experiences that helped shape NBT occurred during my first two jobs which were both in large psychiatric hospitals. During this work, possibly because I was a young professional struggling to find my place in the world, I became aware of the tendency for mental health professionals to hide behind jargon. I did it myself. I noticed that when a client's situation became more complex and harder to address, jargon often increased inversely proportional to the range of practical strategies available to staff. I have since reflected on my own tendency to hide behind jargon when therapy gets difficult with a client, whether it is because I have something sensitive I want to convey, have nothing much to offer, or suspect my agenda is not palatable to the client. Sometimes this jargon is subtle, such as responding vaguely to a client's specific questions such as, *What do I need to do to change?* with something like, *change is a process* or *Why can't I see my file notes?* with something glib like, *It's against the agency's policy.*

A rather unpleasant experience in 1986 helped me appreciate the subtle and sometimes not-so-subtle abuses of power that we mental health professionals can inadvertently and sometimes advertently exert over our clients. In the psychiatric hospital, one of my roles was to comment on psychological issues as part of a small multi-disciplinary team that reviewed the progress of each patient in the locked admissions ward. Although each member of this team was well intentioned, I doubt that all the patients experienced us collectively in this way, for which I jointly take responsibility. During one review meeting, the consultant psychiatrist, who was not a clear communicator at the best of times, conducted an informal assessment interview with a young male patient who wanted to be moved out of the locked admissions ward into one of the open rehabilitation wards. The consultant psychiatrist explored the patient's request in a provocative and clumsy manner and when the patient legitimately responded with frustration and anger to the interview, the interviewer turned to us and indicated that the patient's anger was proof that he should remain in the locked ward. Regardless of the correct assessment, the obfuscation and abuse of the consultant's (and the silence and hence complicity of the team of which I was a member) power over this man was covered up by psychiatric jargon, professional status, and institutional power.

I suspect all of us have silently witnessed and most of us have been implicated in abuses of power, at least subtly, as we have tried to discharge our professional duties. Given the vulnerability of our clients, health professionals need to be particularly aware of our power, even if we intend to be helpful, and especially because we want to be helpful. We need to be particularly careful when our clients face difficulties that are not easily solved, when clients are not open to being helped, when our good intentions amount to nought, and we feel wounded by our failure to help. NBT has provided a framework to help me minimise inadvertent abuses of power inherit in my professional therapeutic work by providing encouragement to make the rules and progress of therapy transparent, and to avoid the temptation of hiding behind professional jargon.

I was tempted to hide behind whatever I could when I was asked to see Gary, who I introduced at the start of this book, because I knew from the referral information that he was likely to be angry. I knew enough about his situation to suspect that therapy could get ugly. The only reason Gary attended therapy was because he wanted to have greater access to his two children, and he thought therapy and I might advance that goal. Although I was feeling more nervous than powerful, Gary saw me as having the power to either facilitate or inhibit access to his children. I was asked to see him by a colleague who had seen his ex-partner and children, as part of a family therapy training program. My colleague had learnt from his ex-partner that she and Gary had experienced a vicious divorce 18 months earlier. My colleague, informed by her work with the mother and children became concerned that Gary may take the children and move interstate. Because of the level of conflict, several sessions into my work with Gary I met with both parents individually, to explain how I would proceed. I explained I would meet with the boys and feed back to both parties about what the boys needed from them as parents. I was clear that they didn't have to like each other but they needed to continue operating as effective parents for the sake of the children. When I met with Will and Toby, I found them to be very guarded which suggested to me they had been significantly affected by their parents' toxic separation. I was alarmed when they finally complained that their father and his new partner did not feed them enough during weekend visits. I think it was a test to see how their dad would respond to their complaint and if I would raise their concern directly with him. I can tell you I was not looking forward to sharing this information with Gary.

I learned a lot from my work with Gary and from an interview I did with him about his experience of NBT. I had seen Gary for six sessions over about five months when I conducted an interview with him in preparation for the first NBT workshop, by which time things had begun to improve, especially between him and Toby.

Gary agreed I could show the video of this interview for training purposes and the verbatim transcript is presented below:

Jeff: Thanks for doing this for me.
Gary: That's fine.
Jeff: So, um as I said I'm doing a workshop on No Bullshit Therapy and um as you know I said that early in our work, I said that I practice a form of therapy called No Bullshit Therapy. Can you think back to what you remember when I first said that?
Gary: Yeah exactly! I can remember you … the first time we met, and I was very upset, I hadn't seen my children and err you said this, the no bullshit approach. And I said that's exactly the approach I like. You know I haven't got the timeframe to, to paint a pretty picture. Tell me *as it is* as I said, tell me the bad news and I'll just accept it.
Jeff: And what was it about No Bullshit Therapy that made you think, that's what I want?
Gary: Yeah, I … it's more that I don't have the timeframe to go through the what-ifs and the maybe could have done this because I really needed to

know if I was making a blue here. I may not see my children. I may make a big mistake. And if you get this no bullshit approach, it's cold hard facts that can't be misinterpreted.

Jeff: Right.

Gary: And I think that's good. It's not like you change it around so you don't hurt my feelings, or it can be misinterpreted. It's saying straight out ... in a limited amount of sentences, it's pretty plain.

Jeff: So, could, in a way, the no bullshit approach be less blaming than trying to not hurt your feelings?

Gary: Um... No, I think it could be more honest. I think it could be either ... it could be both less blaming or more blaming. I think it would be just honest you're just telling me exactly what err how you believe this situation is and what is the best way to help me.

Jeff: That's interesting because the workshop is called No Bullshit Therapy: Striving toward honesty.

Gary: Well, there you go.

Jeff: Um the fact that then I was being more honest with you, how did that impact on the way you were with me?

Gary: The fact that um, the fact you were honest, whether you want to call it no bullshit or you were honest with me, I instantly had trust in you. If you are going to be honest with me, I trust you, and it was easier and that err, the guard's dropped, I could tell you exactly what I feel. Rather than if you, you know beat about the bush a bit, play him, I don't know if I can trust him or not, or is he just playing it off to get me to say what he wants me to say. But if you're honest with me ... that's it. I have to trust you. And I said to my kids, he's a good guy, you trust him you know he's...

Jeff: So, in a way being honest then led to trust, and did it also lead you to be more honest with me than you would have between [without the NBT approach]?

Gary: Certainly, certainly, if you can trust someone you've got to build it you, you know...it's a two-way street.

Jeff: What about even when sometimes or did it... in actual fact, to be honest with you now, I think it helped me say things to you that I was a bit worried about saying to you. That by saying that I practice No Bullshit Therapy, it also helped me then to say things directly rather than try to say things that were difficult to try and make them palatable.

Gary: You're right, we have an hour. We could spend 45 minutes beating around the bush and 15 minutes talking about important things. Or we could just forget all that and spend the whole hour without having to go through all the crap.

Jeff: Actually, I think too um once we'd said that up front you used it sometimes. I think I can remember at least two times when I was wanting to say something to you, and I was thinking how best to say it. And I can remember you saying "Jeff, remember, no bullshit," which then helped me to say what I was thinking more directly. Can you remember?

Gary: I can yeah, I can exactly remember, and I could see you stumbling ... and as I say the clock's ticking, don't try and tell me how good it is if it's not. And as I said I really got to know the truth. I don't want to know that things aren't so bad because things are really bad you know.

Jeff: What do you think was going on in my head when I was sort of?

Gary: (*interrupting*) I think you thought that I was as you've said, "He is an intense person" and you thought "How's he going to handle this?" "I don't think he can handle it if I tell him." And I can tell you exactly what it was it was when you asked my kids what I don't do whether I don't feed them this much. Remember?

Jeff: Yeah!

This interview with Gary helped me to appreciate that clients who are highly suspicious of therapist's motives will interpret anything that is vague or unclear in the worst possible light. Hence being honest and direct, and specific, especially about difficult issues, means the therapist is less likely to be misinterpreted and helps create a sense of trust. Gary indicated that my honesty and directness led him to feel that I was listening to what he was saying, rather than playing him, which led to him experiencing me as authentic and hence more trustworthy. Listening to this interview repeatedly when conducting NBT workshops helped me to appreciate some of the beautiful moments or Moments of Being[1] to quote one of my NBT workshop co-facilitators, Jacqui Sundbery, in my work with Gary, such as being able to talk honestly about his behaviour that was not helping his cause. Later in the interview, Gary pointed to the connection he felt from the mutual honesty and directness we'd negotiated, "the bullshit approach it's gotta, you gotta be in tune with what I'm saying … you've gotta be err, it's shoot from the hip type of thing so you can't just do it by the one liners that everyone wants."

The origin of the following chapter was a critique of an NBT workshop, conducted by my long-time friend and collaborator, Pam Rycroft, which I recorded on a paper tablecloth in a café in Mildura, a country town in Victoria, Australia. Pam and I realised that the relevance and application of NBT is very different depending on whether you are working with therapy-lovers or therapy-haters.

Note

1 *Moments of Being* is the title of a book of autobiographical reflections by Virginia Woolf. Woolf (2017) describes moments of being as moments in which an individual experiences a sense of reality, that could be a result of instances of shock, discovery, or revelation.

References

Rickards, L. (2007). *Critical breaking point? An interim report.* Birchip Cropping Group.

Rickards, L. (2008). *Critical breaking point? The effects of drought and other pressures on farming families, final report.* Birchip Cropping Group.

Talmon, M. (1990). *Single-session therapy: Maximizing the effect of the first (and often Only) therapeutic encounter.* Jossey-Bass.

Woolf, V. (2017). *Moments of being.* Random House.

Young, J. (2012). *A no bullshit approach to drought.* PhD thesis, La Trobe University, Melbourne, Australia.

Young, J., & Rycroft, P. (1997). Single session therapy: Capturing the moment. *Psychotherapy in Australia, 4*(1), 18–23.

4 Therapy-lovers and therapy-haters

Talk about a bullshit centre-of-excellence. You live in your airey-fairy world...

— (Disgruntled female client of a community health centre in a disadvantaged suburb of Melbourne)

The challenges are that some of our clients only view contact with us as a means to an end (e.g., payments) and are difficult to engage for alternative interventions.

— (Brief for NBT workshop in * organisation)

It is important to state from the outset, that therapy-haters and therapy-lovers represent extreme ends of the continuum reflecting the community's wide-ranging views about therapy. Most people sit in the middle regions of the continuum and are somewhat open, somewhat uncertain about therapy. Factors contributing to these views include knowledge of therapy, the way therapy is presented, how it has been experienced in the past, a person's cultural, family, and personal environment, together with the local context in which a problem requiring help occurs.

Placing the rich and complex range of client attitudes towards therapy and the helping professions into a crude and somewhat light-hearted and confronting binary distinction, rather than a more complex categorisation, is both simplistic and helpful. I hope the impact of naming therapy-lovers and therapy-haters will build on the field's recent interest in adapting therapeutic approaches to be more simpatico to a client's context rather than dismissing potential clients who don't like therapy. After all, it is the interaction between the client, therapist, the clinical model, and the overall endeavour that typically creates cynicism about therapy – not the therapy-hater per se. I have thought about adding extra categories between therapy-haters and therapy-lovers, such as *therapy doubters* (sceptical but a little open to therapy being helpful), *therapy neophytes* (new to therapy), and *therapy worriers* (wanting help but very concerned about an unfamiliar and potentially scary process), but felt it would be distracting and also politically unsound – it would seem I was trying to seriously account for, and accurately categorise, the complex and diverse reasons why people attend therapy and the attitudes they have towards this work. Instead,

DOI: 10.4324/9781003354925-4

I have maintained the simplicity and clarity of two extreme attitudes and invite you, the reader, to adapt No Bullshit Therapy (NBT) ideas to fit the unique context of your own work and to the diverse range of attitudes towards you and your work that your clients hold.

While therapy-haters have much in common with mandated and involuntary clients, I prefer the therapy-lover–therapy-hater continuum because it provides a more nuanced range of responses to therapy; it acknowledges that a voluntary client may also be distrustful of therapy or therapists, and it gives greater agency to the client. However, much can be learned from early writers such as Rooney (1992; 2009), Ivanhoff et al. (1994), and De Jong and Berg (2001), who have adapted their work specifically for mandated or involuntary clients and argue that most mainstream therapeutic models and clinical strategies are based on people who are open to therapy. Clients who are not open to therapy (towards the therapy-haters' end of the continuum) are typically judged in terms of deficit (resistant, difficult, uncooperative, hostile, or in denial), rather than scrutiny being focused on whether the range of therapeutic models adequately respond to their needs, context, and cultural sensitivities. David Wexler, an expert in working with men, for example, encourages us to adapt mainstream therapies to reflect what he calls *Guy World*. He writes:

> They [men] perceive the decision to use the therapeutic services and the process of using them to be not particularly helpful and not particularly masculine – often even downright threatening. It is our job to adapt our approach to these realities rather than ... try to massage men into being more like women in the ways they express themselves and experience their emotions (Wexler, 2013, p. 20).

Whilst cautious not to stereotype, I think it is apparent that a significant number of people within broader groups such as Indigenous communities, working class clients, rural people, and adolescents to name just a few are typically expected to fit into therapeutic models that are not designed with them in mind. Members of these groups are often considered as cynical, disruptive, unmotivated, in denial, or worse – assigned a pejorative diagnosis when they don't respond positively to therapeutic models that are not designed by them or for them, not sensitive to their existing healing traditions, and not culturally coherent. In many cases, a culturally sensitive approach to therapy will reap significant rewards for both client and practitioner. For example, my PhD study found that drought counsellors who were embedded in rural settings, who understood the impact of drought, were culturally sensitive to rural people and were trained in NBT commonly reported that, *rural people hate therapy until you put No Bullshit in front of it.*

A key point made throughout this book is that we need to be cautious about writing off clients who do not co-operate with our preferred or existing ways of working. Even clients who dropped out of therapy after one session were described in the 1970s, in extraordinarily pejorative terms. Baekeland and Lundwall (1975) reviewed 330 papers referring to therapeutic "dropouts" and discovered that these clients were described as, "apt to deny his (her) illness, to be resentful and distrustful, and to have psychopathic features" (p. 78). Interestingly, later Single Session Therapy research (e.g., Talmon, 1990) showed that rather than psychopathic, not returning to therapy after the first session is not only very common, but *the most* common occurrence, and most people who only attend once find that single contact to be helpful enough that they don't feel the need to return.

Accepting the Single Session Therapy research has had a profound impact on my work and the work of my colleagues at The Bouverie Centre. Essentially, it has helped us to demystify therapy and to make our work more transparent, collaborative, and responsive to client needs.

Exploring what works for *unco-operative* clients rather than trying to work clients into what works for *co-operative* clients has led to significant innovations. Some other models of engagement designed for "unco-operative" clients are explored in the following section.

Other models designed to engage therapy-haters

A major shift in responsibility for failed therapeutic attempts began in the 1980s when the solution-oriented therapist Steve de Shazer signed the death warrant to the idea of client resistance. In his seminal article "The Death of Resistance" (1984), which was the sixth version of a 1979 paper, de Shazer entreated therapists to take responsibility to change their approach rather than blame the client if therapy was not working – his entreaty, at the time, was liberating and confronting in equal measure. de Shazer and his partner Insoo Kim Berg encouraged us to consider the client, ourselves, the context of the therapeutic enterprise, and the relationship between all three when therapy was not working. de Shazer (1988) suggested therapists consider different approaches depending on the client's attitude to therapy and consequently was one of the earliest therapists to theoretically address resistance by categorising clients as *visitors, complainants,* and *customers.* de Shazer defined visitors as clients who do not accept that they have a problem and hence are not interested in engaging with therapy or in collaborating on a therapeutic solution. According to de Shazer, visitors, like therapy-haters, usually attend therapy because they must, not because they want to. Complainants are more likely to accept that they have a problem but believe the solution should come from someone other than themselves, typically the therapist, referring agent, or someone else in their network. de Shazer recommended therapists provide compliments to visitors and simple observational tasks to complainants hoping that over time they would become customers. Unlike the visitor or complainant, the customer is ready to sign up to owning their own problem and co-operating with the therapist to co-develop an acceptable solution (essentially, therapy-lovers). I have been reluctant to embrace this categorisation, concerned it could lead to workers demeaning visitors and complainants, rather than empathising with their situation, even though I suspect de Shazer's original intention was to avoid demonising these reluctant clients.

The categorisation of visitor, complainant, and customer was embraced by many therapists; however, I believe that the suggested responses to visitors and complainants are at risk of fulfilling Frankfurt (2005) and Dessaix's (2020) definition of bullshit – being deceptive about the enterprise – being complimentary not because the therapist is truly impressed with the client, often the opposite, but because the therapist wants to strategically avoid raising the client's resistance to change, or to being engaged. Hoping that unthreatened, the visitor will transition over time to become a customer. NBT takes a different approach to visitors – it makes overt the client's reluctance and responds honestly and directly about the enterprise, the potential advantages to the client, what the client needs to do to benefit from that enterprise, and what the therapist needs to do to help the client achieve this advantage. NBT accepts and makes overt that the visitor may not want to engage in the hard work of therapy, does not necessarily push the client to engage, but will clearly point out the likely or potential consequences of not engaging in the work.

Whilst this direct approach may seem risky, it is typically less likely to raise the hackles of a therapy-hater because at the heart of their resistance to engagement is distrust of the therapist and/or of therapy in general. In keeping with the key definition of bullshit, the therapy-hater expects that the *bullshitting* therapist will attempt to obfuscate the true nature of the therapeutic enterprise, including their intentions, beliefs, and thoughts about the client. I have found that the *internal bullshit* meter of a therapy-hater is likely to detect insincere compliments of any kind. Complimenting a client who is not interested in participating in the therapeutic process is likely to be experienced as bullshit therapy, rather than NBT. Authentic compliments, on the other hand, combined with honesty and directness about the enterprise and challenges of therapy are central to the art of NBT.

Another major approach that grew out of alcohol and drug services with clients reluctant to embrace therapy, or at least change, is motivational interviewing. First described by William Miller in 1983, motivational interviewing explores a client's ambivalence to change by eliciting the client's own change-no change arguments rather than pushing for a particular direction by empathising with the client and the client's change dilemmas and highlighting discrepancies between the client's own goals and values and their *problematic* behaviour. This approach elaborated by Miller and Rollnick (1991) remains very popular in addictions work and has been embraced by therapists working with a wide range of hard-to-engage clients.

Motivational interviewing has been criticised for not having a theoretical underpinning – this does not worry me because it's effective, and NBT doesn't have a respectable underlying theory either. A cautionary note I would pose to therapists using both motivational interviewing and NBT is that whilst the therapist tries not to push for change, they typically hope for change – and this dilemma needs to be handled openly and with authenticity, otherwise trust can be inadvertently compromised. In addition to acknowledging the constraints to change, NBT invites practitioners to both articulate their pro-change position (ideally linked to the client's goals) whilst acknowledging the client's position of not wanting to change. In practice, this may look something like, *I can see you don't think you should be here, and that's fine, but I know you want your relationship to get back on track (client's goal) and to be honest, I can't see how that will happen without some hard work on your behalf.*

In keeping with de Shazer, the motivational interviewer rolls with, rather than against, client resistance and uses change talk to promote client hope and confidence that change is possible. As with motivational interviewing, NBT encourages a business-like discussion about the *real* pros and cons of change without judgement or blame. However, NBT encourages the worker to both share their heartfelt hopes for the client and at the same time indicate they are not emotionally dependent on the client taking up the worker's offer of help. In other words, the NBT practitioner owns their own investment in the situation but does not try to impose this investment on the client. Achieving this delicate balance is an art form and requires practice. In action, it may look something like this:

NBT therapist: If you are really serious about getting a job, you are going to have to really prepare for the interviews.
Therapy-hater: You don't say!
NBT therapist: I would love to see you working because you've got so much to offer young people who are living rough, because of where you have come from, but I can't make you take the interviews seriously. I'll get paid whether you prepare for the interviews or not.

Being armed with models of practice that are designed with therapy-haters in mind has dramatically changed the way I approach my work. I wonder if it is a myth, a persistent myth, that therapy-haters are harder to work with than therapy-lovers! In my experience, this may not necessarily be the case. Take Gary for example. Once we had established an honest and direct way of working together, he was not difficult to work with and in fact he changed quickly once we agreed that I would provide him with very clear feedback. In contrast, I needed to raise the possibility of therapy coming to an end with therapy-lovers Giovanni and Franca, given we had moved into friendship mode and were no longer making any significant therapeutic changes. I felt nervous and tentative even asking an indirect question like, *How would I know that you didn't need to see me anymore?*

It is important to distinguish between therapy-lovers who are difficult to work with and therapy-haters who are easy to work with once an agreeable approach is found. A client who is difficult to work with but not distrustful or suspicious of therapy is not in my definition of a therapy-hater – they are a difficult to work with therapy-lover. The difficult to work with therapy-lover may compete with the therapist, may think they know better, or not respect the therapist's wisdom, skills, advice, or credibility. They may be disappointed in the therapist and ultimately want to see a better therapist, but they are not deeply suspicious of therapy or therapists in general. The following is an example of NBT-inspired work with a therapy-lover who was difficult to work with as opposed to a therapy-hater.

I received a referral from a colleague who was the CEO of a large health service. She felt my direct approach might be needed to assist Olga, her personal assistant, who had been experiencing marital difficulties. To put it simply, my colleague felt that David, Olga's husband, was insensitive and overbearing.

I agreed to see Olga and David and early in our work together I soon realised that I would need to interrupt David to simply hear Olga's account of their situation. My attempts to subtly focus my attention on David and then on Olga did not work – David simply interrupted when Olga was speaking. My attempts to gently hint at, and even my clear indication, that I needed to hear both sides of the story were ignored by David. I noticed I was orienting my chair so that I was facing Olga slightly more directly which meant I was subtly turning my back on David. Desperate, I knew I had to try something different as I was at serious risk of being rude and disrespectful towards David. Using the NBT approach I spoke directly to David and pointed out that I would probably need to interrupt him from time to time to hear from Olga if I was going to be helpful to them both. Inspired by strategic therapy more than NBT, I asked David to instruct me on how I should do this, but being true to NBT, I took his advice seriously. David's advice was simple, "Just tell me to shut up!"

As predicted, I soon had the opportunity to try out David's advice. I asked Olga a question, David interrupted. I took a breath and in a deadpan tone I slowly said, "David, shut up!" David stopped, sat upright in his chair, looked at me slightly shocked and retorted, "That worked didn't it." Although the work remained somewhat difficult, I no longer had to resort to indirect ways of trying to manage David's interruptions and we were all relieved that rather than reacting in an indirect but rude way in response to David's overbearing style of communication, I now had a direct and humorous way of managing it. Ged Smith (2011), a family therapist from Liverpool in England and author of *Cut the Crap: Language, Risks and Relationships in Systemic Therapy and Supervision*, points out tone is everything. My deadpan tone and slight smile allowed my unprofessional and outrageous response to David to deepen respect rather than demean my relationship with him and I imagine it greatly increased Olga's confidence in me and the potential of the therapy to help them both.

As proposed in the introductory chapter, the therapy-hater's common view of therapists is that we are pretentious psychologisers and/or warm fuzzy do-gooders who are out of touch with the common person, who use jargon to manipulate people under the guise of being friendly. The art of therapy itself may be seen as useless talk without action. In the above case example, David needed me to understand his position or just thought he knew better than me – he didn't think therapy per se was useless. My description of a therapy-hater's view of therapy is not scientific, it is not evidence based, nor has it been validated. It has however, resonated with many health practitioners and professionals attending my NBT workshops and who work with clients who are suspicious of traditional therapeutic approaches. Many of these practitioners have developed practical and effective ways to work with these hard-to-engage clients but feel guilty and frustrated about the lack of theoretical or conceptual validation of their work. Simone, for example, had over 25 years of experience helping prisoners adjust to life outside prison. She found that being forthright, direct, and unambiguously clear about her role and her intentions led to greater trust and effectiveness with her clients. But Simone did not talk about her approach because she worried it would be criticised and seen as *unprofessional*.

Often practitioners like Simone worry that their effective approaches are not valid or ethical. One of the more common responses to the NBT workshops is that the model validates approaches that these "closet NBT practitioners" have developed and found effective. This was particularly the case in the 15 workshops I conducted around country Victoria during 2007 as part of my PhD study supporting general counsellors who were working with rural clients impacted at the time by a severe and persistent drought.

Engagement: How is it different with therapy-haters?

Therapeutic engagement is dependent on specific clients, practitioners, and contexts. However, one general theme is that therapy-haters do not afford workers the luxury of time. If the worker is unable to either elicit the therapy-hater's personal wishes, provide a genuine rationale of how the work will help, or acknowledge the difficulties they personally experience upfront, the worker is likely to be dismissed quickly, either with overt anger or covertly with distant politeness. Therapy-lovers on the other hand will allow time for the working relationship to develop and will typically help the worker move closer and closer towards what they want.

Further exploration of the differences between engaging therapy-lovers and therapy-haters reveals that therapy-haters typically respond better if the therapist makes overt the difficulties inherent in the context of the work, putting any suspicions, doubts, and uncertainties about the work *on the table* upfront. In fact, as one winner of a competition to create a *bumper sticker* describing the essence of NBT in one of our early workshops put it, *I (therapist) will be upfront if you (client) front up!*

There are usually good reasons why therapy-haters are suspicious of therapy and therapists. Common reasons include when a client has been told to attend therapy by their partner in order to save their marriage, called *partner mandated therapy* by my friend and colleague Shane Weir; an estranged parent, like Gary, whom you met in Chapters 1 and 3, who wants to have contact with his/her children and expects attending therapy may help their cause; when meeting with the therapist is seen as a way of getting the law or parents off the client's back; when therapy is seen as hurdle requirement to receiving an entitlement; or an opportunity to secure a supportive response in court. Acknowledging the constraints to an open working relationship created by situations like these, in an upfront business-like manner, can reduce the opportunity for misunderstanding and can avoid the trap of *sugar coating* the difficulty of the task at hand.

Preparing to be upfront about the complexities and constraints to the work, by declaring that you prefer to work in an honest and direct way, is often effective. Declaring unilaterally how you like to work might contravene contemporary collaborative practices, but a unilateral declaration inherently acknowledges that the therapist does not have an established contract with the therapy-hater to commence any work. In the early stages of engagement, it is a mistake to assume that the therapy-hater even wants to be involved in collaborating about how the work should proceed. Even a collaborative discussion about the process of therapy or what to work on assumes an interest in working together.

A unilateral declaration of how the therapist would prefer to proceed allows the therapy-hater to see what they might be entering into and makes no assumption that therapy is needed, although a clear and direct business-like rationale of how therapy could help the therapy-hater get what they want is often effective. It is more effective to articulate a clear, simple, and direct account of how the work could benefit the therapy-hater's goals than to seek collaboration. Even the therapy-hater's goals might have to be elicited carefully and sometimes rhetorically, without assuming cooperation, collaboration, or clienthood. A rhetorical account of the process and potential value of the work makes no assumption, nor should it, that the therapy-hater will accept what is on offer, wants to be helped, or accepts the identity of being a client.

A clear and direct rationale and rhetorical unilateral description of how the work will proceed also helps make overt the rules of the therapeutic endeavour or the *rules of the game* and allows the therapy-hater to consider if they want to join *the game*. The *game* analogy came to me after conducting many NBT workshops. Like anyone who is invited to play a board game without being told the rules, therapy-haters who are not familiar with the rules of therapy are likely to give up or be disruptive due to feeling out of their depth, feeling they are not very good at *the game* and not sure *how to win*. In fact, therapy-haters often feel therapy is a game that they cannot win, given the therapist is an expert at the game and they are inexperienced and unfamiliar with the rules. Like learning a new board game, we are all likely to benefit from an acknowledgement that we are new to the game and being provided with a clear, logical, and specific outline of the rules along with some hints about strategies to enhance the possibility of winning. By winning, I mean the therapy-hater getting what they want from therapy. The therapy-hater may need to give something they don't want to give to get what they want, but like all of us, therapy-haters are usually prepared to give something to gain something important.

Harry Frankfurt (2005) argues that:

> the bullshitter may not deceive us, or even intend to do so, either about the facts or about what he takes the facts to be. What he does necessarily attempt to deceive us about is his enterprise. His only indispensably distinctive characteristic is that in a certain way he misrepresents what he is up to. (p. 54)

NBT attempts to be transparent about the enterprise of therapy. This is important in general, but particularly for therapy-haters, because as my colleague and a former director of The Bouverie Centre, Colin Riess points out, therapy is a socially ambiguous activity. Unless clients are well informed or acculturated to therapy, they are unlikely to know for example, whether they are expected to *spill their guts*; can influence what is talked about or more importantly how it is talked about; whether they are permitted to disagree with the therapist or ask about the therapist's family, religion, sexuality, drug taking experience, or parenting successes and failures. It may seem a fine and somewhat abstract point but the ambiguity of this last simple rule (can the client ask about the therapist's personal situation) is exemplified by the observation that most psychiatrists and mental health practitioners do not display personal family photos on their desks whilst many general medical practitioners do.

Given that the ambiguity and nuance of the therapeutic enterprise is confounding or potentially threatening for male or female therapy-haters, providing very specific details of what to expect, as suggested by David Wexler (2013), is a respectful and empowering act:

> Many men (read: therapy-haters) are simply confused and anxious about the strange, mysterious, and – for all they know – occult process of therapy. They worry about what they're supposed to say, worry about what might be expected of them, and worry about when, how, or if they should disclose anything too 'personal'. This is uncharted territory, and they want very specific information and instructions – a kind of user's manual – about just what is going to happen to them, how they should behave, and what exactly this strange 'therapist' person intends to do with them. I understand this because I feel exactly the same way in new and unfamiliar situations. (pp. 20–21)

If the unilateral explanation is accepted by the therapy-hater and the rules of the game are understood, the therapist can cautiously move from being rhetorical to more collaborative, from businesslike to more social and from focusing on the hot spots to a more collaborative therapeutic discussion and problem solving – although the therapist is likely to need to negotiate and to make overt each of these moves. The general approach to engaging therapy-lovers is the reverse. With a therapy-lover, the therapist starts where they want to finish, collaborating on what to work on, how to work on it and on solving problems, using a balance of business and social interactions. In summary, the approach to engaging therapy-haters is almost the opposite of the approach to engaging therapy-lovers.

In line with common practice, the early stages of work with therapy-lovers begins with engaging socially, to put the client at ease and to build a comfortable relationship from which to commence the therapeutic work. In fact, the warmth of this social engagement is often therapeutic. Therapy-haters, however, are very suspicious of therapists being nice, seeing it as a manipulative effort to engage them in work they have no understanding of and no interest in participating in. The reasons that force a therapy-hater to therapy are usually not nice at all; a failing marriage, a drug or drinking problem, violence, neglect, or some other shameful experience of failure. Shame is typically easier to manage if workers are upfront and direct about the business at hand. Therapy-haters prefer that workers don't minimise difficulties or obfuscate with social chatter, touchy-feely indirect rhetoric, or therapeutic jargon. It is not easy for some workers in the helping professions to make overt the constraints to the work or to *cut-to-the-chase* and address sensitive, contentious issues early on without a solid personal foundational relationship from which to launch these difficult conversations. On the other hand, experienced professionals working in areas such as protective services, jails, unemployment support services, and schools are often very comfortable working with people who don't want to be there and are typically skilled with what I am recommending for therapy-haters.

There is no need to draw too heavily on the NBT Clinical Guidelines in the early stages of working with therapy-lovers, other than the principles of respect and authenticity that underlie all therapeutic endeavours. Working with therapy-lovers, beginning with personal experiences, commonalities, and friendly chatter can help build a comfortable and effective working relationship which can provide the foundation for addressing sensitive or contentious issues later in the work. NBT practices can make a valuable contribution to work with therapy-lovers down the track, when the therapist might find it difficult, because of the comfortable working relationship they have built with the client, to raise sensitive issues that might be embarrassing or shameful. Ironically, there are certain constraints, such as reputations to protect in close relationships, that are less impactful in more distant relationships. Consider the freedom to share intimate information that you might not share with a friend or family member when sitting next to a stranger on a long flight (where there is no ongoing reputation to protect).

NBT work with therapy-lovers relies heavily on Single Session Therapy techniques, as will be seen in Chapter 6. At this point, it is enough to emphasise that NBT is used differently and at different developmental stages of therapy for clients at each end of the therapy loving and hating continuum.

However, over time, I've begun to use NBT principles more and more from the start of any work encounter. For example, when I was asked to fill in facilitating a family therapy clinical supervision group for a colleague, I established a context from the get-go that invited and valued mutual honesty and directness. The supervision group consisted of four masters' students who take turns to see families from their own workplace in front of their student colleagues, who act as a reflecting team, commenting on the session. The previous week the supervision group had seen a family where the 15-year-old daughter revealed she had a suicide plan but would not share it. Her parents and the trainee therapist were shaken and desperate to know how best to respond to this information. Because of the seriousness of the situation, the lecturer had taken charge, potentially undermining the trainee therapist. Although there were different points of view in the student group about how to proceed, there was no time for debriefing because the session ran over time.

I knew from a briefing I had received from the regular lecturer that the student differences were largely around whether the suicidal young girl should be sent to hospital or not. The agenda for the four-hour session was relatively clear but very full – introduce myself to the group and the group to me, debrief about the emotionally taxing family session the previous week, prepare for the new family the group was scheduled to see, complete the session with the new family, and debrief about the session. After introductions, I asked what each student wanted to discuss about the previous week's session. The trainees' responses included an update of what had happened since the last session, the protocols for making group decisions about treatment and a discussion about whether the 15-year-old should have been taken to hospital. Rather than start with the least contentious issue and work up to exploring the group differences about whether the 15-year-old should have been taken to hospital or not, I suggested to the group we take an NBT approach and start with the most contentious issue – the group differences. I argued that this would quickly build a culture of openness and diversity in this relatively new group which would be helpful when discussing the other issues. The group accepted my rationale and using the NBT Clinical Guidelines began respectfully but directly discussing their differences, with a meta-acknowledgement that in enacting the guidelines we were contributing to the formation of a group culture of talking specifically, openly, and directly, married up with warmth and care. Starting with the more contentious difficulties created a feeling of robustness in the group, and sharing the NBT guidelines at the start of the group helped create a sense of safety when having the sensitive discussion.

Whilst created for therapy-haters, I am finding the clinical guidelines underlying NBT increasingly attractive to therapy-lovers. I believe that the therapeutic field can be enriched by practice wisdom elicited from therapy-haters. Given that most models of therapy have been designed for therapy-lovers, by therapy-lovers, therapy has been designed for people who voluntarily seek it out. For example, health professionals are more likely to seek out psychotherapy than other professions and trades (Scott & Howk, 1986). Wisdoms gained from understanding what therapy-haters need might help evolve therapies to become more aligned to working class people, men's ways of helping, and with language of colloquial Australia. Culturally, Australians like to think of themselves as direct, unpretentious, and egalitarian. This is reflected in Australian idiom; *if you've got something to say, say it. End of story; Don't get ahead of yourself; Don't put on your airs and graces.* When I graduated with a PhD, the staff helping students gown up all loved the title of my thesis. It had the effect of breaking through the routine humdrum of their task and later, on stage, the stiffness of the formal graduation ceremony. When the Deputy Dean of Health Sciences read out the title of my PhD in front of 500 guests, she prefaced the title with, *I can't believe I am going to say this at a graduation – Dr Young's thesis was entitled* "A no bullshit approach to counselling drought affected rural communities." I received my award with thunderous laughter and applause which, I think, reflects NBT's ability to create a more relaxed mood in professional settings. It is more than a glib colloquial title; it represents a powerful philosophy of striving towards authenticity and *real* relationships in contexts more often associated with fear, tension, and conflict. The model is simple and yet its impact can be profound. In the following chapter, I will explore the clinical guidelines of NBT in greater detail and focus on how to put them into practice with therapy-haters.

References

Baekeland, F., & Lundwall, L. (1975). Dropping out of treatment: A critical review. Psychological Bulletin, 82(5), 738–783.

De Jong, P., & Berg, I.K. (2001). Co-constructing cooperation with mandated clients. *Social Workers, 46*(4), 361–374.

de Shazer, S. (1984). The death of resistance. *Family Process*, *23*(1), 11–17.

de Shazer, S. (1988). Clues: Investigating solutions in brief therapy. Norton & Co.

Dessaix, R. (2020). *On humbug.* Hachette Australia.

Frankfurt, H.G. (2005). *On bullshit.* Princeton University Press.

Ivanhoff, A., Blythe, B.J., & Tripodi. T. (1994). *Involuntary clients in social work practice: A research-based approach.* Aldine de Gruyter.

Miller, W.R., & Rollnick, S. (1991). *Motivational interviewing: Preparing people to change addictive behavior.* Guilford Press.

Rooney, R.H. (1992*). Strategies for work with involuntary clients.* Columbia University Press.

Rooney, R.H. (2009). *Strategies for work with involuntary clients* (2nd ed.). Columbia University Press.

Scott, C.D., & Hawk, J. (1986). *Heal thyself: The health of health-care professionals.* Brunner/Mazel.

Smith, G. (2011). Cut the crap: Language, risks and relationships in systemic therapy and supervision. *Australian and New Zealand Journal of Family Therapy*, *32*(1), 58–69.

Talmon, M. (1990). *Single-session therapy: Maximizing the effect of the first (and often Only) therapeutic encounter.* Jossey-Bass.

Wexler, D. (2013). Shame-o-phobia: Why men fear therapy. *Psychotherapy in Australia*, *20*(1), 18–23.

5 No Bullshit Therapy clinical guidelines: Practice notes for working with therapy-haters

> I was delighted to discover your name and the short-course at La Trobe, when I typed "no bullshit therapy" into my internet browser. My partner … (has) had a bad run with psychologists in the past, falls firmly into the "cynical, suspicious and unsure" category of potential patients – he deplores the use of corporate pop-psychology terms being used at all, not least within a therapeutic context. "Journey", "moving-forward", "holistic" etc are all trigger words, as is the phrase, "Trigger words".
>
> — (Email wanting referrals for no bullshit therapists, February 2023)

In the introduction, I pointed out that whilst the clinical guidelines of No Bullshit Therapy (NBT) are simple and can be used quite quickly, they are not simplistic and can take time to put artfully, creatively, and consistently into practice. I encourage you, the reader, to see these guidelines as a starting point for creating your own NBT style that will allow you to engage authentically with the clients you find most difficult, whatever your context.

Designed to create contexts for mutual honesty and directness in working relationships, the four NBT Clinical Guidelines are:

1 Establish a mandate
2 Marry honesty and directness with warmth and care
3 Be upfront about constraints
4 Avoid jargon

The NBT guidelines are interrelated, each contributes to the development of the other, and ultimately, to the creation of contexts that invite mutual honesty and directness. I have only separated them out for the purposes of clarity. As pointed out in the previous chapter, NBT is used differently and at different times depending on whether you are working with therapy-lovers (Chapter 6) or therapy-haters (this chapter); hence, I have incorporated practice notes for the translation of each guideline into clinical work with clients representing these two extremes. It is largely up to you the reader to struggle with applying them to clients who fall, as the majority will, along the continuum between extreme therapy-haters and extreme therapy-lovers. Whilst a wide range of clinical examples help bring the guidelines to life,

DOI: 10.4324/9781003354925-5

I again encourage you to find your own personal NBT voice, and to adapt the guidelines to fit your context of work.

Creating a context to promote mutual honesty and directness with therapy-haters

Creating a context for mutuality is key. It is easier to be open and honest with some people and not so easy with others. We also experience some contexts where it seems easy to share our thoughts openly and honestly and other contexts where it feels unsafe, unwise, and seemingly impossible. For example, Rochford, a car salesman I know, pointed out that *law abiding honest folk lie like you wouldn't believe when buying a car.* Culturally, some professional disciplines are hierarchical, where experts have the option of honesty and directness, yet people further down the food chain are not afforded this option. Other disciplines make a feature of discussion, collaboration, and mutuality, but maybe not of directness. Some workplaces invite directness, others passively propagate an atmosphere where few people feel safe to be honest and direct.

Whilst organisational culture is an important determinant, over time, individuals can develop a reputation either as someone who is a straight talker or someone who is not. As one of our early NBT workshop participants who worked in domestic violence pointed out, *How can we expect our clients to open up if we don't?*

As my association with NBT grows so does the inherent invitation from colleagues for me to be upfront with them. Recently, I provided a consultation to a national professional body which was having some growing pains as it expanded from a state to a national association. I received a phone call from one of the key members of this association who asked me to comment on a particularly tense meeting that we had both attended. As I began to create a context for straight talking, my colleague beat me to it and said, Jeff *No Bullshit, tell me what you think straight up.* My reputation helped create the context for me to be honest and direct and I just had to behave in a way that was congruent with my reputation.

Clinically, client desperation, pain, suffering, or a relationship hitting rock bottom can also provide a natural context for honesty and directness – if workers are able to validate, acknowledge, and hold the desperation. I often ask how bad things have got as a way of understanding the severity of a client's difficulties. Understanding the severity of a client's lowest point can provide a context that invites greater honesty and directness, to address the desperate situation. People are less likely to change if they don't have to. For example, having identified that Bob's wife Denise was about to leave him due to his gambling, I was able to say, *Given things have gotten so bad and that Denise is threatening to leave you, I want to help but I will need to be pretty upfront about what you need to do if you're going to have any chance at all of saving your marriage. Are you up for that?*

Dr Brad Blanton, author of *Radical Honesty*, points out that:

When we reveal more, we have less to hide. When we have less to hide, we are less worried about being found out. When we are less worried about being found out, we can pay better attention to someone else. In this way, telling the truth makes intimacy and freedom possible.

(Blanton, 2003, p. 80)

Another advantage of revealing more, especially with clients who are suspicious of the practitioner's motives, is that there is less for the client to try and uncover, thus allowing the client to focus more on what is being said, rather than trawling for threat and speculating what hasn't been said.

Workers regularly confront the dilemma of how honest and direct to be with clients and this dilemma is often more challenging when the stakes are high as they often are with therapy-haters. Engaging therapy-haters is complex and the most helpful way forward is seldom obvious. Does the practitioner push for change, whether it is asking a difficult question, challenging the client's behaviour, broaching an unpopular or sensitive topic, suggesting an unwanted way forward, or discussing the working relationship itself? Do you attempt to preserve the status quo by softening your responses, minimising, or avoiding difficulties, obfuscating the contentious, minimising sensitivities, telling a white lie, or by using silence. There are no simple answers! On any given day or any given circumstance, each of these approaches might be a viable way forward. One way of trying to circumvent dilemmas like this is to focus on creating a context that privileges MUTUAL honesty and directness. Pushing a client to be honest and direct unilaterally is likely to have the opposite effect; as Michael Hoyt, author of *Brief Therapy and Beyond: Stories, Language, Love, Hope and Time*, warns, "Insistence produces resistance, imposition produces opposition, push produces pushback" (Hoyt, 2017, p. 296).

If a context is conducive, honesty and directness will be a logical outcome, beneficial and rewarding for everyone involved. Creating such a context, especially for work with therapy-haters, requires the therapist to actively demonstrate honesty and directness themselves. Creating a context for mutual honesty and directness often requires an appreciation of the client's history, including the client's experience of institutions, services, and therapists, the real and perceived power relationship between all of these, and the usual variables of organisational context, presenting problems, and personalities (yours and the client's). Creating a context to invite honesty and directness will be very different depending on your relative and perceived position, including your socio-political status in relation to your client and hence the following ideas are presented here, not as definitive statements, but as ideas to stimulate further reflection, thought, and discussion.

Whilst the navigation of each guideline will depend on whether your client is a therapy-lover or therapy-hater, one general point can be made: you need to display genuineness and a consistency between your stated wishes and how you act, especially as things get difficult. There needs to be a synergy and consistency between one's espoused and enacted values (Argyris & Schön, 1974). Let's begin exploring my practice tips for enacting the NBT Clinical Guidelines when working with therapy-haters.

Establish a mandate: How to work, what to work on

Lying is done with words and also with silence.

– Adrienne Rich (1995, p. 413)

So how do you talk honestly and directly without opening an ugly can of worms or raising a therapy-hater's defensiveness? Well, first you need to establish a mandate to do any work at all (how to work, what to work on and in fact whether to work on anything at all). Therapy-lovers will give it quickly and generously, often implicitly because they have a stronger sense of agency, given that they, generally speaking, have sought out your service. Therapy-haters on the hand have usually been coerced into attending and hence, it is both respectful and realistic to assume that a therapy-hater will not personally, or automatically, give you a mandate to work with them – it is something that needs to be established gradually, layer-by-layer, step-by-step.

Negotiating how to work

One of the easier mandates to establish with therapy-haters is an agreement to conduct the work in an honest and direct way (how to work). Stating that this is the way you like to work is usually received well, typically leads to greater trust, and may be a new experience for the therapy-hater. Once stated that this is how you like to work you need to be true to your word by, for example, being upfront about what you can do and what you can't or won't do, being clear about any reporting requirements, and how your service operates.

Getting an explicit agreement to conduct the session in an honest and direct way also creates an opportunity to draw on this agreement later in the work when the therapist needs to raise a difficult or sensitive issue. Prefacing a difficult question by asking a rhetorical question like, *Remember I said I'd be really upfront and honest with you, well? Can I be direct with you? Can I ask you a really tough question?* This is called *Signposting* because it is not really asking permission – the question, *can I be direct with you* is rhetorical, it acts like a marker. It says, *hold on what I'm about to say might be hard to hear, so get ready. Put your defences in place, so you can hear what I have to say.* Forewarned is forearmed. A similar approach can be used after a sharing something tough for a client to hear, for example, *I told you I'd be upfront!*

There are, however, inherent paradoxes in creating a context for mutual honesty and directness. Working in a mutually honest and direct way often needs to be introduced to the therapy-hater unilaterally by the therapist. The therapist needs to provide a strong rationale for why it is in the best interests of the client to work in this way, whilst at the same time accepting that the therapy-hater may decide to not work in this way or in any way at all. A key task of a No Bullshit Therapist is to convey the potential advantage of mutual honesty and directness. In the case of therapy-haters, this must primarily be about the work and the client's goal. Emphasis on the mutual, not a one-way honesty and directness, is particularly important for therapy-haters – even if the idea of mutual honesty and directness is introduced unilaterally.

Simply explaining that, as a professional, you prefer to work in an honest and upfront way is surprisingly effective and has significant benefits for the work. It is not necessary to use the term *No Bullshit Therapy*; however, the term has some power to break through strong negative perceptions therapy-haters may hold about therapy and therapists.

As pointed out in Chapter 3, I have found that in the very early stages of work with extreme therapy-haters, talking in unilateral terms rather than in collaborative terms, essentially describing *how I like to work,* is effective. This initial unilateral approach is more respectful than assuming the client wants a service, wants to engage in a collaborative working relationship, or even is willing to engage in a collaborative discussion about the work. In extreme situations, I will say that I practice NBT, which usually gets a reaction of surprise and often palpable relief. I then go on to explain that I will be honest and direct and that I will invite, but depending on the context may not expect, the client to be equally honest and direct with me. For people who are very suspicious of therapy, this can be a breath of fresh air and can create a context for productive straight talking – especially if combined with judicious amounts of warmth and care and an acknowledgement of constraints to the work. I have found that the therapy-hater's most common response to my explanation of what I mean by NBT is, *That's exactly the way I like it.*

Negotiating levels of honesty and directness in an overt, formal, and clear way can help transform a vexed working relationship into an effective working one. A starting point is to recognise, acknowledge, and accept that you usually don't have an agreement to work together. The negotiation therefore must start without an expectation that a working relationship exists or will continue. Hence, initially establishing the level of honesty and directness is not really a negotiation, but an explanation, a rhetorical explanation as discussed earlier, about how you as a professional prefer to work.

It is important to take every opportunity to negotiate a mandate for honesty and directness. Sometimes the opportunity begins with a therapy-hater's overly critical, dismissive, or angry response to you or the therapy. For example, a simple negotiation might look like:

Therapy-hater:	This is all shit!
NBT Practitioner:	Good on you for being so upfront, that's the way I like to work too.

Embracing, acknowledging, and accepting a therapy-hater's view as a starting point for gaining a mandate for mutual honesty and directness is a great stance to adopt. A client can't resist if you don't give them anything to resist. Although that sounds strategic, it is just a fact.

Once an agreement for mutual honesty and directness has been established with therapy-haters, an early task is to use this agreement to make overt the context of the relationship (this will be discussed further under making a feature of a constraint). As mentioned already, taking a non-emotional, non-judgemental, matter-of-fact business-like approach tends to work best with therapy-haters. Making overt the context may include acknowledging that the client did not choose to attend and has been mandated or *pressured* to attend the session by someone else or by your institution or some other institution. Acknowledging that the therapy-hater did not want to attend softens the need for them to demonstrate their lack of enthusiasm for the work and can begin to create some confidence in the therapist. Acknowledging the difficult context may be the first thing to do. It will demonstrate your capacity to be fearlessly honest and direct.

Sometimes, mutual honesty and directness is not possible or wise. An NBT workshop participant working in an organisation that assessed unemployed people's eligibility for funding support found an innovative way of overcoming organisational constraints to negotiating high levels of mutual honesty and directness. She would say to her clients, *[My organisation] does not reward honesty and directness, so I don't expect you to be honest with me, but I will attempt to be as honest and direct as I can be with you.*

Negotiating what to work on

Having an agreement to be honest and direct provides the wherewithal to begin to establish a mandate about what to work on – this is not so easy. A challenging but important task is to seek *motivational congruence.* As far back as the 1990s, Ronald Rooney (1992) and André Ivanhoff and her colleagues (1994) pointed out the need to create a fit between what the client wants, and what you and your service can provide. Put simply, people, but especially therapy-haters, are motivated to achieve what is important to them, not what's important to you or referrers. Therefore, it is essential to identify the therapy-hater's goals and link your work directly to achieving their goals. Scott Miller and his colleagues' research (e.g., see Miller et al., 2010) found that successful client-therapist relationships require a mutually agreed goal, agreement about what is being talked about, as defined by the client and genuineness and unconditional positive regard shown by the therapist.

In the absence of client investment in exploring anything, a practical tip is to utilise the referrer's investment in the therapy-hater attending and gradually find a link between the referrer's goal or problem definition (external pressure) and the client's goals or problem definition (internal pressure). In essence, explore, with permission, why the referrer has pressured the therapy-hater to attend, without siding with the referrer, and gradually explore if the therapy-hater shares any of these concerns (illustrated later).

Another practical tip I've found surprisingly helpful is to not be overly invested in the relationship continuing. Being prepared to forgo the working relationship is powerfully engaging to therapy-haters if a little unsettling for a therapy loving helping professional like myself. Adopting the stance and possibly stating that *I don't want to waste your time and to be honest I don't want to waste my time* is counter cultural for many therapists but paradoxically allows therapy-haters to engage with the work on their own terms. I have learnt the power of this approach repeatedly via role-plays conducted with participants playing the role of therapy-haters in our workshops. I make no apologies for using role-play examples, as it is difficult to get feedback from therapy-haters in real time about the effectiveness of the NBT approach because they are not usually inclined to fill out research surveys or evaluation questionnaires early in the work. The participants of a recent NBT workshop created Sam, a fictitious client, and I role-played an Alcohol and Other Drugs (AOD) counsellor. I was out of the room when the participants created Sam's story, which was based on the workshop participants' collective experiences with therapy-haters.

Sam is a 28-year-old man mandated to see me, (an AOD counsellor) because he has been charged with assaulting a police officer, resisting arrest, and using speed. Sam does not think he has done anything wrong – the police officer was aggressive, and Sam reports that he has simply popped a pill for a bit of fun. Sam expects to attend counselling, tick the box with his community corrections officer, and return to his usual life. He is clear he doesn't have any problems and certainly doesn't need therapy. I ask questions and make comments that utilise the energy from the referrer, given Sam doesn't have any investment in exploring anything himself.

Jeff: Hi I'm Jeff Young, I'm the counsellor who will be seeing you today.
Sam: I don't need counselling.
Jeff: You're not keen to be here.
Sam: No.
Jeff: I understand that you have to see me.
Sam: Yeah, but I don't know what I'm doing here.
Jeff: Let me tell you how I like to work. I practice what I call No Bullshit Therapy.
Sam: Oh yeah!
Jeff: Which means I'm going to be as straight as I can be with you. You seem to talk straight too.
Sam: I don't want to waste your time.
Jeff: Great, I certainly don't want to waste your time and to be honest I don't want to waste my time either. I said I'll be upfront with you. I know from your community corrections officer that you assaulted police, resisted arrest, and tested positive to speed so you're potentially in a serious situation. [external pressure]
Sam: What's the problem with just popping a pill – I was just having some fun. I was just walking, minding my own business when the cops asked us for ID and then got a bit pushy and I may have said something, but I didn't do anything wrong.
Jeff: I know you don't want to be here but given you are here is there anything you would you want to get out of it?
Sam: I haven't got any problems.
Jeff: I said I'd talk straight so if you don't want to work with me that's fine, but I will need to let your community corrections' officer know [external pressure]. Sometimes things can build up and can lead to these things. I'm happy to talk about what's important to you but I said I'd be honest. I'm not prepared to just tick the box. That would be a waste of your time and mine.
Sam: But I haven't got any problems.

Jeff:	Can I ask then why you think your corrections officer thought you should see me? Understanding what they are concerned about might help me help you get them off your back or maybe more supportive. I'm not necessarily going to agree with them (corrections officer).
Sam:	I don't know. Maybe they thought I needed to get some support.
Jeff:	Use to having to look after yourself, hey.
Sam:	Yeah, who else will?
Jeff:	What if I ask you some questions and you can decide to talk about it or not. But I'm a therapist and so I'm pretty nosey. Is that ok? I'll let you know if I think anything might be helpful to you. I know you're used to doing everything yourself, but maybe some support could help you get through this. But I'm also happy to just let your community corrections officer know that you didn't want to talk to me.
Sam:	Yeah, that's alright.
Jeff:	So, are you in a relationship?
Sam:	Nah.
Jeff:	Who's in your family?
Sam:	Parents and a brother.
Jeff:	I could talk about all the good things with your family but what's the worst thing? I told you I'd wouldn't waste your time.
Sam:	Dad gets pretty aggro (aggressive) at times [internal pressure].
Jeff:	Can I ask a bit more about your dad? I'm happy not to.
Sam:	Yeah, I guess.
Jeff:	What would your dad say about your current situation? [internal pressure]
Sam:	He wouldn't care but he'd think I was a dickhead.
Jeff:	Have you got anyone who is in your corner? Anyone helping you with the police? [starting to link the external and internal pressure]

Explaining the process of therapy and the "rules" of the encounter provides clarity for people who approach therapy with bad faith and don't see themselves as clients and certainly don't share the referrer's definition of their problems. During the debrief about the role-play, the workshop participant Andrew, who played Sam, reported that he had wanted to be more disruptive but couldn't because I had been clear about the process of the therapy, I had accepted that he didn't want to be there and that I was not invested in us working together. Andrew, who works in an AOD service with mandated clients who, like Sam, are very reluctant to engage in any real work, confided that he would try to join with the client against the community corrections officer and agree just to talk about anything hoping something useful would happen. Role-playing Sam, he realised that it was more effective to be very upfront and clear about the vexed context and to push for a useful outcome, whilst accepting that the client had the power to not co-operate. As Sam, Andrew found my genuine offer to work or equally not to work with him very powerful.

What helps me to adopt an *I can take it or leave it* stance is to realise that this is the reality. I no longer adopt it as a therapeutic strategy – but as naming the situation as it is. I acknowledge and accept that realistically I can only be as helpful as a client will let me. But I need to give them the best chance I can to see how they might benefit from the work. Ironically being non-attached to whether the therapy-hater engages or not allows me to state my personal and/or professional hopes and dreams for both the work and for the client, more directly because I make it clear that they are my hopes and dreams and not necessarily the client's. This helps the client understand that the relationship will only continue if they allow it to, and this is more likely to occur if they can see that the working relationship is likely to be beneficial to them. A clear and convincing rationale must therefore be put forward by the therapist, in a way that acknowledges the difficulties of the task and in a way that is understood and accepted by the client.

An important warning for the NBT therapist here is not to commit to anything that you cannot stay true to or deliver throughout the work. Don't fall into the trap of avoiding, underestimating, or obfuscating what you as a therapist will need to do at some stage in the work, to help the person, achieve their goals. In fact, a skilful NBT practitioner makes a feature of overtly naming the challenges to the work, including anything unpopular a therapist may need to do later in the therapeutic contract, such as notifying authorities if the client is not prepared to do any *real work* as was the case, initially, with Sam.

Many mandated clients do want something from therapy, it is just difficult for therapists to provide them with what they want. For example, if a partner mandated therapy-hater wants to save his marriage, the therapist may provide a convincing rationale by pointing out that *doing some real work rather than just showing up is more likely to save his marriage.* In doing so, the NBT therapist must not under-estimate the difficulty of what will be involved to make that goal possible. For example, emphasising, *I will need to ask some pretty direct questions and ask about some really tough things if I am going to have any hope of helping you to save your marriage.* The NBT therapist also knows the power of being specific rather than general in these warnings. If the situation demands it, *I will need to talk directly about your wife's fear for her safety if I'm going to be any use to you* is more powerful than simply saying, *I may need to ask some tough questions,* but timing and clinical judgement are crucial here.

What helps me to be both bold and specific in these situations is to remind myself that whilst trust often increases by being nice to therapy-lovers, the opposite is true for therapy-haters. A therapy-hater's starting position of bad faith means that vague niceness raises suspicion and causes the therapy-hater's internal bullshit meter to increase in sensitivity. Specifics are harder to misinterpret than generalities, as Gary in Chapter 3 told us. In the eyes of the therapy-hater, generalities provide room for a manipulative therapist to hide their real intentions!

Partner mandated therapy is one of the most common vexed scenarios raised by participants in our NBT workshops. Aryan agreed to play a therapy-hater called Tom. Tom did not want to attend therapy but was worried his relationship may be over if he didn't – that's what his wife had warned. Having been out of the room when the workshop participants had created Tom's scenario, again from actual therapy-haters they collectively found difficult to manage, I only knew that Tom wasn't keen to see me.

Jeff: Hi, I'm Jeff, I'm the therapist who will be seeing you today.

Tom: G'day. (*not looking too enthusiastic*)

Jeff: Were you keen to come today?

Tom: Not really.

Jeff: So, I know you aren't that keen to be here but is there any way I could be useful to you at all today?

Tom: I'm not sure you can be – my wife thought I should come.

Jeff: But you didn't have to come – how come you decided to turn up anyway?

Tom: Well, we are having a few problems at the moment, she's just a bit stressed and always complaining.

Jeff: The way I like to work is to be pretty upfront and direct.

Tom: Yeah, that's fine by me.

Jeff: Can I ask what your wife's name is?

Tom: Mandy.

Jeff: I said I like to be pretty direct so can I ask you straight up; do you want things to be better between you and Mandy?

Tom: Don't know.

Jeff: I know you're not so keen on being here, so I don't want to waste your time and to be honest I don't want to waste my time either.

Tom: Yeah, I guess it'd be good if she didn't complain so much.

Jeff: Things must have gotten pretty bad if your wife has suggested you speak to me.

Tom: Yeah, it's not pretty at the moment – she said that if I didn't speak to someone, she'd have to think about things pretty seriously.

Jeff: I don't know you, but I get the sense that you are keen to try and save your marriage. I don't want to put words into your mouth, but have I got that right?

Tom: Yeah, you've got that pretty right.

Jeff: If I'm going to help you, I'll need to ask you why your wife thought you should come to see me. I'm not saying I'll believe her side of things, but if I'm going to help you get what you want, I need to understand her view of what's not working for her. And so do you. I told you I'd be pretty upfront, didn't I!

Tom: Yeah. She thinks I drink too much, but I just like having a drink or two with the boys.

Jeff: Do you think you drink too much?

Tom: Nah, I work hard and a drink or two on the way home isn't too much to ask for, is it?

Jeff: If I'm going to be any use to you, I'm going to have to ask some pretty direct questions. Is that ok?

Tom: Go for it, mate!

Jeff: What is it that Mandy hates most about your drinking? As I said, I'm not necessarily going to take her side, but I need to ask you about her view otherwise I won't be much use to you.

Tom: I get, I can lose my cool sometimes, nothing much, but the complaints just drive me nuts!

Jeff: Good on you for being upfront too. We won't get anywhere if we don't tackle things head on. How bad has it got, have you ever put Mandy in hospital, or hurt her?

Tom: No, I haven't put her in hospital, never.

Jeff: Have you pushed her or touched her?

Tom: Yeah, I pushed her a couple of times.

Jeff: I guess you're not too proud of that – but good on you for not bullshitting. It means I'm going to be a lot more helpful to you. How serious are you about trying to save your marriage?

Tom: I wouldn't still be talking to you if I wasn't.

Jeff: Ok, we'll need to talk more about those times when you've lost your cool, but can I ask what pressures are on you at the moment?

The excerpt from the role-play session provides one example of how I might begin to establish a context for mutual honesty and directness that allows shameful and sensitive issues to be discussed without judgement or blame. The role-play focuses on how to create a working contract that allows for Tom to be both supported and held accountable for his violent behaviour.

Having introduced NBT early in the work, established a rationale based on the client's goals, and the challenges to the work made overt, the therapist needs to obtain a mandate for the level of honesty and directness required to achieve the outcomes that the therapy-hater wants to achieve, in Tom's case to save his marriage. In vexed situations, the therapist needs to be very direct about what they need to be able to do to help the therapy-hater with their goal. Again, what helps me to articulate what needs to be talked about and what doesn't is to ask myself *Realistically, what do I need from the client for me to be able to help them get what they want?* Therapists are unlikely to be effective if they are left with the responsibility but not the power to address a client's wishes.

Because the therapy-hater does not understand the rules of therapy, it can be very helpful to explicitly explain the rules as you enact them, rather than just proceed as you would with a therapy-lover. For example, I explained to Tom that I had to ask about his wife's views, if I was going to help him save his marriage. I also explained that by asking about his wife's views, I was not necessarily agreeing with her. It was just logical that if Tom wanted me to help him save his marriage, I needed to understand his wife's concerns, and so did he. Explaining the rules of the encounter, as therapy unfolds, helped Tom understand where I was heading with my questioning and why I was asking such intrusive questions, which provided him with a sense of safety and over time, trust. Having created this context, I was gradually able to explore what pressure Tom was under whilst not excusing his violence. Debriefing from playing Tom, Aryan reported that the explicit commentary of what I was doing and why, helped Tom feel safer in engaging with a real conversation about his situation, although he remained somewhat cautious and cynical.

To get a mandate or agreement in principle to address the areas that are realistically required to achieve the therapy-hater's goals, the NBT therapist may need to be prepared to call it quits if a workable agreement is not possible. I have had some success in pointing out (after taking a deep breath) that I will get paid whether I work with a client or not – but I also provide a clear description of what would be required and a heartfelt but realistic rationale of the benefits for the therapy-hater of doing the hard work.

Ironically since exploring NBT I have concluded that honesty is not always the best policy and that you need a good reason and a mandate for honesty or directness, in the therapeutic relationship. NBT is not *off-the-cuff honesty* (you retain a duty of care), it is not *honesty at any cost* (as Dr Brad Blanton's radical honesty movement would have it), it is not *provocative therapy* (Dr Frank Farrelly's therapeutic model, see Farrelly & Brandsma, 1974), it is not *unilateral honesty and directness* (Dr Phil), and it should not be condescending or patronising – it should be simply a realistic approach required to address the negotiated purpose of the therapeutic encounter.

If you state that you prefer to work in an honest and direct manner, then your actions absolutely need to reflect this stated preference. A No Bullshit Therapist needs to be genuine and consistent. Put simply, saying one thing, and doing another is poisonous to trust. As a colleague of mine is fond of saying, *you cannot talk your way out of somewhere you acted your way into!* For example, you cannot advocate for mutual honesty and directness and then get defensive or overly compliant when a client is questioning or critical of the therapy or you. Your capacity to accept and respond to client honesty and directness can be a test of your word and of your capacity to practice what you preach.

Once the level of honesty and directness has been mutually agreed, trust is built by being true to this agreement in attitude, language, behaviour, emotion, and non-verbals. As argued by Virginia Satir (1972) so many years ago, when what we believe, what we say and how we say it are truly in alignment, we give trust an opportunity to emerge even in the most difficult of situations.

My friend and colleague Mark Furlong taught me a lot about dealing with confidentially, and many of my ideas about negotiating and monitoring honesty and directness with therapy-haters have come from this vexed area of mental health. Like confidentiality, honesty and directness should be seen as flexible and dynamic, re-visited at different times during a working contract. A drought counsellor who was part of my PhD project adjusted her approach when working with someone who was very cautious by stating, *I like to work with 100% honesty – you may not want to be so honest.* She had found that when working with families where a child is seen as the problem, the child often starts cautiously by saying they'd prefer to use 80% honesty but down the track typically agrees to 100% once sufficient trust is established. Drawing on ideas from managing confidentiality in mental health services, Furlong points out that trust is not gained by giving a person everything they want, it is built by being true to what you say you will do and what you will not do. An important element of NBT is the degree to which a therapist can instil trust. Whilst authenticity and consistency are likely to promote trust, hypocrisy will destroy it. Hence, NBT can be quite challenging for a therapist because you need to say what you mean, mean what you say, and even feel what you think. This is particularly difficult and particularly powerful in vexed and highly charged situations.

It is important to track how the client is responding to your NBT approach. Risk is a necessary component of working with clients in difficult, sensitive, and complex situations no matter what approach is used. It is often perceived that *an out there approach like NBT* requires greater risk management. Whether this is true or not, it is important to have a range of safety strategies available to provide the NBT therapist with the confidence to be bold. Various practical safety strategies are provided in Chapter 8.

Marry honesty and directness with warmth and care

It is easy to be honest and direct. It is easy to be warm and caring. What's difficult is to be both honest and direct and warm and caring.

The seamless integration of honesty and directness with warmth and care is the art or heart of NBT, but it is also the most difficult skill to articulate. I describe this skill as an art because it is so hard to operationalise in tangible, clear, or progressive steps. The most effective integration is driven by a belief in the interconnectedness of the two and is operationalised on the micro level, weaving honesty and directness with warmth and care within the one sentence or as part of the same issue. It is not the old strategy of saying something nice, then something tough, and finishing with something positive, sometimes referred to as the *shit sandwich*. Instead, moving deftly between genuine warmth and care and authentic honesty and directness, called *pat, slap, pat, slap therapy* by a colleague of mine Ross Mortimer, is an art that takes time to perfect.

Kristan Baker delivered a heartfelt speech at the 2014 Bouverie Alumni and Friends annual celebration where he credited SST and NBT as being significant influences on his personal and professional development. In a moving description of how marrying honesty and directness had informed his approach to parenting, Kristan shared his 4-year-old son's assessment of his parenting style, *I like it that you're firm, Dad. Not too grrr and not too la la.* In one of our many discussions, Moshe Talmon, who is credited with promoting SST to the world, shared with me his metaphor of the opposite forces in tai chi movements to convey the importance of holding whilst at the same time pushing clients.

In my NBT teaching, I resort to images and reflective exercises to help participants find their own ways to integrate these dimensions; integration that is true to their personality and compatible with their own therapeutic style. Some therapists, because of their demeanour, can convey great care and acknowledgement of a client's experience with small expressions of warmth whilst for others the same level of positive expression may go unnoticed. My NBT colleague and workshop co-presenter Jacqui Sundbery points out that heartfelt direct feedback from a good place is a gift, which helps provide the ethical reason for directness.

Providing critical feedback from a caring place can lead to profound personal development. I ask NBT workshop participants to recall occasions when they have received critical feedback, that resonated. Apart from the fact that it doesn't happen very often, a common theme is that they somehow knew the person giving the feedback had their best interests at heart. Giving critical feedback to clients, family members, friends, and associates requires not only to have their best interests at heart but to ensure they know you have their best interests at heart. Linking the feedback to the heart-felt positive rationale for giving it, will go a long way to the feedback being well received.

To authentically integrate honesty and directness with warmth and care I personally draw on ways of understanding the world (hermeneutics) that encourage complex rather than simple dichotomous appreciations of people and their actions. For example, the *unity of opposites* articulated, although not very clearly, by the pre-Socratic Greek philosopher, Heraclitus in the 5th Century BC, helps me to see that negative behaviour often helps make sense of more acceptable behaviour and vice versa rather than seeing these dimensions as mutually exclusive or unrelated (see Graham, 2007). I have found that often a positive intent or motive such as protection can be found at the source of a family member's negative behaviour such as criticism, frustration, or anger – and sometimes an extreme positive behaviour such as protectiveness can have an unintended negative consequence – such as conveying a lack of confidence.

A 1991 article in *Family Process* by Susan McDaniel and Judith Landau-Stanton introduced many family therapists to *both/and* thinking. Their epic article challenged the previously polarised views that *either* family-of-origin work *or* family therapy skills training was the best way to train family therapists (*either/or* thinking) and proposed *both* the use of family-of-origin work *and* family therapy skills. Since their article was published, *both/and* thinking stance has had a profound impact on clinical practice as well as the training of family therapists. A *both/and* stance allows the move from simplistic dichotomous thinking to embracing complexity. For example, a client can be both hurting and hence need support as well as needing to be held accountable for behaving badly. Therapeutic effectiveness often requires us simultaneously to hold a client and to hold the client to account; to be warm and caring whilst being honest and direct. In her pioneering work with couples who choose to remain together despite intimate partner violence, Virginia Goldner (2004) from the Ackerman Institute for the Family in New York found ways to hold men who were violent 100% responsible for their actions whilst seeking to understand their own emotional pain, such as, *In order for you to take responsibility I need to understand how you got to this point.* On a more recent visit to the Bouverie Centre, her colleague, Fiona True, built on Goldner's work pointing out that if you see a client as more than just an abuser, it can help open space for the client to empathise with others, including the target of their abuse.

I was introduced to a very powerful image for combining apparent contradictions by a workshop participant whilst delivering training in family sensitive practice to mental health workers in a rural town in the north of Australia. I was explaining to the workshop participants that in my view it is important to acknowledge carers' sense of shock, grief, and feelings of incompetence in the face of the traumatic effects of mental illness at the same time as acknowledging the family's resilience and pride in having survived these traumatic experiences. As I shared how I explore feelings of failure and pride as part of the same experience, I was

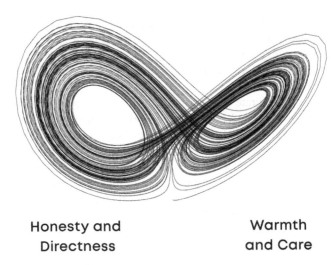

**Honesty and
Directness**

**Warmth
and Care**

Figure 5.1 The Lorenz Attractor: A metaphor for combining honesty and directness with warmth and care.

moving my hands back and forth in an image not unlike the infinity symbol. One of the workshop participants called out that I was enacting the *Lorenz Attractor* with my hands. On my return to Melbourne, I researched the Lorenz Attractor and discovered that the iconic image, (depicted in Figure 5.1), is the result of an attempt by American mathematician and meteorologist, Edward Lorenz, to use nonlinear equations to plot and predict the weather, which culminated in a 1963 paper, entitled *Deterministic Nonperiodic Flow*, a paper which provided the foundation for Chaos Theory. The plotted lines move back and forth between two foci, never repeating the exact same path, and never crossing over itself. I use the Lorenz Attractor as an image for how therapists can move between honesty and directness and warmth and care, in a seamless and beautiful way.

Like most art forms, enacting warmth and care, at the same time as honesty and directness, can be frustratingly difficult in the early stages of a therapist's NBT career, but it can also provide a life-long goal to be able to do it comfortably, effectively, and naturally.

Whilst some therapists are naturals, in my experience, the successful integration of honesty and directness with warmth and care takes time and often requires self-reflection and personal development. Being a family therapy agency, The Bouverie Centre's NBT training uses a guided imagery exercise to help workshop participants reflect on the way honesty and directness and warmth and care were viewed in the family context in which they grew up. Within the family therapy tradition, it is recognised that the views we encounter growing up can have a profound influence on our later life, including on our professional life. For example, a therapist who has grown up with a strong family injunction that *if you haven't got anything good to say about someone, say nothing or directness is rudeness or be careful, words can hurt,* may have to overcome a visceral anxiety about breaking these family-of-origin rules when needing to be direct as part of plying the NBT art. On the other hand, if a therapist has grown up with a strong family value such as *honesty is always the best policy, whether it hurts someone or not or if you can't cope with honesty, it's your problem or warmth equates to weakness,* then they may need to work harder to convey sufficient warmth and care when they are being honest and direct.

Occasionally participants in NBT workshops thump their fists on the table and proudly say, *I'm a no bullshit therapist, I tell them what I think*! This is not NBT – it's simply being rude, blunt, or even worse, aggressive. NBT can be a useful framework to help these participants improve the effectiveness of their work by developing greater warmth and care, the shadow side, in Jung's terms, of their assertive nature (e.g., see Jung, 1964). Possibly even more participants, especially therapists who only work occasionally with therapy-haters, find being honest and direct more challenging. Jung believed that our strengths can be likened to a tower that inevitably casts a shadow. Our lifelong task, Jung believed, is to develop our shadow side, as well as celebrating our tower of strength. For example, some of us may have well developed social engagement skills by being naturally warm, accommodating, and empathic, but these strengths create a shadow or underdeveloped skill in being able to challenge and confront.

You, the reader, can consider using the following family-of-origin guided imagery to help reflect on your personal context and the area you may need to develop to fully integrate honesty and directness with warmth and care. This exercise comes with a warning that reflecting on our upbringing can raise intense emotions, which for some readers may be overwhelming. The power and responsibility lie with you to manage how much, or how little, you enter into this exercise, even if it is in the privacy of your own home.

The exercise is designed to help you reflect on the messages you were given whilst growing up – either in your family-of-origin or with early care givers – and how these messages have influenced your approach to honesty and directness, as well as warmth and care in your working relationships as an adult. Whilst our practice is also informed by our professional training, work context, and the clients we work with, our upbringing can instil strong messages, legacies, and values that may be less than conscious to us. I will use the term family as shorthand to represent the diverse range of intimate contexts for readers. The reader could also conduct a similar reflective process to the one below to interrogate the impact that workplace cultures and professional training have had on your capacity to integrate honesty and directness with warmth and care.

Part one (Guided imaginary)

Get comfortable, close your eyes, and take a few deep breaths. Imagine yourself as a child – notice the age you are. Recall a typical family scenario or situation you experienced at this age. You may recall a particular event or have a memory of a family occasion. Picture each member of your family or group. Reflect on the values that were important in your family especially in relation to ideas of honesty, directness, warmth, and care. Each person in your scenario may have a different view about these values: *How were these values expressed in your family? How did family members show warmth? What situations invited warmth, and which didn't? What were people honest and direct about? How were honesty and directness expressed? What were the consequences of this honesty and directness? What were people indirect about? What was the consequence of this indirectness?*

You may want to virtually place the members of your family on a continuum from most direct to least direct. *Where would you place yourself on this continuum?* Now place the members of your family on a continuum from who showed the most warmth and care to those who showed the least warmth and care. *Where would you place yourself on this continuum?*

Do you notice any relationships, themes, patterns, or contradictions about the two continuums? *Who in the family was most able to combine honesty and directness with warmth and care? Who was least able to do this?* Perhaps some other significant person in your life comes to mind when you consider who had a natural ability to integrate honesty and directness with warmth and care. *Who are you most like in relation to the ability to marry honesty and directness with warmth and care?*

Part two (Reflection on the impact of your early upbringing on your work)

Take a moment to reflect on how these experiences growing up has influenced you, your work, or your work/therapeutic style. *In what ways have these early/family experiences impacted on your professional practice? How might these personal wisdoms influence, if at all, your work? Is there an area of NBT (warmth and care, honesty and directness or the combination of honesty and directness with warmth and care) which you find comes easy? What area do you find difficult or requires you to overcome early messages, legacies, or values to enact? If you find it difficult to combine honesty and directness with warmth and care, consider how your practice would change if you adopted some elements of the person you thought has or had a natural ability to combine these qualities?*

Part three (Completion)

Complete the exercise and notice how you feel. If you are emotional, accept that this is ok and natural when reflecting on early personal experiences. If you find it difficult to get things out of your head, maybe try writing down your thoughts or recording them in some way. Try doing some gentle exercise, or a simple or pleasurable activity. If you still find it difficult to move on from this exercise, consider talking to a friend or even a professional counsellor.

Participants in our NBT workshops have found this exercise challenging and productive, both personally and professionally. One participant recorded the following observation in her evaluation sheet, *Made me think about my own personal/family history. What I bring to work with clients/fellow workers – how honest I am willing to allow myself to be.*

Another participant spoke to an even broader integration of NBT thinking:

> Be more honest with the families and clients I engage with. Be more honest
> with services and decrease the jargon. This has been a powerful day and I
> love the principles and will tread lightly to ensure it is done in a sensitive,
> non-blaming or shaming approach. Next step – practice sensitively looking
> after both clients, families, co-workers and most importantly, self.

Central to the art of NBT is being able to combine honesty and directness with
warmth and care in a combination that suits the specific client with whom you are
working and in a way that is relevant to the context of the work. Again, for the purposes of clarity I will apply this task to the extremes of therapy-lovers in Chapter 6
and to therapy-haters now, because there is a significant difference in application of
this guideline, depending on where clients fall on this continuum.

Marrying honesty and directness with warmth and care when working with therapy-haters

As emphasised, therapy-haters are very suspicious of warmth and care dished out
by a therapist, or by anyone that they do not trust, especially if the person is in a
position of authority and especially if it is not specifically relevant to the task at
hand. Hence, in the early stages of engaging a therapy-hater, the No Bullshit Therapist should emphasise honesty and directness and minimise demonstrating warmth
and care, as reflected in the adaption of the Lorenz Attractor in Figure 5.2. Warmth
and care maybe as subtle as, *You've had the decency to front up which is not easy,
so I'm going to be upfront with you!* Or *good on you for being so straightforward.*

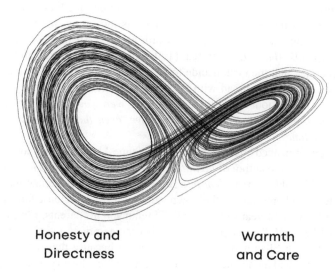

Honesty and   **Warmth**
Directness   **and Care**

Figure 5.2 The Lorenz Attractor metaphor for working with therapy-haters.

Especially in the early stages of the working relationship small amounts of warmth and care go a long way for a therapy-hater – too much warmth and care and the therapist will be in danger of being seen as attempting the art of manipulation.

Warmth and care may be simply expressed by sharing your authentic and personal hopes for the client but without being invested in whether the client acts on your hopes or not. In this way NBT has some similarities to motivational interviewing (neutral to outcome) but is also different, in that the therapist can actively indicate both what they want for the client and that the client has the power to decide what to do for themselves. In a recent role-play in an NBT workshop, participant Tanya's motivational interviewing approach was made more compelling and emotionally powerful by her being asked to add her authentic hopes for her client without being invested in the outcome.

Expressing warmth and care in a cognitive rather than in a feeling way tends to work best for therapy-haters. A cognitive expression of warmth and care may include comments such as *I can see you want the best for your kids,* or *Good on you for being able to hear this stuff, or I get the impression you are keen for things to improve, no matter what it takes.* An observation made by Mark Furlong (2020, p. 61) about working with men and emotions is that the therapist "can be direct about emotions if not directly emotional" helps me to think about how to address emotions such as warmth and care with therapy-haters. Initially, it is possible to talk about warmth and care without oozing warmth and care but over time as the work progresses, warmth and care can be expressed more directly emotionally rather than just directly.

American psychiatrist Stephen Bergman (1996), a leading researcher on male psychology uses the term *relational dread* to describe the challenge a considerable number of men have in addressing emotional and relational issues. Bergman, who writes under the pen name, Samuel Shem, points out that providing subtle support after having acknowledged this dread can facilitate engagement – acknowledgement that David Wexler describes as indicating that you think "his heart is in the right place even though his words aren't" (2013, p. 22). In his book *I Don't Want to Talk About It*, Terry Real (1998) complements Bergman's terminology with the idea that men can decide to also create acts of *relational heroism* to overcome their relational dread with those close to them. Competency questions can elicit acts of relational heroism such as *How were you able to step into your partners shoes, and see it from her perspective, even though you were hurting yourself at the time?*

I have been influenced by my Australian colleague Alan Jenkins, a social worker, narrative therapist, and author of *Invitations to Responsibility: The Therapeutic Engagement of Men Who Are Violent and Abusive* (1990), to challenge male clients and some female clients against their own values. I recall an intense family therapy session I had with a 22-year-old man called Stefan and his parents, Eliza and Tony. I had seen Eliza and Tony together on six occasions prior to seeing them all as a family. Although Eliza and Tony sought therapy because they were concerned about Stefan who had mental health difficulties and a long history of abusing drugs. They had struggled to convince Stefan to attend therapy until they used the *NBT self-supervision for clients* tool (outlined in Chapter 9). Stefan was cautious but surprisingly open about both his serious drug use (marijuana, speed, and mescaline) and his ambitions to work. However, not studying or working, Stefan felt he was so behind in his aspirations compared to his peers that it was easier to return to drugs than to begin to catch up the eight years he estimated he was behind in life. Using an NBT approach I had made a reasonable connection with Stefan, but I was not sure if he would agree to return for a second session, and so I articulated my dilemma, which conveyed to him that it was his decision.

Jeff: Can I ask you a really direct question?
Stefan: I guess so.
Jeff: Do you reckon you will come back or not?
Stefan: I'm not sure.
Jeff: If you don't think you will come back, I've got a couple of extra questions, but if you are prepared to come back, they could wait until next time.
Stefan: Yeah, the questions can wait.
Jeff: OK.

Stefan returned for a second session with his parents at the scheduled time. This time I met with them altogether and amongst other things we decided that the next step was for Eliza and Tony to work on Stefan's plan, rather than their plan, to help restart Stefan's life. Adopting Stefan's plan seemed to work well, and Stefan agreed to return for another family session. In this session, he talked more about his failed aspirations. I asked if he felt like a failure and he responded, *I feel like a silent success but a failure on the outside. I know I've won in this life – I know Dad's intimidated by me! Mum gets more upset than intimidated!* At this point, Stefan stood up and walked behind his seated father. I responded in a heartfelt way, *I can see that your father is intimidated, but I don't believe that is what you really want – it isn't true to who you really are – is it?* After an intense exchange, he shared that he was not living true to his values. He had sat down. In the following family session, Stefan talked about giving up marijuana and we talked about detox referrals as part of a longer-term plan. Stefan didn't return after this session, his fourth. I kept seeing his parents on 14 further occasions to help them support each other in the face of Stefan's fluctuating progress. In their last session, Eliza and Tony, who were divided on how to respond to Stefan when they began therapy, told me they were getting on well and thanked me for being able to take their sense of failure seriously without shaming them.

Challenging a client can be a validation of their basic decency. In the spirit of the unity of opposites, I often challenge a client because I know he or she is ethically decent and emotionally strong enough to withstand the challenge. I believed that Stefan was a decent person even though he wasn't acting in line with this decency. Not challenging therapy-haters can have the reverse effect – conveying that you think they are neither decent, strong, nor emotionally resilient enough to be able to talk about difficult things.

Be upfront about constraints

> I see you are naming constraints before they become constraints
> – (NBT workshop participant, Melbourne)

During my family therapy training in the 1980s, I was taught that being upfront about constraints is one way to soften them. As a young family therapist, I made overt the most obvious constraints to my work, whether it was helping a client parent before I had children, problem solving accommodation for a client sleeping rough when I had secure housing or challenging a high-status male client in my first year of work. Making overt the challenges was also helpful when I was trying to introduce family therapy approaches to hostile organisations, when family therapy was new and viewed with suspicion. I raised constraints as a technique or as a strategy. As I became more practised, I became less strategic and made overt constraints as part of genuinely exploring what might get in the way of a client achieving their goals.

I found myself again being drawn to acknowledging constraints as a strategy in the early days of working with therapy-haters, such as making overt that fact that they didn't want to be in therapy. I initially made difficulties overt because it was an effective technique. Over time as I began to develop the framework around NBT, I increasingly appreciated constraints as real things that got in the way of good work and hence should be respected – rather than acknowledging them as a strategic technique. The difference between the strategic or pragmatic use of acknowledging a constraint and a genuine understanding and respect for a constraint is largely attitudinal. A genuine understanding and respect for the influence of a constraint is more compatible with building authentic relationships with clients, and hence is more likely to build trust in the long term.

Simply being curious about constraints can be a very effective way of finding ways around them. Creative ways of identifying constraints such as *What is going to make it hard for me to be helpful to you?* Researcher-like inquiry about constraints that have been identified are equally helpful, such as *Out of 10, what's the likelihood I'll be able to overcome these constraints? What will help? What will make them worse? What did other workers do that made them stronger or weaker?* The same questions can be asked of the client, *What's the likelihood of you overcoming this difficulty?*

Whilst my family therapy training taught me to address and utilise the therapeutic value of constraints, it was working with an experienced film director, Nancy Black, that taught me to make a feature of them. Nancy shared an industry secret that goes something like this: *If you can't hide it (a problem) make a feature of it.* For example, if there is a problem with the lighting of a scene being filmed and this problem can't be remedied, trying to hide it tends to draw the eye of the viewer to the very problem you are trying to hide. Likewise, I have noticed that trying to hide, for example, my lack of credentials or lack of knowledge in a particular area seems to simply draw greater attention to these deficits. In therapy, I found that making a feature of a constraint is typically more effective in overcoming that constraint than trying to prove one's credentials and is certainly more effective than trying to ignore the constraint.

The difference between making a feature of constraints with therapy-lovers and therapy-haters tends to be a matter of emphasis and timing rather than requiring a particularly different approach.

Being upfront about constraints when working with therapy-haters

Early on, constraints to successful work are often the most significant thing you have in common with therapy-haters. Therapy-haters have usually been mandated in some way to meet with you and unless this is addressed directly you are unlikely to get anything other than stand-offish politeness or outright hostility. The context of the work may also be vexed; your host agency may have policies that make establishing an effective working relationship difficult or the client may have had unpleasant or unhelpful experiences with your agency or similar agencies in the past. As well as a greater emphasis, it is not uncommon to spend a lot more time talking about constraints and over a longer period when working with therapy-haters. Without wanting to put a positive spin on it, talking about constraints can be an effective way, and often the only way, to begin building a relationship with a therapy-hater. This was the case with a 13-year-old boy whom I saw with his foster carer. Like with many therapy-haters, as I have mentioned earlier but need to continually restate, the context of this working situation would turn anyone into a therapy-hater. Tim grew up in an extremely violent family which he escaped by living on the streets, in an inner suburb of Melbourne. Tim attended our Centre with Joseph, a 41-year-old man who had befriended and looked after him. Prior to this friendship, Tim was using considerable amounts of marijuana, was violent to others, and was not attending school. As a result of this friendship, Tim had reduced but not completely stopped using marijuana, had started playing football, was no longer violent (although I noted he had tipped a cup of hot chocolate over his previous therapist!), and had started going to school although somewhat irregularly. Though Joseph had been a heroin addict in the past, he was now clean and there was no evidence he had exploited Tim in anyway. The only problem was that a prominent politician in opposition had used Joseph's past heroin use to publicly deride the government's handling of this case (I learned this from the referrer). To their credit, the state protective services had not broken up Tim and Joseph's relationship but had managed the public criticism of their handling of the case by implementing a very rigorous monitoring program which infuriated both Tim and Joseph.

The referral to me was in lieu of some of this monitoring, but as Tim clearly stated in our first, second, and third meeting, *Why should we come to see you – it is just replacing one big brother with another?* I simply made a feature of this constraint and was completely honest in my interactions with both Tim and Joseph; mainly Joseph actually, because Tim had stated he did not want to participate in therapy. I accepted Tim's stridently stated position that he didn't want to talk with me and talked with Joseph, who wanted some support to help *parent* Tim, especially around his anger. I emphasised the fact that it was totally unfair that they had to endure intense monitoring, when all the outcomes from any measure was that Joseph had had a significantly positive impact on Tim's life. I repeatedly acknowledged that they were simply trading time having to work with me instead of having protective services in their home. I acknowledged that they had to travel to see me whereas they could be seen by protective services without leaving their own home. I accepted that Tim did not want to work with me, but that Joseph did. Gradually, accepting that only Joseph wanted to work with me, led to Tim saying in the fourth session, *Why are you talking to Joseph about me rather than asking me directly?* I simply replied honestly and directly, *I would prefer to talk to you directly, but you said that you didn't want to work with me, and I've respected that.* Gradually we began working all together and made some progress. I still remember two poignant moments in the work. One was how both Tim and Joseph responded as if I was speaking a foreign language when I asked how we might celebrate the progress we had made after about the eighth session. The other was Tim bringing in a resume he'd prepared in readiness for seeking part-time work after school. I was moved then, and I still have a copy of that resume.

Whilst I wanted to work with both Tim and Joseph, I had appreciated that the constraints to the work were so great, that they may never want to work with me. As Nancy Black had advised me whilst making the training films all those years ago, if I couldn't successfully hide the fact that I was just a replacement of protective services and potentially another inconvenience, then I may as well make a feature of it. In NBT terms, I gave this constraint the respect it deserved and focussed on the constraint to the intensity that reflected Tim and to a lesser extent, Joseph's, experience of me as an inconvenience.

Avoid jargon

> When there is a gap between one's real and one's declared aims, one turns as it were to long words and exhausted idioms, like a cuttlefish spurting out ink.
> – George Orwell (1946, p. 137)

> How can we create an ideal speech situation when those who are engaged in dialogue do not share equal access to speech resources?
> – Virginia Goldner (1993, p. 161)

Avoiding jargon is about managing the power differential between therapist and client, not the language per se. Putting a client at ease, especially in a vexed or complex situation where bad faith exists, requires clarity about every aspect of the endeavour: Purpose, process, goals, techniques, strategies, options, redress, and potential outcomes. The language test of a No Bullshit therapist is not whether their language is sophisticated or simplistic – but whether it conveys information and message clearly and effectively. NBT is not anti-intellectual; it is simply anti-obfuscation. Hence, the language of NBT is neither academic nor non-academic, it is simply clear, unambiguous, and non-obfuscating.

All professions must manage the balance between employing standardised language to facilitate communication between peers, the development of ideas and professional identity, and the over or inappropriate use of standardised language, consciously or unconsciously, to empower the professional at the expense of others outside the profession. In Richard Dawkins' 1998 review of the book *Intellectual Impostures* by Alan Sokal and Jean Bricmont (1998), Dawkins congratulates the authors in their attempt to expose jargon designed as self-enhancing for a profession or professional as opposed to facilitating the development of complex and nuanced professional knowledge. In his review, entitled *Postmodernism Disrobed*, Dawkins articulates the challenge of knowing what thoughts are so profound that many of us cannot understand them versus what descriptions simply obfuscate the true intention of the speaker. Dawkins warns that lucid literary styles potentially risk exposing a lack of content and more seriously points out that language designed to be unintelligible to conceal an absence of honest thought, is an abuse of power.

The extent of jargon in our professions is exemplified by the well-known hoax perpetrated by one of the authors of *Intellectual Impostures*, Alan Sokal, a physics professor at New York University and University College London, who successfully submitted a purposefully nonsensical paper for publication called *Transgressing the Boundaries: Towards a transformative hermeneutics of quantum gravity* to *Social Text*, an American postmodern cultural studies journal.[1] I have reproduced verbatim, a much-quoted commentary on this hoax written by journalist Gary Kamiya (quoted in Dawkins, 1998, p. 143), because I don't think it can be improved upon:

> Anyone who has spent much time wading through the pious, obscurantist, jargon-filled cant that now passes for 'advanced' thought in the humanities knew it was bound to happen sooner or later: some clever academic, armed with the not-so-secret passwords ('hermeneutic', 'transgressive', 'Lacanian,', 'hegemony', to name but a few) would write a completely bogus paper, submit it to an au courant journal, and have it accepted ... Sokal's piece uses all the right terms. It cites all the best people. ... And it is complete, unadulterated bullshit – a fact that somehow escaped the attention of the high-powered editors of Social Text, who must now be experiencing that queasy sensation that afflicted the Trojans the morning after they pulled that nice big gift horse into their city.

Whilst the hoax sparked furious debate between the humanities and the physical sciences, my main interest in the hoax is that it highlights how we are all vulnerable to being seduced by status-giving jargon. The Sokal affair is one of many similar hoaxes targeting a wide range of professional disciplines perpetrated by a range of people, including software programmers, and even a chimpanzee called Brassau, who received favourable reviews from several critics for a painting exhibited in an art gallery.

Don Watson, ex-speech writer, biographer, and ex-friend of Paul Keating, prime minister of Australia (1991–1996), wrote *Death Sentence: The Decay of*

Public Language in 2003 and its companion book *The Dictionary of Weasel Words: Contemporary Clichés, Cant and Management Jargon* in 2004. In this latter text he points out that the term *weasel word* first appeared in the US around the end of the nineteenth century and was mentioned in 1916 by Theodore Roosevelt who declared that the tendency to use weasel words was "one of the defects of our nation." Watson argues that weasel words suck the meaning out of communication – in fact he notes that this is their purpose; to hide truth and slew or complicate meaning to exercise and maintain power. To emphasise his point, he draws on a quote by Primo Levi that public language that defies normal understanding is "an ancient repressive artifice, known to all churches, the typical vice of our political class, the foundation of all colonial empires" (Watson, 2003, p. 3). Watson goes on to add sociologists and deconstructionists to Levi's list of *obfuscating types*. Therapists and health workers seem to have narrowly escaped his gaze! However, Watson's description of these purveyors of jargon is a little close to the bone, "They will tell you it is in the interests of leadership, management, efficiency, stakeholders, the bottom line or some democratic imperative, but the public language remains the language of power. ... To take power is to win speech" (p. 3).

It may be heavy handed on my part to reference Hannah Arendt's extraordinarily detailed analysis of Eichmann's Jerusalem trial during which this architect and logistics expert was investigated on his culpability for Nazi war crimes. But one certainly comes away from reading her 312-page epic, *Eichmann in Jerusalem: A Report on the Banality of Evil (1963),* aware of the dangers of turning language into a purely political technology. Arendt described how Eichmann evaded culpability by speaking only in *clichés* and *officialise* and at best merely simulating thought through misplaced quotations of authorities. He did not think or reflect. Her famous quote from this work, *the banality of evil*, refers to how Eichmann was able to continue playing a key role in the extermination of people by just doing what he was told, day-to-day, efficiently, and without question.

In a very different context, and in a more subtle but equally banal way, workers need to be cautious of blindly and blithely following a stereotyped professionalism or organisational protocols without actively thinking about how one's actions may impact on clients. To draw on Sokal and Bricmont's evocative use of words, one wonders what honest thought is left when the verbal veneer covering weasel words is stripped away. It could be argued that the intentional or unconscious use of jargon to obfuscate rather than to clarify is particularly harmful in the human services, where situations can be subjective and complex, and where the consequences of a professional's actions can profoundly affect peoples' lives. Whilst most helpers would support the need for the helping professional's language to be clear and accessible to the person they are employed to help, when we feel boxed in, challenged, fearful, protective, powerless, or incompetent, resorting to jargon can be an attractive, if short term, solution. To be upfront if a client fronts up angry, upset, or traumatised requires real courage. Part of that courage may be to be open to gaining support from a colleague or a framework such as NBT – as it can be hard to *do it alone* (strip away the protection of jargon).

Early in my career, I would have found it quite confronting to rigorously ask myself what I had to offer if I stripped away the veneer of professional jargon. In an interview about jargon that I conducted with well-known Australian couple therapist, the late Tom Paterson, pointed out how the other accoutrements of the professions can also empower workers at the expense of disempowering clients, especially therapy-haters. Tom's comments raise the question – W*hat purpose do gilt framed qualifications, leather couches, formal bookshelves, suits, and ties play in creating confidence, trust and credibility and do these accoutrements affect therapy-lovers and therapy-haters differently?* I think so.

The overriding emphasis of the NBT guideline to avoid jargon is really to match your client's language rather than to speak in a particular way: too simple and it may come across as condescending, too sophisticated it may be experienced as disempowering. It can be confronting, but possibly also very productive, to seek feedback from our clients about every aspect of how they find their encounters with us and our work environment; the tone of the waiting room, our professional accoutrements, what's hanging on our walls, the style and tone of our communication, and the processes and procedures of our host agency – essentially the cultural safety of the service. The Bouverie Centre's work with the original inhabitants of Australia has given my organisation and I a deeper appreciation and richer understanding of the importance of cultural safety for our Aboriginal and Torres Strait Islander colleagues and clients. Acknowledgement of the Traditional Custodians of the land as part of our work, images celebrating Aboriginal culture on our website and in our waiting areas, participation in cultural events and the Aboriginal and Torres Strait Islander flags flying alongside the Australian flag in the car park, all indicate that our centre appreciates that many Indigenous families will be suspicious of a mainstream organisation like ours, because mainstream Australia and mainstream organisations have treated Aboriginal communities horribly.

Cultural safety for rural clients, for example, may translate into client appointments and professional workshops that start late and finish early to allow for travel time. Cultural safety and managing power are not about pretending to be the same, they are about seeking an understanding of the other, in order to be transparent about power. A major hurdle in seeking feedback from therapy-haters, especially in the early stage of the relationship, is that they are likely to be either too angry to give you constructive feedback or too fearful to say anything other than what they think you want to hear. Hence, I have provided some tips collected from my work with therapy-haters who have stayed around long enough to provide me with some honest and direct feedback.

Avoiding jargon when working with therapy-haters

When he speaks like this you don't know what he's after
                                    – Leonard Cohen (1977, *The Stranger Song*)

In the early stages of working with therapy-haters, the tone of business is often more effective than the compassionate tone of therapy or the emotional supportive tone of the helping professions. Given the therapy-hater does not want to enter a working relationship at all, but especially not a relationship where they must take on the vulnerable position of a client in order to receive help, business language may empower the client as customer, deciding whether to purchase the goods you have to offer – or not! It can be easier to be black and white when guided by the metaphor of business language rather than the subjective language of therapy. As we learned from my interview with Gary, any shade of grey is open to misinterpretation when the client, for whatever reason, comes in bad faith. Any interpretation from a position of bad faith is always going to be negative.

As discussed in Chapter 2, the definition of bullshit most relevant to us is the concealment of the enterprise – jargon is commonly the way we conceal or obfuscate the real purpose of the therapeutic enterprise. The irony is that the temptation to obfuscate increases in proportion to a client's anger and cynicism about what we have to offer. I met with Esther and Moshe who have spent over $100,000 battling the family court, protective services, and therapists, trying to seek contact with Esther's two children. Both Esther, the children's mother, and her new partner Moshe, felt powerless, angry, and frustrated. They are not therapy-haters but find themselves so embattled with several different services that they now share the therapy-haters' distrust of all helping agencies, including my own. A colleague from our centre is seeing Esther's children and their father Redmond, which is why Esther and Moshe want to meet with me – to insist we facilitate contact between Moshe, Esther, and Esther's children. I know from my colleague's work with Redmond and the children, that the children do not want any contact with their mum. Knowing the meeting with Esther and Moshe will be difficult, my colleague Colleen Cousins and I prepare for the encounter by consulting our colleague who is seeing Redmond and Esther's children. They say Esther and Moshe must agree to a therapeutic contract.

When Colleen Cousins and I raise this requirement in our early discussions with Esther and Moshe, things become tense. Colleen and I reflect that this seemingly harmless and very familiar phrase (therapeutic agenda) is jargon, obfuscating what we can offer, what we can't, and what we require of Esther and Moshe. It also obfuscates other practical details including likely timeframes and guarantees of the service we can offer. Considering the simple but challenging NBT guideline of avoiding jargon, we eventually clarify what Esther and Moshe must do, in a clear step-by-step process, for us to work with them. We make overt several difficulties and what we expect from the couple. Esther and Moshe, who are upset, angry, and distrustful, respond well to the clarity.

Stepping into the shoes of Esther and Moshe was an important step in being able to provide a clear and transparent formulation for the work. Colleen and I imagined that Esther and Moshe found being told they needed to agree to a therapeutic agenda as implying that they had a mental health problem; that they were the problem. Esther's and Moshe's problem was that they wanted to have contact with Esther's children, but her children didn't want to have contact with them. I said to them, *What I can offer you is that once my colleague establishes a trusting relationship with your children and their dad, and with their permission, and on the*

recommendation my colleague's views about what's in the children's best interest,
I will share the children's concerns with you, so you can address them. I am happy
to work with you to help you to respond productively to their concerns. If you can
do this, I imagine they will be more likely to agree to have contact with you. I can't
provide any guarantees, or be specific about how long this will take, or if it will be
successful. So, I can also understand if you decide not to work with us.

An ethical use of power in therapy-hating situations requires a clear, simple, and
specific use of language. I think it is easier to communicate clearly if a worker has
and feels they have legitimate authority. Clear communication likewise leads to
greater legitimate authority. Therapists are not always trained in being overt about
the power they have and the power they do not have. A more theoretical analysis
on NBT and power will be presented in Chapter 10.

In the case of therapeutic relationships, it is ethical to be clear about what authority the therapist as well as clients have and don't have – especially when therapists are working with therapy-haters. A therapy-hater will see therapist power in
the unstated, the vague, and the unclear. A therapy-hater will also see the potential for the therapist to use his or her power, without accountability, if it remains
hidden, invisible, or unspoken. With George Orwell's words in mind, be aware
when your client's hopes, thoughts, or behaviours "do not square with your hopes
and make sure you do not succumb to the temptation of reverting to euphemism,
question-begging and sheer, cloudy vagueness" (Orwell, 1946, p. 136). Esther's
hope was that I would instruct her children to have contact with her and her new
partner. My hope was that she would understand that she had to rebuild the children's trust and that this could only be done by eliciting and listening to their concerns non-defensively and responding in a reparative way. I was initially tempted
to hide behind the subtle jargon of requesting that Esther and Moshe agree to a
therapeutic agenda, whatever that means, because I knew they would not like the
details hidden within the jargon *therapeutic endeavour*.

The art of NBT is to be upfront about power and business-like about the
rationale for the work without being emotionally disengaged, dismissive, or un-
caring. In essence, it embraces a *kind use of power*. The interconnectedness of
power and love and the relationship between these dynamics is explored in Carl
Jung's much quoted, but hard to locate reference, "Where love reigns, there is no
will to power; and where the will to power is paramount, love is lacking" (Jung,
2014, p. 53).

Jung's quote was in response to Nietzsche's paper on the will to power (Nietzsche, 1968). A simple reading of Jung's quote begs the question, *Can love and*
power co-exist? From an NBT perspective, without power there is little capacity
for love, only submission, or patronising compassion. A therapist requires legitimate power to have the confidence and capacity to combine honesty and directness
with warmth and care in therapy. Therapy-lovers grant the therapist power; therapists working with therapy-haters must take it but use it with kindness. Without
legitimate power, therapists are likely to either strive to recruit any self-preserving
power they can, relevant or not to the task at hand, or avoid the difficult issues and
acquiesce as an equally unhelpful way of preserving one's safety.

Articulating the respective authority and responsibilities of our clients and ourselves, with simple real-world clarity, can be extremely helpful to therapists working with therapy-haters. It may be particularly helpful for therapists who favour a warm fuzzy mode of working and who may be at risk of inadvertently obfuscating their own professional authority, and under-representing the authority and responsibilities, of their therapy hating clients.

Keeping my warmth and care (wanting the best) for Esther and Moshe in the forefront of my mind allowed me to be clear and non-abusive in using my legitimate authority at the time, as the Director of The Bouverie Centre, to state how my colleague and I would and how we wouldn't work with Esther and Moshe's family. I also communicated that I was aware of Esther and Moshe's authority to choose to work with us or not.

Note

1 The editors of *Social Text*, Andrew Ross and others won the 1996 Ig Nobel Prize for literature, based on the acceptance of Sokal's fraudulent paper.

References

Arendt, H. (1963). *Eichmann in Jerusalem: A report on the banality of evil.* Viking Press.
Argyris, C., & Schön, D. (1974). *Theory in practice increasing professional effectiveness.* Jossey-Bass.
Bergman, S.J. (1996). Male relational dread. *Psychiatric Annals, 26*(1), 24–28.
Blanton, B. (2003). *Radical honesty: How to transform your life by telling the truth* (rev. ed.). Stanley, Virginia, Sparrowhawk Publications.
Dawkins, R. (1998). Postmodernism disrobed. *Nature, 394*, 141–143.
Farrelly, F., & Brandsma, J.M. (1974). *Provocative therapy.* Shields Publishing.
Furlong, M. (2020). Neither colluding nor colliding: Practical ideas for engaging men. In P. Camilleri (Ed.), *Working with men in the human services* (pp. 54–67). Routledge.
Goldner, V. (1993). Power and hierarchy: Let's talk about it, *Family Process, 32*(2), 157–162.
Goldner, V. (2004). When love hurts: Treating abusive relationships. *Psychoanalytic Inquiry, 24*, 346–372.
Graham, D.W. (2007). Heraclitus. *Standford Encyclopedia of Philosophy.* https://plato.stanford.edu/ENTRIES/heraclitus/ Accessed, 01/05/2023.
Hoyt, M.F. (2017). *Brief therapy and beyond: Stories, language, love, hope, and time.* Routledge.
Ivanhoff, A., Blythe, B.J., & Tripodi. T. (1994). *Involuntary clients in social work practice: A research-based approach.* Aldine de Gruyter.
Jenkins, A. (1990). Invitations to responsibility: The therapeutic engagement of men who are violent and abusive. *Australian and New Zealand Journal of Family Therapy, 11*(4), 201.
Jung, C.G. (1964). Civilization in transition, In H. Read, M. Fordham, & G. Adler (Eds.), *Collected works of C. G. Jung* (Vol. 10). Routledge.
Jung, C.G. (2014). *Two essays on analytical psychology.* In H. Read, M. Fordham, & G. Adler, (Eds.), *Collected works of C. G. Jung* (2nd ed., Vol. 7). Routledge.
Lorenz, E.N. (1963). Deterministic nonperiodic flow. *Journal of Atmospheric Sciences, 20*(2), 130–141.

McDaniel, S.H., & Landau-Stanton, M.D. (1991). Family-of-origin work and family therapy skills training: Both-and. *Family Process, 30(4), 459–471.*

Miller, S.D., Hubble, M.A., Duncan, B.L., & Wampold, B.E. (2010). Delivering what works. In B.L. Duncan, S.D. Miller, B.E. Wampold, & M.A. Hubble (Eds.), The heart and soul of change: Delivering what works in therapy (2nd ed., 421–429). American Psychological Association.

Nietzsche, F. (1968). *The will to power* (W. Kaufman, ed.). Vintage.

Orwell, G. (1946). Politics and the English language. In S. Orwell & I. Angos (Eds.), *The collected essays, journalism and letters of George Orwell.* 4(1), (pp. 127–140). Harcourt, Brace, Jovanovich.

Real, T. (1998). *I don't want to talk about it: Overcoming the secret legacy of male depression.* Simon and Schuster.

Rich, A.C. (1995). *On lies, secrets, and silence: Selected prose, 1966–1978.* Norton.

Rooney, R.H. (1992*). Strategies for work with involuntary clients.* Columbia University Press.

Satir, V. (1972). *Peoplemaking.* Science and Behavior Books.

Sokal, A. D., & Bricmont, J. (1998). *Intellectual impostures: Postmodern philosophers' abuse of science.* Philpapers.org.

Wexler, D. (2013). Shame-o-phobia: Why men fear therapy. *Psychotherapy in Australia, 20*(1), 18–23.

Watson, D. (2003). *Death sentence: The decay of public language.* Random House Australia.

Watson, D. (2004). *The dictionary of weasel words: Contemporary clichés, cant and management jargon.* Random House Australia.

6 No Bullshit Therapy clinical guidelines: Practice notes for working with therapy-lovers

Scared is what you're feeling. Brave is what you're doing
— Emma Donoghue (Irish-Canadian, playwright)

Creating a context to promote mutual honesty and directness with therapy-lovers

No Bullshit Therapy (NBT) with therapy-lovers is a more subtle process and could easily go unnoticed. The approach may be driven more by the attitude of the therapist than by a set of tangible techniques. Gently creating contexts for honesty and directness in the early stages of the engagement process can usually be done simply and easily through a transparent collaboration, providing a legitimate rationale within an atmosphere of warmth and care. Levels of honesty and directness can be negotiated openly early on or over time as part of a much broader collaborative discussion about preferred ways of working. An agreement about accommodating both client's and therapist's wishes can usually be done with relative ease because the therapist can work on the assumption that an ongoing contract is desired by both parties. Moments of greater honesty and directness can be signposted as needed, and unlike working with therapy-haters, are facilitated by early expression of genuine warmth and care.

Since practicing NBT I have been surprised how enthusiastically most clients, therapy-lovers and therapy-haters, respond to an invitation to join me in working honestly and with directness, especially if this offer is clearly linked to achieving the mutually negotiated goals of the encounter.

The techniques of SST provide useful guidance on how to make overt client and worker goals for the encounter. Gentle business engagement adds power and purpose to social engagement: *What brought you here today? How can I be most helpful to you today? What would you like to walk away with at the end of the session?* The techniques and questions of SST, derived from thinking that if this session is the last, what should I ask, explore, share, and do, helps to create a culture of directness. When both client and therapist consider that each session *may be* the last, there is a natural tendency to *cut to the chase*. And the single session structure provides an obvious boundary which provides safety; essentially the framework *this*

DOI: 10.4324/9781003354925-6

could be our last session – so let's make the most of it allows clients to determine how deeply to go and how quickly to cut to the chase.

If not adopting an SST approach, embracing an attitude *I can be gentle and caring and still talk about the most important things* is one way to create a general culture of directness. Promoting a gentle culture of openness can be achieved by creatively combining explorations about what brought a client to therapy with questions about the hard stuff such as *What problem, if solved, would make the biggest difference to your life?*

If a client is cynical about the likelihood of success, but is not a therapy-hater, Barry Mason's (2012) *Not the Miracle question* can be useful. Barry, who passed away in 2021, was an internationally recognised family therapist who lived with ankylosing spondylitis (the fusion of the vertebrae) for many years. Possibly because of his own experience, he worked with clients also affected by chronic conditions who would often come to therapy disheartened, without much hope of getting the help they desired, but feeling the need to do something. Barry created what he called, *Not the Miracle Question*, in reference to the Miracle Question made famous by Insoo Kim Berg and Steve de Shazer. The Not the Miracle Questions goes, *Suppose I worked with you for a number of sessions. What would I have to do to be of no use to you whatsoever?* The question can *be f*ollowed by *What would be helpful?*

The techniques of NBT may play a more obvious role later in therapy if there is a requirement to shift the rules that have been established during the early working relationship. It can be surprisingly difficult to shift from the established (often unstated) rules governing a relationship to another set of rules, especially to set more demanding rules. Introducing a change of pace, depth of feedback, or degree of challenge is a key role NBT can play in working with therapy-lovers. For example, because of a good working relationship a therapist may find it difficult to raise sensitive issues. Therapists who are good at engaging clients by accommodating to their style can then find it difficult to challenge the client later in the process of therapy – it is as if the therapeutic relationship has a course of its own. Like a river it can be difficult to re-direct. Sometimes, as Ged Smith points out, the need to move things forward requires the therapist to "challenge and to raise uncomfortable questions within a frame of respect" (Smith, 2011, p. 60). The role of introducing honesty and directness with therapy-lovers tends to translate into the need to establish moments of greater honesty and directness, whenever a particular need arises (see Figure 6.1).

Moments of honesty and directness may be needed to overcome a constraint (see later), to raise a particularly sensitive issue, or to give some critical feedback. Even the simple task of *exiting the relationship* long enough to check how it is going by asking meta-questions about the working relationship itself can seem difficult or rude once an intense intimate therapeutic relationship has been established. Helpful meta-questions such as: *Is this what we should be talking about right now? How will we know that we are approaching the end of our work together? Is this helpful? Should we be talking about something else?* allow a change to the natural

SIGNPOSTING: Creating a marker to indicate and imminent shift in the rules for the relationship/conversation

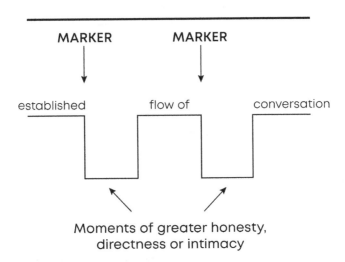

Moments of greater honesty,
directness or intimacy

Figure 6.1 Signposting: Marking moments of greater honesty, directness, or intimacy. (Used with permission of The Bouverie Centre, La Trobe University, Australia.).

flow of the conversation and are described by my colleague Pam Rycroft as *talking about the talking* (see Chapter 8). NBT strategies can be used to change the inherent level of honesty and directness that has developed over time, when a deeper or more direct conversation is required. It is helpful to be aware that a close working relationship can both facilitate openness and can also restrict openness. As I have mentioned, just think of those times a stranger has sat next to you on a long plane or train trip and shared things they have never revealed to their family or closest long-term friends. A close relationship, including a close working relationship, might place reputation ahead of honesty; sharing shameful material might be easier with a stranger. Whilst NBT strategies may be helpful to create a moment of required honesty within a close working relationship, NBT strategies, when working with therapy-lovers share a lot in common with the techniques of SST.

A subtle difference used when introducing honesty and directness to therapy-lovers is that rather than a rhetorical statement such as *I prefer to be honest and direct,* the therapist can ask a rhetorical *cutting to the chase* question which comes directly from our single session work (Rycroft & Young, 2021; Young & Rycroft, 1997), such as: *Can I be honest with you? Is it alright if I offer you some direct feedback? Can I be really direct with you? Are you interested in hearing what I'm thinking?*

Although in the form of a question, it is difficult to say no to such questions when posed by an *expert* and hence they are best seen as signposting. I used to think I was being respectful by asking this question and offering clients a choice but thanks to some direct critical feedback by one of my early NBT workshop participants (part of the value of creating a workshop context that promotes mutual honesty and directness), I now appreciate that it is more of a marker indicating that the rules of the relationship are about to change. Indicating that there is going to be a change in the rules is helpful as it allows the client to figuratively sit down and get ready and prepare themselves for the challenge, maybe by enacting their favoured defence strategies. I now find myself using markers in many of my sensitive day-to-day work encounters. For example, I recently employed a gifted colleague to work on a major feasibility study conducted by The Bouverie Centre. This colleague, who was paid at an appropriate rate for a short-term high-level consultancy, played a key role in the preparation of the study's final report. Following the completion of the report her role merged into ongoing project management work on a related project. Several weeks into the ongoing work it was brought to my attention by my business manager that our Centre could not afford to pay the same initial high consultancy rate for the ongoing work, which she had already started, at the higher rate. The fact that I needed to raise the payment issue directly after a very successful meeting, only complicated my task. Marking a change in the tone of the conversation from positive debrief to talking about reduced pay rates was made easier by stating, *I have something that is a bit sensitive to raise with you.* Before I could add, *Can I be really direct with you?* my colleague, almost impatiently responded, *Spit it out!*

Therapy-lovers are more open to the therapist acknowledging their strengths and this can also be an effective way to introduce a shift in the rules of the relationship or conversation, especially later in the work when the therapist genuinely knows the client's strengths. For example, the NBT therapist may simply say, "Given you have risen to all of the challenges I have dished out over the past three months we have been working together, would you be up for some pretty direct feedback, even if it was a bit hard to hear?" or "Given you are so committed to your daughter, can I share something that I think is getting in the way of your relationship with her?"

If the therapist is concerned about how the client will respond, they can gently link this marker to the rationale, purpose, or contract for the work. For example, *I know you want to help your daughter get back to school* (presenting problem), *so can I be really honest about what I think may help?* (marker of greater directness) or *Can I be direct with you* (marker of greater directness) *given you want to feel less depressed?* (presenting problem), or *Are you interested in hearing what I'm thinking* (marker of greater directness) *about how you can feel stronger when you're communicating with your dad?* (presenting problem).

Therapists will no doubt have their own way of making changes in the conversational rules. Colin Riess (a former Director of The Bouverie Centre) has a natural ability to get away with raising difficult issues. He is fond of signposting a change in the conversational rules by simply saying, *I'm going to take my therapist hat off for the moment and speak to you as a person or friend!* Penny, a participant in an early NBT workshop, used the following signpost when providing challenging advice, *You're going to think I'm crazy when I tell you what I think you should do!* It can be helpful to think of ways to maintain a deep level of honesty and directness, once depth has been achieved, with markers such as *I have been really direct with you so why stop now, hey?*

In negotiating levels of honesty and directness with therapy-lovers, clients may opt for the therapist to be honest and direct in some areas and more cautious in others. A colleague of mine, Jenny Dwyer, negotiated with a client who had survived significant abuse in her past that she could be direct about the process of therapy but not about the details of the sexual abuse itself. Making overt this arrangement facilitated the work in both areas.

Establishing a mandate when working with therapy-lovers

> You cannot mandate productivity, you must provide the tools to let people become their best
>
> – Steve Jobs (American, co-founder of Apple Inc)

A mandate will often occur naturally as part of creating a context or even culture of mutual honesty and directness. Therapy-lovers typically offer therapists a generous mandate; they attend therapy in good faith. Unlike therapy-haters, they have voluntarily chosen to attend and hence have greater power to decide how to work and what to work on. Therapy-lovers also have greater capacity to sack the therapist; in short, they have greater legitimate power to determine the course of service than therapy-haters.

Negotiating what to work on

I have found it productive and respectful to ask therapy-lovers what they want to work on first, followed by how they like to work (to achieve their goal); the opposite order to how I work with therapy-haters. However, in practice, these tasks are integrated and can be flexibly and openly negotiated. What to work on is less contentious because therapy-lovers typically come to therapy wanting help, and often with a problem they want addressed.

Sure, problems may need to be specifically articulated, clarified, and operationalised, and the path to a workable, implementable, solution is seldom straightforward, but there are many approaches and techniques in the literature designed to assist work with voluntary clients. I've already mentioned SST as one of my preferred models (e.g., see Hoyt et al., 2018; 2021). SST is so compatible with NBT, I think of it as NBT for therapy-lovers.

My colleague, Pam Rycroft, and I have articulated the following ten core elements of single session work (Rycroft & Young, 2021, pp. 46–51):

1 Negotiating a client-led outcome

  • *What would you like to walk away with at the end of our session?*

2 Establishing clients' priorities

  • *Of the concerns you've raised, which is the one we should work on first?*

3 Finding a focus and talking about the most important things ("cut to the chase")

- *Of all the things we've talked about which is the most important?*

4 Checking in with the client(s) at regular intervals

- *Is this what we should be talking about right now?*

5 Interrupting respectfully, when necessary, to help the client(s) get what they want

- *Can I just jump in there because I'm so keen to help you get what you wanted from today that I need to ask you this question ...*

6 Making time your friend

- *We've probably only got about ten minutes left, which not much time, so can I ask ...*

7 Sharing your thoughts openly with clients

- *(Feedback, even advice, guided by the question, "What would I want to share with the client if I knew I'd never see them again?")*

8 Preparing to end well (reaching closure if not solution or resolution)

- *Before I share what I'm thinking, Is there anything I should have asked but haven't yet?*

9 Leaving the door open (an "open door" policy)

- *See how you go but feel free to contact me at any time.*

10 Listening to client voices (following up, seeking feedback, and utilising it)

- *(Using follow-up phone calls to check out what the client got from the session and what they want to do next. Putting into practice ideas gained from client surveys and questionnaires)*

Negotiating how to work

Establishing a mandate how to work, can usually be achieved by simply asking therapy-lovers straightforward questions such as *How do you prefer to work? What works best for you? What advice would you give me that would allow me to be really helpful to you?* Asking questions like these is a useful way to start negotiating how to work. Given the usual level of co-operation and good faith, additional more challenging questions can be asked to provide more detailed direction on how to conduct the session, such as *What has allowed you to change in the past? What obstacles have you overcome in the past, and how did you do it? What do I need to do to be most helpful to you? What's the biggest trap I could fall into in my efforts to help you? What do you think is the most likely thing to get in the way of us working well together? Honestly, how likely are you to put these ideas into practice?* (Once a way forward has been proposed)

The lessons from therapy-haters have been helpful to make my work with therapy-lovers efficient: linking all of the work to the client's goal, providing a clear explanation of how therapy works (rules of the game), even if the client is familiar and open to therapy, and providing a rationale for the questions asked, such as *the reason I'm asking you these uncomfortable things is solely to help you get what you wanted from coming to see me.*

Marrying honesty and directness with warmth and care when working with therapy-lovers

Happiness is not a matter of intensity but of balance and order and rhythm and harmony

– Thomas Merton (Author)

Therapy-lovers are not put off by direct displays of warmth and care in the early stages of a working relationship, and in fact genuine and direct expressions of warmth and care typically create a strong foundation for the collaborative negotiation about how to best work, including the negotiations about how to address uncomfortable issues. In fact, if the therapist shares authentic warmth and care right from the start, this is modelling a context of honesty and directness, which can facilitate a therapy-lover's preparedness to venture into difficult territory. Therefore, the Lorenz Attractor is unbalanced in a different way (Figure 6.2) when engaging therapy-lovers early in the work. The decision about how to express warmth and care is not so vexed with therapy-lovers – if the expression is authentic and

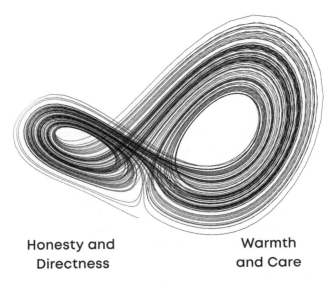

**Honesty and   Warmth
Directness   and Care**

Figure 6.2 The Lorenz Attractor metaphor for working with therapy-lovers. (Used with permission of The Bouverie Centre, La Trobe University, Australia.).

consistent with the context of the work, warmth and care is usually met with positive acceptance.

I have learnt a lot from my work with therapy-haters on how to be honest and direct with therapy-lovers. The principles are similar – just implemented more subtly and usually more easily. A convincing rationale helps gain a mandate for honesty and directness, but due to the comfortable working relationship, this may go unnoticed or may not even be visible, as mentioned. As with therapy-haters, the rationale is strongest when it links the need for honesty and directness to achieving the client's goal or the goal of the therapy and when accompanied by an acknowledgement of the constraints to the work. For example, *I want to share some thoughts* (subtle honesty and directness) *with you that I think will really help you to respond more effectively with your son given I know that's want you want* (linked to presenting problem and with a hint of warmth and care), *I know everyone has been giving you advice* (acknowledging constraints), *I'm a bit worried you might feel I'm picking on you* (acknowledging constraints), *but would that be ok?* (signposting greater directness than usual).

Using an NBT approach with therapy-lovers is often but not always subtle. At times I have been drawn to what I call my finger wagging therapy – a heart-felt plea to a client to change. Donna is stuck in a critical cycle with her 15-year-old daughter, Deb. Donna is worried about Deb's messy and inconsiderate behaviour around the house which appears to me to be within the normal realms of adolescent behaviour. I genuinely feel that whilst motivated by wanting the best for Deb, Donna is at risk of alienating her daughter permanently, because things had got that bad. When my gentle efforts at effecting change come to nought, I tell Donna, I'm going to do what I call my finger wagging therapy and I launch into an emotional speech along the lines that you only get one go at life and it is not worth putting a relationship that is so important at risk by getting caught up in the little things that don't matter. I can get quite emotional and quite intense during finger wagging therapy, when I genuinely see the potential damage of an interaction like the one Donna and her daughter were caught in. Smiling, I finish my emotional plea and say to Donna, I told you I was going to do my finger wagging therapy! Although it breaks all the rules, I have found that when introduced and framed thoughtfully, clients are typically thankful and find *finger wagging therapy* powerful, authentic, and empathic. It certainly clears the air and stops me from asking indirect and somewhat blaming questions or trying to push for an outcome indirectly.

Being upfront about constraints when working with therapy-lovers

> It's not that I'm so smart, it's just that I stay with problems longer.
> – Albert Einstein (Theoretical physicist)

Many of the ways to make a feature of constraints when working with therapy-haters is equally relevant to working with therapy-lovers, usually delivered in a more subtle way and maybe at a different time. This is in line with the practice of family therapy and motivational interviewing; all are facilitated by the therapist speaking openly and with an open mind about what might get in the way of an effective working relationship or of change. Whilst early family therapists strategically made a feature of a constraint, No Bullshit Therapists do the same thing with sincerity and with a straightforward attitude that for any action there is often an equal and opposite reaction.

Each therapist will have their own unique constraints to overcome. I use the following structured exercise in our NBT workshops to help participants find their own ways to overcome what gets in the way of them doing their best possible work. The exercise is done individually, guided by the following steps.

The first step is to choose a piece of work or collaboration where you feel you are struggling to achieve the results you would like. Reflect on your own situation and note down what is getting in the way of you being the best worker possible (biggest constraint, in this particular situation). It may be that you feel that not having children of your own is getting in the way of you working robustly with a father who wants advice on how to manage his active child or it may be that you feel being a male therapist is a problem given it has emerged that your female client has a sexual abuse history. It may be that you feel that not being knowledgeable about the Middle Eastern culture is embarrassing and gets in the way of you being more challenging towards your Iranian client or that you are intimidated working with a family in which the mother is a high court judge.

The second step is to imagine making a feature of this constraint. Imagine naming it boldly, rather than trying to overcome the constraint, or avoiding it altogether. Run through how you would do this, imagining the actual words you might use.

Thirdly, add a mixture of the three-Hs: Humility, Humour, and Honesty.

Fourthly, add warmth – if you haven't done so in the previous steps. Adding warmth may translate to you being gentler toward yourself or more understanding towards your client or colleague.

Finally, practice your new imagined approach and choose a good time to try it out. Good luck.

Combining all the NBT guidelines discussed so far, establishing the level of honesty as part of creating a context for mutual directness, marrying honesty and directness with warmth and care, and making a feature of constraints, can lead to powerful ways of promoting change. For example, if an NBT therapist is concerned that their client may inadvertently get upset or feel blamed by honest feedback, the therapist can resolve this dilemma by making everything overt; *I would like to share some pretty direct feedback with you* (establishing the level of honesty) *because I admire your wish to be the best parent you can be and I think you are strong enough to take it on board* (marrying honesty and directness with warmth and care), *but I'm worried that you will feel so blamed by what I have to say* (making a feature of a constraint) *that you will not even hear it.* If these comments reflect the therapist's genuine view and the therapist takes any client response seriously, the combination of these comments inspired by three of the four NBT guidelines is likely to be a powerful facilitator of change – especially if communicated without jargon, which brings us to our final guideline.

Avoiding jargon when working with therapy-lovers

> We've all been on the other end of an infuriating customer service call and heard these insulting words, "I'm not authorized to solve that problem. I don't make the rules, I just have to follow them. Sorry, but that's our policy."
>
> – Ron A. Carucci (2021, p. 74)

It is helpful to be conscious of the subtle effects of institutional power on our clients even when working in relative comfort with therapy-lovers. I became aware of this personally when completing my PhD. I, along with five colleagues, facilitated regional *co-operative inquiry groups* (CIGs) of drought counsellors and related professionals. CIGs were an opportunity to co-develop ideas and share practice wisdoms, engagement strategies, resources, and practical information about drought issues across a local area. All regional CIGs were conducted in a professional but friendly manner. When I formally evaluated my own role in the CIG I facilitated, I was flattered but surprised by the emphasis the CIG members placed on their experience of me as being friendly and not talking down to them. This feedback was more significant given the rural members had greater experience in rural issues and drought than I, and had joined the CIG with an open mind and in good faith. And yet they were still relieved that despite my formal authority (University appointment, Director of an urban centre of excellence, PhD candidate) I had not used jargon and other accoutrements of power to bolster my authority at their expense (Young, 2012). For me, this experience reminds me to be sensitive and to be consciously aware of the institutional power and authority that my position affords me – even if, or particularly if, I don't take this power seriously myself. It is the privilege of power not to notice it.

Given our *taken for granted* approaches to our work are unlikely to be critiqued by therapy-lovers, we need to use personal discipline to reflect and interrogate our language and attitudes, our professional context, and our host organisation's policies, procedures, and environments for their potential to disempower compliant clients. The use of feedback, a culture of a learning organisation, including client audits, and virtual walk throughs of each step of your service are valuable accountability mechanisms and ways to create transparent workplaces.

In the following chapter, you will see a verbatim transcript of the early part of a simulated session, which will provide one example of what the NBT Clinical Guidelines look like in the hurly burly world of practice.

References

Carucci, R.A. (2021). *To be honest: Lead with the power of truth, justice and purpose.* Kogan Page.

Hoyt, M.F., Bobele, M., Slive, A., Young, J., & Talmon, M. (Eds.). (2018). *Single-session therapy by walk-in or appointment: Clinical, supervisory, and administrative aspects.* Routledge.

Hoyt, M.F., Young, J., & Rycroft, P. (Eds.). (2021). *Single-session thinking and practice in global, cultural, and familial contexts: Expanding applications.* Routledge.

Mason, B. (2012). The personal and the professional: Core beliefs and the construction of bridges across difference. In I-B. Krause (Ed.), *Culture and reflexivity in systemic psychotherapy: Mutual perspectives.* Routledge.

Rycroft, P., & Young, J. (2021). Translating single session thinking into practice. In M.F. Hoyt, J. Young, & P. Rycroft (Eds.), *Single-session thinking and practice in global, cultural, and familial contexts: Expanding applications* (pp. 42–53). Routledge.

Smith, G. (2011). Cut the crap: Language, risks and relationships in systemic therapy and supervision. *Australian and New Zealand Journal of Family Therapy, 32*(1), 58–69.

Young, J. (2012). *A no bullshit approach to drought.* PhD thesis, La Trobe University, Melbourne, Australia.

Young, J., & Rycroft, P. (1997). Single session therapy: Capturing the moment. *Psychotherapy In Australia, 4*(1), 18–23.

7 No Bullshit Therapy first session – With commentary

How could I talk in a way that increases others' desire to listen and how could I listen in a way that increases others' desire to talk?

— Jorma Ahonen (Finnish Social psychologist)

The following 12-minute verbatim transcript is taken from the start of a 36-minute simulation which can be viewed in full as part of the No Bullshit Therapy (NBT) self-paced online learning suite offered by The Bouverie Centre, La Trobe University (www.bouverie.org.au/nbt). The commentary explains the application of the clinical guidelines, in the early stages of an NBT session. You will notice from the transcript that in practice, all the clinical guidelines are interwoven and do not occur in order or in isolation. (Used with permission of The Bouverie Centre, La Trobe University, Australia).

Sarah, a 35-year-old therapy-hater, is pressured to attend counselling by doctors at a psychiatric hospital from which she has been recently discharged, as well as by her mum Louise and sister Mary. Everyone wants Sarah to address her drug use and failure to hold down a job. They also want her to stay out of hospital. Sarah has had frequent admissions and the doctors want her to attend counselling to reduce her stresses, which they feel will help her give up the drugs and reduce the likelihood of readmission. The doctors have threatened to make her stay involuntary if she doesn't seek counselling and returns to hospital.

The early and most challenging part of NBT is to engage someone who doesn't want to work with you. In this early part of the interview with Sarah, I acknowledge that she doesn't want to work with me and has been pressured by her doctors and her family to attend. I introduce the idea of NBT early, get agreement to be honest and direct, signpost when I intend to ask a sensitive question, and link these questions to the original contract of mutual honesty and directness. I repeatedly acknowledge that Sarah does not want to see me so that she doesn't have to demonstrate her reluctance. Because Sarah doesn't come with a therapeutic agenda, I inquire, with permission, why people have pressured her to seek counselling, making sure she knows that I'm not accepting their views. I gradually link the reasons that the doctors and her family want her to attend (*external pressure*) to her own goals (*internal pressure*). I then intensify Sarah's goals and use them as the rationale and mandate for the work.

DOI: 10.4324/9781003354925-7

You will notice I gradually get a mandate on how to work and what to work on, asking Sarah's permission to ask questions in small progressive steps (*layering*) that will allow me to help her. Managing the power, role, and responsibilities later in this session is discussed using more of the transcript in Chapter 10.

Jeff:	Sarah, is it?
Sarah:	(*looking down*) Yep.
Jeff:	I'm Jeff, your counsellor today.
Sarah:	Hi.
Jeff:	How you doing?
Sarah:	(*disinterested*) I'm here.
Jeff:	I get the sense that maybe you don't want to be here.

> Making a feature of the constraint that Sarah doesn't want to see me

Sarah:	Nope. Nah.
Jeff:	So, how come you had to come here. It sounds like it wasn't your choice.

> Making a feature of the constraint, emphasising that I know Sarah doesn't want to see me

Sarah:	Augh, I've just come out of hospital. Um, again! And the doctors pretty much told me if I don't turn up and I end up in hospital again, err I'm going to be made involuntary.
Jeff:	(*slightly surprised*) Oh, Ok. Right.

> My tone shows subtle warmth, acknowledging that Sarah feels that she has been given an ultimatum

Sarah:	Yep. I've met a few people on the ward who fit that bill and it doesn't sound nice.
Jeff:	So, you're sort of here involuntarily, in a way.

> Making a feature of the constraint that Sarah doesn't want to see me and demonstrating directness

Sarah:	Pretty much.
Jeff:	Pretty much.
Sarah:	Yeah. Yeah.

Jeff: Well, let me tell you how I like to work. Which is to be really upfront and direct. I don't want to bullshit you and err, I'll try and be as straight as I can with you and hope you can be straight with me too.

Unilaterally introducing the NBT clinical guideline of mutual honesty and directness – because Sarah doesn't want to collaborate at this stage

---

Sarah: Yeah, look, I appreciate that, err Jeff, but I sort of feel like I've been through this process before.

Jeff: Right.

Sarah: I've been involuntary before and err look, err I don't want to say the wrong thing and end up back in there.

Jeff: Right, ok. One, you're cautious if you say the wrong thing and end up being made involuntary. And also, you've been through this and probably had other counsellors like me say they are going to do the best thing for you, and it hasn't always worked out. Is that true to say?

Making a feature of Sarah's lack of trust – stating an assumption but checking to see if it is correct – to give Sarah a sense of control

---

Sarah: Yeah, and look I've gotten on well with some people too and you know they have left and gone to other jobs and all those sorts of things too so. It's sort of hard to repeat yourself over and over again and yeah.

Jeff: OK, well good on you for being that upfront. I appreciate that. And I'll try to be like that too. So, can I ask you, umm you didn't want to be here, like who pressured you to come?

Using Sarah's directness to begin to get a mandate to work in a mutually honest and direct way; given Sarah doesn't want to be here I start with asking permission to see why others think she should be here. There would be no point asking what Sarah wants from counselling at this stage because she doesn't want anything, so I start where there is energy – her experience of those who have pressured her to attend

---

Sarah: Umm Yeah, so the doctors on the ward, and you know my mother and my sister really wanted me to be here too. So, err yeah. They get pretty worried about me, and I wish they'd back off a bit, but I do love them you know, sort of, yeah.

Jeff: And what's your mum's name?

> Subtle warmth and personalising her mum

Sarah: Louise.
Jeff: Louise. And your sister?
Sarah: Mary.
Jeff: Yeah, ok. And um, what do they, can I ask. Sounds like you're not here because you want to be here, but your mum and sister want you to be here and also the doctors on the ward. Can I ask maybe firstly why the doctors on the ward thought you should be here?

> Layering is asking permission for each small step in the process of gradually getting agreement on what to work on. I reiterate that I know Sarah doesn't want to be here and ask permission to inquire why others think she should attend. There is external pressure on Sarah from the referrers wanting her to attend but at this stage Sarah doesn't want anything from me. My task is to gradually link what Sarah wants (internal pressure) to what others want for her (external pressure)

Sarah: Umm, I've had a couple of admissions you know pretty quickly. Sort of, umm I went in then spent a couple of weeks out and then I was back in – so I think they thought some community help might be a good thing. I haven't, it's been a while since I've had a case manager or therapy and Mum, she's sort of worried about me and so is Mary. I haven't been working for a while umm, and they say they are not happy about me using. So yeah.
Jeff: So, they are worried about you but want you to be doing things differently, and that's a bit of a pressure on you.

> Subtle cognitive warmth and care

Sarah: Yeah, yeah, yeah, but then again, yeah, you know it's my life, I'm 35 now, umm yeah, I've been through all this before. Yeah, yeah.
Jeff: Ok. Can I ask um then, like I said I'd be upfront and so I will. Um, you've been though all this in the past. What's been most unhelpful about all the help people have tried to give you and probably, to be honest, they're probably trying to be helpful.

> Using our agreement to be upfront, I signpost that I want to ask a question about being helpful, but without too much attachment to being helpful, so I decide to ask what would be helpful in the negative. I'm also being honest when I say, "I think people have tried to help," rather than strategically aligning with Sarah against the doctors and her family

Sarah: Yeah. That's right I'll give them that.

Jeff: But it hasn't been helpful, let's be honest. So, what hasn't been helpful. And the reason I'm asking that is that I don't want to do the same things that haven't been helpful in the past.

> Continuing to emphasise my agreement to be honest and direct. I'm also explaining why I'm asking a complex question so Sarah knows "the rules of the therapy game" which I hope will gradually build trust

Sarah: Um. Well, um.

Jeff: And feel free to say. Like, I know that sometimes it feels like you shouldn't criticise other professionals in front of a counsellor, but I'd really appreciate you being really straight.

> Inviting mutual honesty and directness, whilst acknowledging the constraint to Sarah being honest

Sarah: There are a probably a few things. I'm just not used to talking to start with, it's just not my thing. Umm. You know being, my experience of Indian mental health you know, it's not ok. It's pretty, yeah, it's something that's not talked about. I'd rather deal with it on my own. Yeah! I feel that when I've come in before [to helpers] I've been pretty honest about stuff and then you know I've either been told off or I've been put in hospital because other people think what I'm saying is pretty crazy. Um and so it feels like shit, like why should I come in and you know I'm trying to get help but then if I say the wrong thing I land back in there. When I do finally feel some trust, those people have left, so yeah, I think there are all those things and I get that Mum and Mary want me to get help, but I think it's hard for them to accept that I've just got issues.

Jeff: So, in the past when you have been honest about things it hasn't worked out for you and here I am asking you to be upfront and direct, so you're going to be very cautious and you're not going to trust me, so I guess I've got to earn that. And um, although you're here voluntarily but really with a pressure, a pressure, over you.

> I'm enacting honesty and directness and making a feature of the constraint that Sarah doesn't trust mental health professionals, and by implication me, yet

Sarah: Yeah, feels like it yeah.

Jeff: So, um I'll ask some questions, as I said I'll be pretty direct, so it I might seem a bit pushy, and you can say if you don't want to answer them.

> I'm signposting that I will, as agreed, ask direct questions, but I'm giving and acknowledging that Sarah has the power not to answer them

Sarah: Yeah.
Jeff: So, but can I ask what your mum is worried about? No, no, let's start with um, you said you'd rather deal with the issues that you have on your own. Because in the Indian community it sounds like it is seen as really negative or...
Sarah: Yeah, it's um...
Jeff: Stigmatised and ...
Sarah: We don't talk about it. It's sort of like, if there is something wrong with me, I think people are going to judge Mum.
Jeff: Right. So, in some ways you're almost protective of your mum.
Sarah: Yeah.
Jeff: Oh ok. Right and I can see that, that is sort of important to you because you know, you are pretty emotional about it.

> Subtle warmth and care

Sarah: (*crying*) Yeah. I feel really guilty about putting her through the wringer.
Jeff: So, it sounds like you do see there is some problem because you want to deal with it on your own, but you do see there is some problem. Is that right? Would that be fair enough to say? I don't want to put words into your mouth.

> Trying to get a genuine mandate from Sarah on what she wants to work on – I take the lead in suggesting she sees a problem but ask her to confirm it. I'm starting to link the external pressure Sarah is under to an internal pressure

Sarah: Um, I suppose so. Like I've landed back in hospital a couple of times, and it's been pretty awful, and I don't want to go back.
Jeff: Ok, so you actually don't want to go back to hospital, um, but you don't want to talk about it because it might be shaming for your mum.

> Starting to elicit a problem that Sarah defines, not others, whilst continuing to acknowledge her concern for her mum

Sarah: Yeah.
Jeff: And do you find it difficult to talk about these sort of things just personally or...
Sarah: Yeah.
Jeff: ... or is it more about protection of your mum?

Sarah: I think both. I um, I sort of I don't see the point of talking. And um, I'm not sure how helpful it is anyway. Like, if I end up back in hospital anyway like um, has it really made a difference.

Jeff: So, is staying out of hospital one of the most important things for you?

Sarah: (*quite determined*) Yep. Yeah, I don't want to go back. It's horrible.

Jeff: (*surprised*) Ok, ok, so that's something you would want to work on.

> Motivational congruence- I've managed to link Sarah's internal goal to the external goal of those wanting Sarah to seek help

Jeff: Um and your mum? What would, and by asking what your mum's worried about, and what she would hope for you, I'm not going to take her side. But just to understand what she's worried about.

> Again, explaining the rules of the therapy game – so Sarah knows the reason I am asking the question. Being transparent to build trust

Sarah: I don't know, you'd have to ask her.

Jeff: Yeah, sure but you're here.

Sarah: Of what she's worried about?

Jeff: Yeah.

Sarah: Arrh, I don't know, she says she's worried about me, but. Um, probably the drugs and not being in hospital. And not having a job at the moment. Yeah.

Jeff: So, they are some pretty big things. Stop the drugs is that a fair assumption?

> Being direct and avoiding jargon. Still focusing on what Sarah's mum wants because Sarah is still reluctant to engage on her own terms

Sarah: Yeah.

Jeff: Um not going to hospital. And she'd love you to be working.

Sarah: Yeah, and just doing more with myself, I'm sort of not doing a whole lot during the day she says, and so she keeps nagging me about it.

Jeff: So that is what your mum wants, but which of those, which go closest to what you want? Obviously staying out of hospital, is that something you sort of both want?

> Linking Sarah's goal and her mum's goal, which was the initial focus of my interview

Sarah: Yeah, I suppose, yeah, I suppose we both want that. Yeah, yeah.
Jeff: Right, ok, um and again I said I'd be really upfront so – the drugs – is that something you see as a problem too or is that just a problem for your mum?

Signposting a confronting question and then asking it directly and being open to whatever answer Sarah gives

Sarah: Um, I think it's mainly Mum who sees that. I um, look I do it with friends. It relaxes me. If I get stressed, it's nice to know it's there.
Jeff: Right, so. And getting a job? Is that something you're interested in or is that more your mum?

Being genuinely curious, clarifying what Sarah sees as a problem and again open to any answer Sarah gives

Sarah: Um, I'd like to get a job again, yeah that would be good. Um, yeah, I think that would be good.
Jeff: You might have different ideas about how to go about it or what sort of job, or whatever. But something you both want is to stay out of hospital and ideally get a job.

Continuing to strive towards motivational congruence – to ensure that I know what Sarah wants from therapy

Sarah: Wouldn't you?
Jeff: Yeah. Well, um.
Sarah: Surely that's not too much to ask for, is it?
Jeff: Yeah, and in some ways I'm lucky I'm not in hospital and I've got a job so I can see why you would want the same.

Acknowledging openly and non-defensively that I'm in a lucky position rather than downplaying my privilege and acknowledging that what Sarah wants is understandable. Demonstrating honesty and directness

Twelve minutes into the interview, Sarah is still cautious but starting to look more engaged than she did at the start. I have moved from a focus on why others wanted her to seek help to what Sarah wants to change. I will continue to acknowledge that Sarah didn't want to attend counselling with me, signpost any tough questions, and make overt that my questions are designed to help her get what she wants: To get a job and stay out of hospital. I will continue to be upfront and direct, in line with the way I said I would work, especially about any sensitive issues.

My work with Sarah continues in Chapter 10, to illustrate the importance of being upfront and direct about power, role, and responsibility.

The ideal No Bullshit therapist

Effective NBT therapists acknowledge the complexity of the task they face and start by being honest and caring with themselves. They act with the directness of the pragmatic business world and the warmth and care of the counselling and therapeutic community. They embrace a lifetime of wisdom about the realities, extent, and paralysing impact of unwanted events that disrupt how we would like to act. Experienced NBT therapists integrate all the skills described above in a sophisticated way and communicate clearly, driven not by strategy but by guileless honesty. As part of my PhD research, I asked participants affected by severe drought, *what makes an ideal therapist*? A female farmer's response was, "Someone who has the skills, knowledge, and people skills to tell it as it is and the discretion to treat you like a person with hopes and dreams that have been very bruised" (Young, 2012, p. 184).

An ideal NBT practitioner aspires to maintain an awareness of power and the integrity to not abuse it, obfuscate it, or explain it away. An NBT practitioner embraces the authority of their position to help people live the best possible life they can – no matter who they are. When working with clients who have acted abusively or criminally, the NBT therapist is sufficiently self-reflective to be able to hold the client whilst holding them to account. Engaging with the good in people while directly challenging bad behaviour can be one of those beautiful moments in therapy.

My colleague, Ken Wolfe, has unique insights because he was an ardent therapy-hater who became a therapy-lover and a natural No Bullshit Therapist, counselling fellow inmates. Let me tell you Ken's extraordinary story.

Ken, now in his 60s, was a promising sportsman in his teens but developed a serious gambling addiction in his 20s. Ken joined the police force, continued gambling, and eventually resigned from the force to use his entitlements to pay down crippling gambling debts. He subsequently got work in the planning department of a local council but continued to gamble. Depressed, in debt and desperate, Ken started taking bribes to facilitate building permit approvals, for which he was eventually charged and imprisoned.

Prior to sentencing, cynical and distrusting, Ken saw a counsellor to help his impending court appearance, not to address his personal issues. However, in prison, he trained as a counsellor and evolved into an effective and compassionate no-bullshit therapist helping fellow inmates.

In 2017, I interviewed Ken and towards the end of the hour-long discussion, I asked him to reflect on his own experience and to describe what he thought a counsellor needs to do to engage people who are suspicious of therapy:

Ken: Relax, a touch of skin, so a shake of the hands, maybe a pat on the shoulder, "good to see you, have a seat." The preamble about honesty, integrity, this is about you, not about me. "I'm going to be as honest with you as I can." It's ok for the counsellor to be flawed. Don't be afraid to use the honesty thing, because the more you use it, the more he's going to get used to it. I'm relaxed, I'm assertive, I'm sympathetic when I need to be sympathetic. I have empathy when I need to show empathy, but I have passion, and I have power. Every single client who comes in will sit down opposite you as the counsellor and his first thought is, *you're a sign of authority*. So, the first thought is, *I'm going to clam up. What could a counsellor do!* Then it's up to you to relax them. To bring them into your world, what you want, and what you want to talk about. What they can say. They can say anything they like. Language is no issue; speak how you would speak at home. And that sets off, and a bit like today, it sets the tone of the next two or three sessions. And if you've gotten him, you'll know it, you'll feel it. They'll reach for you, or you'll see their body language, and you'll see that they want to be rid of their burden. And they're all carrying a burden, Jeff. Every single one of them is carrying a burden that they need to put in their knowledge and wisdom drawer. I'm big on this wisdom and knowledge drawer. "Remember when you were drug dealing and you were sleeping with one-eye open because the coppers are only one-step behind you, and they are! Just one step behind you. Do you need to live like that?"

Jeff: So, show some warmth and bit of a connection. Have the spiel and discussion around setting up the context for honesty and directness. Being upfront about your power and be passionate. Recognise that the person is burdened by this and link the honesty, in a way, to lifting the burden. That, it's going to be a bit a bit tough, and you'll be a bit challenging. Anything else?

Ken: That it will need courage. They think they've been brave before; this is the bravest thing they are going to do. This is the thing that's going to change their lives; Talk about changing your reality. Here is an opportunity. Between us, we can change it, we can change it.

Jeff: You're showing you are there for them. And that you see the good person that they can be. But they are not living true to their core values. There's a lot in it!

Ken: Yeah.

Jeff: Anything else?

Ken: The gambling addict is going to be the worst liar and obfuscator and will try to deflect you at every turn. So, you have to be pretty strong with him.

Jeff: So, you've got to be a bit persistent, and not be pushed away. You've got to use some personal authority?

Ken: You do, you really do.

Jeff: And talk their language and not obfuscate and use jargon.

Ken: Yeah, talk their language. And the other thing, at the end of it, leave it like when you first met. Say "It's been a good conversation" And that's what it is, it's not a session, it's a conversation.

(Interview used with permission from Ken Wolfe and The Bouverie Centre, La Trobe University, Australia).

Put another way, the greatest compliment an NBT therapist could get from a client, paraphrasing an NBT workshop participant, is, *if I needed to talk about a difficult, complex, or shameful issue, I'd like to talk with you, and if I had to hear bad news, I'd like to hear it from you.*

In the following chapter, a range of NBT safety strategies are provided.

Reference

Young, J. (2012). *A no bullshit approach to drought.* PhD thesis, La Trobe University, Melbourne, Australia.

8 No Bullshit Therapy
safety strategies

This approach (NBT) also embodies a truly 'humanistic' approach to the counselling relationship, which seems to motivate clients to want to invest in their own capacity to change

— (NBT Workshop participant, Melbourne)

The truth might set you free, but it can also get you into trouble. Therefore, it is reassuring to have a range of safety strategies and remedies if you do get into trouble. Knowing you have a range of safety strategies also provides greater confidence to take the risk of applying No Bullshit Therapy (NBT) ideas. Having a range of safety strategies at your finger tips also helps inform a recovery action plan if your initial efforts don't work out well. It is important to remember that vexed and complicated contexts are always full of risks, and sometimes the most unhelpful thing to do is to play it safe or to "cover-your-arse" by doing what is expected.

The most effective way to promote safety is to integrate and implement all the NBT Clinical Guidelines. If stuck, it can be helpful to stop and explore if one of the NBT guidelines has been neglected or needs greater emphasis. Therapists are therefore advised to develop a self-reflective consciousness about which NBT guideline they might struggle with most, possibly using the guided imagery exercise framework presented in Chapter 5. In addition, it is important to be familiar with a range of safety strategies which may help you both to take calculated risks in your clinical work and *get back on track* if it feels it is all going awry. The following list of safety strategies was developed in response to participants in our NBT workshops asking, *What should you do if your honesty and directness makes things worse?* Whilst these safety strategies may seem grossly inadequate, they are aimed to stimulate you to develop your own ideas that will work for you, your clients, and your unique work role.

Remember risks are part of effective clinical practice

In considering the negative impacts of directly addressing sensitive issues and hard to raise topics, it is also important to consider the impact of not addressing them. In an article called, "Cut the Crap: Language – Risks and Relationships in Systemic Therapy and Supervision*,"* Ged Smith (2011) makes the following points about therapeutic safety in relation to speaking up about the seemingly unspeakable: "Too

DOI: 10.4324/9781003354925-8

often we can be paralysed into avoiding certain topics for fear that we might offend somebody" (p. 63); "Not voicing them does not make them go away" (p. 67). He goes on to argue that:

> The art and the beauty of therapy is in creating a space where things can be said that are so countercultural, and occasionally so challenging that people would never accept them in any other context...words that would otherwise create conflict can turn out to be helpful. It is as if the normal rules of social discourse do not apply. Generally, in therapy we have a licence to do the unusual, by asking questions that would be unacceptable in any other context.
>
> (pp. 67–68)

It is important to create a warm and caring foundation for the directness to be received well. But at the end of the day, one must take a risk to authentically engage, especially in situations where there is significant tension.

About ten years ago Simon, the physiotherapist I was attending on a semi-regular basis, asked me about my therapeutic work. I had been attracted to Simon because he practised Single Session chiropractic work; he would have a vigorous session and then say only come back if you need to. I'd been reduced to leaving my diary in the car on purpose to foil the assumption made by previous chiropractors I'd seen that I would automatically continue to make appointments. In the context of the discussion about my work, Simon, who looked very robust and had a very successful practice, revealed that he had been hospitalised with anorexia nervosa in his late adolescence. (Global Lifetime prevalence rates of eating disorders range from 0.74% to 2.2% for males compared to 2.58% to 8.4% for females and cost the Australian economy between 2007 and 2017, an estimated $84 billion from years lost due to disability and death, and an annual loss of earnings of about $1.646 billion; Hay et al., 2023.) When I asked Simon what had helped him recover, he matter-of-factly told me that an older nurse had remonstrated with him, "What the fuck do you think you are doing to your parents!" I assume Simon's recovery was much more complicated than this and that he was ready to respond to this nurse's response in a productive way. No matter the deeper story, Simon attributed the beginning of his recovery to this seemingly outrageous comment.

There, but for the grace of God, go I

The most powerful and effective safety strategy is to be sympathetic to the plight of people; sympathetic but not patronising and certainly not naive. It is powerfully therapeutic to adopt a non-pathologising, non-blaming stance, even towards people, or especially towards people who may be acting in unhelpful ways, either towards themselves or others. Many models of practice and their underlying philosophies can provide guidance to help therapists to adopt and maintain a non-blaming attitude when situations become frustrating and difficult – the simplest is to truly believe that: *There, but for the grace of God, go I* when interacting with *"difficult"* clients. Adopting such a humanistic stance transforms a *difficult client* into *a client facing a difficult situation*. I personally draw on the philosophy underlying systemic family therapy to generate what I call *contextual compassion* towards clients – I step into the shoes of my clients and try and appreciate the world from their perspective. Family therapy inherited a post-war II optimistic view that clients can change. It sees all individual behaviour in a context and appreciates the powerful impact of interaction and relationship on individual behaviour. When I feel like I am drowning, feel frightened by a combative client, or impatient with an unco-operative client, I try to manage these uncomfortable feelings. For example, I accept that these feelings are likely to make blame attractive to me, either towards myself or the client. I check whether my approach may be contributing to the problem. I metaphorically step into the client's shoes and explore their relational, structural, social, economic, historical, or family context for explanations of their behaviour. This tends to create a contextual compassion, not a patronising compassion, which helps me to come from a good place and hence allows me to be more honest and direct about a client's problematic behaviour – which includes holding them accountable for their actions.

Authenticity and therapeutic alliance

Indirectness or insincerity is likely to be experienced as bullshit and hence will typically elicit greater anger or suspicion from unhappy clients. Authenticity linked to the client's goals or the task at hand is an NBT therapist's best friend. If things begin to go awry, restating or stating more clearly the rationale for your honesty and directness may help. As I have mentioned earlier, there is only one way to be authentic, but there are many ways to express authenticity – try conveying your genuineness in ways more consistent with your client's ways of communicating – maybe your authenticity is not coming across. Remember the client needs to experience your authenticity; it is not enough for you to simply feel it. I learned this lesson from Nancy Black, the film director I've mentioned, and whom I worked with on four training videos that I produced in the mid-1990s for mental health workers and families dealing with mental illness. I was struggling as the narrator in these films to translate to camera the genuine warmth I felt for these families. At about the 17th take filming my introduction for the first video Nancy told me the following story in a desperate effort to avoid hitting me over the head with the clapper. Nancy shared how she had interviewed an actor friend who was playing a character in a Bertolt Brecht play, about his extraordinary ability to hold the audience in a trance as his character contemplated, in silence, an impossible dilemma – probably a choice of evils. Nancy revealed that her friend had admitted that whilst appearing to be wracked with emotional indecision, he was simply counting the number of lights at the back of the theatre. As a professional actor, he'd discovered what he had to do to convey to the audience the intensity of the emotion he felt. To this day, I know I need to be careful whilst filming training DVDs that I don't come across as stuck up – it is just something about the physical structure of my face – my feelings of warmth don't translate to film naturally. So, I need to feel like I am having fun, even if it is talking about loss and grief, to come across as warm and empathic on video. Essentially, Nancy's message to me and it is now my message to you, was, that we need to read our audience; how are our clients experiencing our efforts to be warm and empathic?

Seeking direct feedback

The NBT therapist can call on the mandate of mutual honesty and directness created early in the work, to ask for direct feedback from the client, if things go off track. If you have not established an agreement about mutual honesty and directness – pause to do this as a prelude to addressing difficulties in the therapeutic relationship. Once you elicit feedback – take it as a gift rather than a personal attack. To this day, I benefit from an experience that occurred in my second job. Together, with a hospital chaplain John Mackley, I established a family therapy team in a large psychiatric hospital. We had installed a one-way screen so that colleagues behind the screen could provide additional advice to families and feedback to the therapist. On one occasion, I was the therapist and John was behind the screen. The father in the family repeatedly questioned the value of the therapy and I struggled to respond in a productive way. Once the family left, John provided some useful feedback to me about my response to the father's criticism. He reflected that when the father criticised the therapy, my voice went soft, and I looked pathetic and defeated. John pointed out that it was a critique of the therapy – and not of me. I have never forgotten John's words. Now if a client criticises the therapy, I don't take it personally, which frees me up to inquire openly and directly about why a client feels the therapy (not me) is not going well. Tone is important here – as is your response to the feedback. Inquiring about a client's concerns in a non-blaming, straightforward tone and responding actively, practically, and non-defensively to what you find out will go a long way to creating a productive response to a potential crisis. Ged Smith, whom I've introduced earlier in the book, describes a similar stance:

> If we have a good enough therapeutic relationship with a family then they are unlikely to be offended by a mistake we might make or a false assumption we might arrive at. If, however, they can inform us of this, and we can take it with grace, then that for me is a sign of the best kind of alliance, where people can correct us without fear, and we can accept such comments without defensiveness.
>
> (Smith, 2011, p. 63)

I am aware that there is a dilemma here. Sometimes clients are unable to share critical feedback with their practitioners (let's face it, it's challenging enough for professional therapists to share critical feedback with clients) even if we ask genuinely, with a non-blaming, straightforward tone. My family therapy and NBT colleague Pam Rycroft, gets around this by asking, "I have this idea that you're worried about what I might be thinking of you right now. Would it help for me to tell you openly?"

Talking about the talking

Exiting the relationship to talk about the relationship itself – its rules and its effectiveness can be a powerful and pragmatic way of addressing difficulties when the NBT approach seems to be missing the mark. Making overt your intention, rationale, and purpose and seeking advice and feedback about the usefulness of how the relationship is unfolding can be a way to get back on track, as demonstrated in the following fictional account:

Jeff: Can I ask how I am coming across? I really want to help you. That's why I'm being so pushy, as I said I would be, but I get the feeling I'm not helping.
Client: No, it's not helping!
Jeff: What would work better for you?
Client: Going a bit slower and asking what I've tried to do in the past.
Jeff: Ok let's try that – but we will still have to talk about some sensitive issues at some stage if I'm going to be helpful to you.
Client: Yeah, I know.

Checking in with clients (from Single Session Therapy)

I hold the view that therapy should be productive, useful, but also efficient. Most therapists including myself have experienced what my colleague Mark Furlong calls *therapeutic drift*, where over time the clarity and effectiveness of early sessions are gradually lost. The work may feel comfortable – maybe too comfortable – but the work has lost touch with its purpose. Clients are more likely to be able to tolerate uncertainty, discomfort, and tension if it is in pursuit of what is important to them. The pioneering family therapist, Jay Haley, was fond of saying that client cooperation fades the further away therapy veers from the presenting problem. Staying on track and linking the hard work to the client's goals or the mandated task is likely to create greater authority in the worker and hence greater safety in the working relationship. The following fictitious dialogue demonstrates a simple example of how this could be done:

Jeff: Can I check in to see how this is going for you – I know we agreed I'd have to ask some tough questions if I was going to help you get on better with your son. But do you think we are talking about the things that are most important to you?
Client: Yeah, it's hard, but I want to be there for my son.
Jeff: If I am going to really help you be there for him, we need to be able to understand why he is so angry with you. Does that make sense to you?
Client: Yeah, I know I need to know why he is so angry with me.

Therapeutic drift is not always obvious. I was working with Sophie, a woman in her 60s who felt torn between looking after her 28-year-old son Steve who was severely incapacitated by chronic schizophrenia, her elderly infirm mother, and her second husband, who was supportive but feeling neglected by his wife. Sophie, a therapy-lover, was a very compassionate person who had trouble saying no and as a result was running herself into the ground. Exploring Sophie's family-of-origin had helped me to understand some of the reasons why she found it so hard to say no. I discovered that her father, a charismatic man, had been involved in the intelligence field and saw Sophie as his *little helper* which, along with her caring nature, had led her to always help others in her adult life. Whilst this family-of-origin work provided Sophie with a context for her difficulty in saying no, and seemed to contribute to strengthening the therapeutic relationship, I decided to *check in* to see if the work was on target. The work seemed so intimate, it took all my discipline to *interrupt the conversation* and simply ask, *Is this what we should be talking about right now?* I still vividly remember Sophie's response, even though I finished seeing her many years ago. *Well, it would be good to talk about how my cancer is affecting me!* Since that experience I have never assumed I am talking about the most important thing in a client's life – I know that I don't necessarily know – so I practice the discipline of regularly *checking in* to test if I am on track.

It is similarly helpful to check in about the process of therapy, not just the content. For example, *I said at the start of our work together that I was going to be pretty direct. Is that still, ok?* Alternatively, *I said I'd be pretty direct, but I want to check that it is working for you or whether I need to tread more carefully?*

Intuition and judgement

Therapy is an art rather than a science and hence intuition and judgement are important and cannot be replaced by simple recipes. I told David to shut up and he loved it. I could have been wearing a black eye if I'd told another client the same thing. Or told David to shut up using a different tone. If it doesn't feel right – it may not be – but it might be right. How do you solve this dilemma? Often our reluctance to challenge is due to our own fear, not because of the client's vulnerability. Taking a risk knowing you are motivated by good and knowing you can apologise if things go awry is one way forward. Combining the techniques of NBT with your intuition such as remembering to create a marker – when you're going to take a risk – when you feel directness will help – is another way forward. Talking aloud about your internal dilemma – *I'm wondering if I should take a risk and share my thoughts openly, because* (rationale) *but I'm afraid you might get upset*, is yet another way forward. These and other ways forward are likely to be enhanced by having a good understanding of your own internal world, achieved through self-reflection, and possibly using the NBT principles in the pursuit of personal development. But at the end of the day, taking a risk is taking a risk.

Apology

The truth emerges more readily from error than confusion.

— Francis Bacon

The tyranny of the novice is the feeling of needing to know everything, while the liberation of the veteran is knowing that we don't have to!

— Ged Smith (2011, p. 63)

Apology is one of the most under-used and under-rated therapeutic techniques. If we take risks as therapists, we are likely to make mistakes. Only one thing is worse than making a mistake – never making one. Clients come to us because people in their social network have not been helpful – therefore we often need to break the mould, provide something different, and respond in non-predictable ways – not an easy brief. Knowing that we don't need to always get it right, as Ged Smith reminds us, can be as liberating as is knowing that if we do get it wrong, we can offer a sincere apology and start again.

Stop and start again

When all else fails it can be an option to formally give up and start again, learning from what worked and what didn't the first time around. Rather than a failure, stopping and starting again should be seen as a responsible and responsive thing to do when nothing seems to be working. Being upfront about what's not working is a powerful component of NBT, especially when raised in a matter-of-fact, non-defensive, non-emotional, and non-blaming tone. Starting again allows for re-negotiation of how the work will commence, proceed, and finish – including how differences, difficulties, and dilemmas will be addressed and managed, in a better way.

The following chapter describes tools that I have created, informed by the NBT Clinical Guidelines, to provide a structure to facilitate productive outcomes in a range of challenging situations. Hopefully, these tools encourage you to develop your own.

References

Hay, P., Aouad, P., Le, A., Marks, A., Maloney, D., Touyz, S., & Maguire, S. (2023). Epidemiology of eating disorders: Population, prevalence, disease burden and quality of life informing public policy in Australia: A rapid review. *Journal of Eating Disorders, 11*(23). http://doi.org/10.1186/s40337-023-00738-7.

Smith, G. (2011). Cut the crap: Language, risks and relationships in systemic therapy and supervision. *Australian and New Zealand Journal of Family Therapy, 32*(1), 58–69.

9   No Bullshit Therapy tools

The most important persuasion tool you have in your entire arsenal is integrity
— Zig Ziglar (Author, salesman, and motivational speaker)

I have used the No Bullshit Therapy (NBT) Clinical Guidelines to generate a range of tools to help supervisees stuck in their work with clients, to help clients raise difficult issues with their family members, friends, or work colleagues, and to help anyone who needs to make a sensitive request of another. These tools can be used verbatim or used as inspiration to develop your own tools. The self-supervision tools can be used directly with clients or supervisees or as the name *self-supervision* implies, can be passed onto clients or supervisees to guide their own self-reflection in the comfort and privacy of their own home. The NBT "hand" provides a simple image, mnemonic, and structure, to make everyday requests more effective.

Self-supervision for workers

Self-supervision is a five-step process to assist workers who are feeling stuck in their work with a client. In fact, this is the origin of the NBT self-supervision process, which is why it, maybe strangely, has supervision in the title, although it can be used by clients. The process came together in a group supervision session I facilitated in a community health centre many years ago, mainly because I found it difficult to provide useful advice to Jenny, an experienced therapist in the group who was working with Barry, a 48-year-old client. I asked Jenny five questions based on NBT and then integrated her responses to all five questions into one response, using her own words as much as possible, that she could use to provide direct feedback to Barry. The exercise was helpful and I have since used the NBT self-supervision tool to help clients have the difficult conversations they need to have with other family members (see next section).

Jenny is struggling with Barry because he is sexually suggestive during their work together in a gambler's help program. Jenny reports that Barry, a solicitor, looks her *up and down* during sessions, and asks, "How did you feel after the last session?" in a way that makes Jenny feel uncomfortable. Jenny describes how Barry's seemingly innocent comments, such as, *I really enjoyed today, I think it's really working for both of us,* comes across to her as sleazy.

DOI: 10.4324/9781003354925-9

Barry had sought therapy because he felt traumatised following the breakup of a three-month relationship with Vanessa, whom he had met at a social club. Barry's mother had died after a long illness around the time Barry and Vanessa first met. According to Barry, Vanessa had pursued him relentlessly and became very possessive as they got to know each other. After several months, Barry discovered that Vanessa was having affairs with other members of the club. When Vanessa began telling her other boyfriends about him, Barry began to fear he may be bashed by her other partners.

Jenny had gradually realised that swinging was part of the social club. She had sought advice from an external private supervisor who advised her to set concrete goals, but this had only partially helped. The verbatim NBT self-supervision for workers' process with Jenny is presented here:

1 What would you say to Barry if you "said it, as it is," "shot from the hip," or said what you would like to be able to say?

   Jenny: I don't know whether to believe you or not, I don't know whether you want to change anything. You strike me as a sleaze-bag.

2 How would you say this in a non-blaming way? It can be useful to explore if there is anything about the client that may push the supervisee's buttons such as family-of-origin issues or other past experiences that might get in the way of responding directly, but without anger or resentment. Without going into details, a gentle discussion revealed Jenny had experienced inappropriate attention from sleazy men during her adolescence. This led Jenny to fear that if she raised Barry's sleaziness directly, he would get angry or aggressive.

   Jenny: I may not understand your whole situation, but I have some understanding how the break-up with Vanessa affected you. I can understand why you would be frightened about the other men at the social club. We need to move on and work out what you want to do about it because we only have six sessions (*host agency policy*). If I'm going to be helpful to you, I really need you to focus on what you want to change and not on how we are getting on, which feels a bit sleazy to be honest.

3 Acknowledge any difficulties or constraints that make it hard for Barry to do what you would like him to do.

   Jenny: I know you are upset about the loss of your relationship with Vanessa and that was on top of losing your mum very recently. I understand you are frightened about the other blokes at the social club. I know you would like to feel really safe with me before you start addressing these big issues.

4   Articulate Barry's strengths that will help him change.

> *Jenny:*   You are a very a bright man and are able to address difficulties head-on when you put your mind to it. You are a solicitor who understands about contracts and working relationships.

5   State what you want to happen in specific and tangible terms.

> *Jenny:*   I need you to genuinely look at your part in the situation. If I am going to be helpful, I need you to focus on what you want to be different. I want you to stop looking at me up and down and commenting on how you feel about me and the sessions – I need you to respect me professionally if I am going to be able to help you address your problems.
>
> I integrated Jenny's responses (to steps 1–5) and read them back to her, trying to use her own words as verbatim as possible:
>
> *Jeff:*   I may not understand your whole situation, but I know you are upset about the loss of your relationship with Vanessa and that was on top of losing your mum very recently. I understand you are frightened about the other blokes at the social club. I know you would like to feel really safe with me before you start addressing these big issues. But we need to focus on what you want to be different because we only have six sessions, and if I'm going to be helpful, I need you to focus on what you want to be different and for you to genuinely look at your part in the situation. You are a very bright man and you're able to address difficulties head-on when you put your mind to it. You are a solicitor who understands about contracts and working relationships. For me to be helpful to you I need you to respect me professionally. I want you to stop looking at me up and down and commenting on how you feel about me. If I'm going to be helpful to you, I really need you to focus on what you want to change and not on how we are getting on, which, to be honest, feels a bit sleazy.

Although Jenny felt relieved to have a structure to provide a way forward, that was consistent with her views about Barry, she eventually decided to refer Barry onto another therapist.

Whilst the NBT tools can be helpful to negotiate vexed situations, they remain vexed situations, and no approach, and certainly no tool, is going to ensure smooth or successful outcomes in all situations. Sometimes the outcome is naught but achieved in a respectful way (that is why the final step [little finger] on the NBT hand [see later] is called an *honourable conclusion)*. Sometimes the best outcome is to refer the client onto someone or some organisation more suitable.

Self-supervision for clients

The NBT self-supervision process can also be used to help clients stuck in their relationships. I have used this tool for example, to help parents find a way to ask their reluctant son with major drug problems to attend therapy with them, to help a father respond to a physical attack by his son-in-law, to provide guidance to a grandmother who was being taken advantage of by her angry but dependent granddaughter, and to help a client address a difficult work relationship. The self-supervision tool helps clients have the hard conversations they want to have, with other family members, or colleagues. The only significant difference to the NBT self-supervision for workers is step two, where the client's task is to describe how they are affected personally by their family members behaviour, using "I" statements. I have found that this is the step that clients, especially parents, find most difficult.

I introduce NBT self-supervision to Eliza and Tony, who I've been seeing in couple therapy for six months. Eliza and Tony's attempts to get their youngest son, Stefan, whom you met in Chapter 5, to family therapy has failed repeatedly. Eliza and Tony swing between avoiding the topic of Stefan seeking help altogether and exploding in frustration; neither approach works. Stefan, a major drug user, flies into unprovoked rages, steals from his parents, swings between being reasonable and aggressive, and lives in a bungalow at the back of Eliza and Tony's home.

In the absence of Stefan, I had helped Eliza and Tony respond in more helpful ways to their son. Our work together addressed their feelings of loss, grief, guilt, and anger and helped Eliza and Tony join forces more effectively as a parenting team. However, the effectiveness of the couple work had gradually petered out and we all agreed we needed to find a way of getting Stefan to join the sessions.

I suggest NBT self-supervision and Eliza and Tony agree to give it a go. I explain that the tool consists of five steps. I encourage Eliza and Tony to fully embrace each step, one at a time, reassuring them that each step softens or moderates the previous steps. I point out that the aim of the self-supervision tool is to integrate all the steps into one nuanced and effective request.

The five steps of NBT self-supervision and Eliza and Tony's verbatim responses are reported below:

1 What would you say to Stefan if you "said it, as it is" or "shot from the hip?"

  a Eliza: I want, need you to come because I need you to tell me how to help you!
  b Tony: You need to take more responsibility for your illness and life. We're here to help but we can't do it for you.

2 Describe the impact of Stefan' actions on you, using "I" statements

  a Eliza: My distress is because I don't know how to help.
  b Tony: I feel powerless, distressed.

3 Acknowledge any difficulties or constraints that would make it hard for Stefan to do what you want him to do.

  a Eliza: You feel there is no point, it'll be more of the same, more talk and because we are in therapy we will talk, and you won't.

b Tony: The situation goes around and around. There is no progress. It'll be another same old same old. It's not going to work, and you'll feel pushed into a corner and ganged up on.

4 Articulate Stefan's strengths that will help him change (in the area you want him to change)

a Eliza: Stefan, deep down you are a caring person.
b Tony: I know you really want things to get better. You're warm and care about others. You're curious about things.

5 State what you want Stefan to do, in specific, tangible, and measurable terms

a Eliza: I want you to come to therapy so we can talk.
b Tony: I want you to attend therapy with us.

To help Eliza and Tony integrate these steps, I write down their responses and then read first Eliza's and then Tony's responses almost verbatim, modelling how their respective invitations to Stefan to attend therapy may sound if they are able to fold their responses to each of the five steps into one integrated request.

I tell Eliza and Tony that their request can commence at whatever step seems appropriate. For example, if a situation is particularly vexed, clients might start with strengths (step 4) or the difficulties (step 3). Whilst I use Eliza's and Tony's words, I also take the liberty of adding a few minor *therapeutic tweaks*, to make their invitation to Stefan even more compelling.

Eliza's responses, when I integrated them, went like this: *I know you feel there's no point coming to therapy because you think it'll be more of the same, just more talk, just us talking, but I really want you to come because I need to know what's important to you and how I can help you! I know you're a really caring person deep down, and I'm just so distressed because I don't know what will help us as a family. I really want you to come to therapy so we can talk and see what might work for us all.*

Eliza was surprised by the power of her own words, as was Tony, whose responses I read back as: *I know you really want things to get better. And I know you're frustrated that the situation just goes around and around and there's no progress. I just feel so powerless and distressed because I don't know what to do. You're curious about things and to be honest, I feel you can take more responsibility for your life. We're here to help but we can't do it for you. I know you probably feel we'll gang up on you or you'll feel pushed into a corner, but I want to help, but we can't do it for you. I really want you to attend therapy with us, so we can all stop doing the same old same old.*

I provide Eliza and Tony with a copy of their responses and invite them to practice at home until they feel they can deliver their personal integrated response confidently to Stefan. Although I do the self-supervision process with both Eliza and Tony, we discuss who might be the most likely to be successful in getting Stefan to attend therapy. I also advise Eliza, who they thought would have the best chance of succeeding, to choose a good time (e.g., not during an argument, not too early in the morning, not when Stefan was high) to deliver the invitation to Stefan.

At the next family therapy session, Stefan arrives with his parents.

I realise the power of the NBT Self Supervision Tool when Beryl, 61 years of age, breaks down in tears of relief having a structured process that she can use to communicate with her 38-year-old daughter, Amy. Beryl is one of the most anxious, tentative, and unconfident women I've worked with in my career, and I found Beryl's uncertainty frustrating (It reminds me of my own mother's uncertainty). Looking over the DVD recordings of our work together, my efforts to help Beryl rebuild her relationship with her daughter Amy and communicate her needs to her more clearly, verge on impatience.

Beryl's tentativeness, although fuelled by her worry about her daughter, leaves Amy increasingly frustrated with her mother. Amy feels her mum is indulgently focusses on herself, rather than expressing grief about the loss of her husband, who had died 18 months earlier. Amy also feels her mum is not interested in her experience of losing her father. Amy's frustration makes her mum even more anxious, which further paralyses Beryl and confirms Amy's feeling of isolation.

I introduce Beryl to NBT self-supervision after a particularly unproductive and frustrating discussion during which I encourage Beryl to be genuinely curious about her daughter's experience. The structured process helps us both; me, to be less frustrated with Beryl's capacity to be clear about her position in relation to Amy and Beryl, to communicate more effectively with Amy. The rambling transcript reflects my hypothesis that Beryl's uncertainty protects others, and maybe herself, from her underlying anger. It also demonstrates my frustrations with Beryl's tentativeness. After reviewing the recording of the session, I realise how hard it would have been for me without the self-supervision structure to keep me focused.

Jeff: This is something a little different [from curiosity], it is helpful when you feel a bit stuck.

Beryl: Yes, I am feeling stuck.

Jeff: There are five different steps, so the idea is that when I ask you about each step you can get fully into it as there will be other steps to modify it. So, the first step is – and you mentioned your tendency to pussy-foot-around – if you were to absolutely say what you thought to Amy, if you didn't pussy foot around, or if you were going to shoot from the hip and not worry about the consequences, just be really direct, how would you put it?

Beryl: I'd want to know what is wrong between us, there seems to be a lot of, of um, er, I don't know ... something there. Um, we don't seem to be able to talk, and when we do, we seem to be angry with each other.

Jeff: Ok, now, are you angry with her?

Beryl: No!

Jeff: (*impatiently*) Ok. So, in a way that is not exactly right, so

Beryl: (*interrupting*) And that frustrates me because I don't feel anger and I don't know why she feels that way. So obviously I'm doing something that is making her angry. We don't really see each other that much.

Jeff: So just go back to what would you say to Amy if you were to be really upfront with her. So, if you were to shoot from the hip.

Beryl: What's going on? What's making you angry with me? I don't know what I've done to upset you.

Jeff: That sounds good. So, you would like to know what is making Amy angry with you.

Beryl: Why are you angry with me type thing?

Jeff: Yeah, something like that. Why are you angry with me? Is that what you are wondering?

Beryl: I don't know what I've done to upset her, (*pause*) I don't know what's going on. I'm wondering why are you so cross with me?

Jeff: Ok. So, you're wondering why you are so cross with me. Now the next step is to say what is the impact of this is on you. How does it impact you, is the next stage?

Beryl: How will it or how does it?

Jeff: How does it?

Beryl: It just makes me feel um (*pause*) oh, hurt that she is angry with me for no particular reason.

Jeff: Hurt in what way?

Beryl: Just my feelings are hurt, I can't, I don't want to talk to her, I just go quiet, and I'd rather not talk then … and that sort of annoys me too, because I sort of go quiet rather than get angry.

Jeff: And when you go quiet how do you feel? Because hurt is a pretty general thing?

Beryl: I genuinely feel hurt. Why is she, um I just get hurt. How do I explain it. I don't get angry. I don't get angry.

Jeff: Maybe um bit more explanation. People get hurt and …

Beryl: Well, I don't want to talk.

Jeff: Makes you feel hurt, and you go quite and you go quiet because?

Beryl: I feel that if I say anything it will be the wrong thing.

Jeff: So, you lose confidence.

Beryl: Yes, yes.

Jeff: So, then what we start doing is add these together. So, something like, Amy I want to know what's wrong between us, we don't seem to be able to talk so well and it just feels like you're really angry with me and this makes me feel hurt and then I close up and then I lose confidence. You could even say, and then I waffle or whatever.

Beryl: Yeah, well I do and that's what she goes crook at me about.

Jeff: The next step is to say why it would it be hard for Amy, what would she be thinking, why would she be angry and frustrated and why would it be hard for Amy to change that.

Beryl: For Amy to change that?

Jeff: Yeah, in relation to what you want her to do. Why do you think it would it be hard for Amy to change?

Beryl: Um.

Jeff: Why would it be hard for her not to be angry?

Beryl: I would probably need to change the way I present myself or something. I don't know. She has, I don't know if she has expectations of me, or whatever um.

Jeff: Just think for a moment of what it would be about your presentation that would make her angry and make it hard for her to not be angry.

Beryl: I'd be better off not saying anything. Um, because it seems if I talk or say things to her and it's not the things that she's wanting to hear that, I'm not quite sure.

Jeff: Yeah, just try and step into her shoes for a moment. And think …

Beryl: Yeah, I'm just imagining her walking in the door.

Jeff: Why do you think it would be hard for her, you know, not to be angry with you? Because that's what you are wanting changed.

Beryl: Obviously it would be something that I would do that would make her not get angry.

Jeff: You've been angry with her, or it could be that other people have been angry with her or she's had a hard life, like if you were just to think, whatever, you talk a lot and it annoys her, you've got different personalities, or that you drive her nuts, or like whatever, what do you think would make it hard for her to shift. (*pause*) I've been pretty blunt in my options haven't I. (*laughing*).

Beryl: Yeah, I can't quite work out how, if I'm in her shoes. Um and er …

Jeff: (*interrupting*) Just knowing her and knowing you.

Beryl: I don't know her very well.

Jeff: Oh well that's why this might be useful because if you are not sure why it would be hard in a way, usually it can be helpful to understand why it might be hard for someone to change. And if you can acknowledge that …

Beryl: That's what she says sometimes that you don't even know, more or less that you don't know me. Maybe it's sort of wanting to get to know her.

Jeff: Right, ok well is it that something that you can feel …

Beryl: That I want to get to know her better or whatever.

Jeff: Yeah, but that's what you want to happen, but what we are trying to work out is why she might find it hard, like. (*pause*) Put it this way, why do you think she is angry with you?

Beryl: Um.

Jeff: It sounds like she's irritable, she's angry with you.

Beryl: Yeah, she's angry with me. She wants to have a go at me.

Jeff: Ok. Have a guess. What's your best guess at why?

Beryl: I annoy her. I don't know why. The only stupid things I can work out is that maybe I might say, I've said don't put the such-and-such thing there and I don't know why. I just say or do the wrong thing. Even if there isn't anything really to have a go, she wants to have a go. And I don't know why.

Jeff: That's why I'm asking you to guess.

Beryl: Oh.

Jeff: It doesn't matter if you get it wrong. It's just having an idea that you are thinking about it and you're thinking what it might be. Maybe let me say some things we've talked about. She gets annoyed that you're asking questions that aren't really interested questions, you waffle, you're indecisive, that you don't know her, that, those sorts of things.

Beryl: Yes, there are all those things, but she knows that but (*pause*) she knows that, it's just me.

Jeff: Just remember that this is a way of letting her know that you know that there are some things you do that annoy her.

Beryl: I've said that to her.

Jeff: This isn't everything. This is just the next stage. Out of all those things we've discussed, which do you think annoys her the most?

Beryl: (*long pause*) I don't know if it would be that not knowing her or not listening.

Jeff: The next step is then what do you think her strengths are, what do you really enjoy about her, that will help her to be able to do what you want?

Beryl: She's very calm. She's intelligent but she's bit of a, she's slightly airy fairy. But she's intelligent. I don't know, there are a lot of things about her I like, she's different to [her sibling] but they're best of mates.

Jeff: Especially, what do you think will help her have this chat to sort things out with you?

Beryl: That she can sort of talk things out in a really calm way. This is why it is interesting to see her get really angry with me.

Jeff: And finally, what would you like her to do? She's frustrated with you or annoyed and angry with you. What would you really like her to do?

Beryl: Probably be able to have conversations, to communicate without her getting ... as a companion, maybe, looking after the baby, just popping in.

Jeff: So, what is it you'd like to happen? So, you would like to communicate in what sort of way?

Beryl: More mother to daughter, more things in common. But we don't seem to have very much in common, not that I ...

Jeff: This is not really, if you don't have much in common, this is not going to make that happen. But you'd like to communicate in a ... What sort of way?

Beryl: Friendly terms rather than just in convenient terms, I suppose.

Jeff: So, they are the steps and what you would do now is to put them all together and you can look at the video, or look at my notes, I can give you a copy of my notes. And what you do is to add them together, so they become one ...

Beryl: (*interrupting*) They follow on type of thing.

Jeff: So, it would be something like this, I'll give you an example using your words: [Amy, I know that there is something wrong between us, we just don't talk much and I get the feeling that you are angry or cross with me, which just makes me feel really hurt and then I lose confidence and then I start to waffle which probably annoys you because you feel that I'm just not listening and hence I don't really get to know you really well. You're a really calm intelligent person, you're really good at talking things through in a calm way so that's what I'd like to be able to do, for us to talk, communicate in a real way, in a friendly way. But I just, and you might go through it a couple of times, but I just feel you're angry all the time so I lose confidence and then I probably don't listen to what you say, and I can understand that makes you angry. But I'd really like to communicate better because you're my daughter.]

Beryl: It comes together, I don't know how you got that.

Jeff: (*insistent*) I got it, I got it from what you said.

Beryl: (*laughing*) I know, but it makes more sense, when you say it than what I …

Jeff: I was just putting that together, I just made a few changes, but not many.

Beryl: No. But it all comes together a bit and you could build on that sort of thing.

Jeff: And you practise it first. So, this is called self-supervision, you don't go straight into it, you practise it, and you refine it a bit. It's real but it's not blaming. That's where I made it a little bit less blaming. And you practise it until you feel comfortable with it and then you find a good time to raise it. Um, and you do the whole lot, and you might check before you start, *Is now a good time?* And you can even have a little marker that I want to say something straight to you, or I want to say …

Beryl: (*interrupting*) It's really important to me.

[We discuss a little more about how Beryl might convey her thoughts directly to Amy and the importance of being open-minded about whatever Amy raises in response. Beryl raises her wish to improve her relationships with her other children. She feels she is not living up to Amy's or her own expectations of being a grandmother. She assumes everyone else can do this naturally without needing to seek help. I normalise seeking help and suggest applying the self-supervision process to help Beryl become the mother (and grandmother) she wants to be for her other children too.]

Beryl: … If I get stressed or whatever if she comes up with something that I don't want to hear, I don't want to feel upset.

Jeff: That's where the curiosity comes in. Just try and think, I really want to know. Just because you hear about it doesn't mean it's true.

Beryl: No, no.

Jeff: But you want to find out her perspective. You might even say I need to think about it, and I'll get back to you.

Beryl: Rather than …

Jeff: Rather than feel it is all your fault and then start apologising. Or getting defensive or fluffing around.

Beryl: Fluffing around. Yeah, well that's what happens, and I know that annoys them.

Jeff: Fluffing around. So that's the sort of thing you can add. It makes me lose confidence, I start fluffing around and not making sense. And I imagine that it drives you nuts. But you're really calm, and we can sort this out and what I want to do is to communicate in friendly terms, where we get to know each other more.

Beryl:	Well, that's not too, it's fairly to the point in a way without being sort of angry and so forth.
Jeff:	Yeah! That's exactly right, good one, that's a good summary.
Jeff:	And that's why it's designed to be upfront, but it's based on idea of being honest and direct with warmth and care.
Beryl:	Thank you.
Jeff:	Right. You're very warm and caring, and adding the honesty and direct-ness is a ...
Beryl:	But to them, they don't think so.
Jeff:	Maybe being honest and direct and adding that, ... maybe they might see your warmth and care a bit clearer. Who knows. (*pause*) Alrighty!
Beryl:	Thank you.
Jeff:	Now, er ...
Beryl:	Homework! (*laughing*)
Jeff:	Yes, homework. Something to practise. (*laughing*)
Beryl:	This is really odd, but this is helping, and I find it, it's stupid I was going to say I enjoy it, but I suppose I really enjoy trying to learn what to do. It gives you a basis not just for home, but it helps in your whole, just the way you go about things. It just gives me a bit of, er something to go by. (*crying*) I've been falling apart lately.
Jeff:	That's alright. It's emotional.
Beryl:	I feel it's sort of heavy stuff, but I um I want to do something about it – and not being involved with the family and so forth is hard for me.
Jeff:	And um in a way and it is so important to get on well with your kids. It's tough and, I've been a bit direct and tough with you.
Beryl:	No, no, I need to know how, because what I'm doing and have been doing for a long time obviously isn't working. And I can see that I'm in some ways becoming a bit crumbly and yet me being stronger is helpful and I need to work on it.
Jeff:	What I've found is that sometimes the advice you get is to just be tougher and stronger and not put up with it. But the value of this I think is that it's a mixture of being upfront but still being warm and acknowledging.
Beryl:	With a softness sort of to it.
Jeff:	And if you can combine the two it becomes even more powerful than just ...
Beryl:	Some people could have a real big blue and not see each other and that's not for me and I don't think they want that either. No, no.
Jeff:	Alright, then.
Beryl:	Are you going to give me a copy of your notes?
Jeff:	I can give you a copy of that.
Beryl:	It will help me go about things.
Jeff:	And what I could also do is to make a copy of that video and you can or you could have a go – what would be most helpful?
Beryl:	Um, er ...
Jeff:	Have my notes and have a go and you know the video is here if you want it. (*walking out, chatting*)

The NBT hand for making everyday requests

A particularly enjoyable part of our NBT workshops includes experimenting with different ways of making requests or giving feedback in everyday life. In the workshops, we focus on a minor workplace infringement. I came to recognise my own avoidance of providing feedback about annoying workplace incursions, when demonstrating one of these approaches. The workplace gripes we suggest exploring include the failure of a colleague to fill up the company car with petrol after using it, a colleague not washing up their lunch dishes, or a colleague leaving coffee mugs and other paraphernalia on your desk; all seem to be instantly recognisable to participants. Whilst minor, not addressing them can lead to major frustrations.

We get NBT workshop participants to pick a minor workplace irritation and apply three different approaches to addressing them. Using hands as a metaphor and mnemonic, the first two, the "Beat About the Bush Hand" and "The Direct-Hit Hand," are not recommended, but may feel familiar. The third, the "NBT Hand," provides a more helpful guide for making timely and thoughtful requests or providing critical feedback, at work, with your family, or friends. (The hands concept is used with permission of The Bouverie Centre, La Trobe University, Australia).

The Beat About the Bush Hand (see Figure 9.1) is illustrated with an offending colleague, Deni, who has failed to fill up the company car, goes something like this:

Jeff: Hi Deni! How was your weekend? [Long rambling preamble – often overly positive and irrelevant]
Deni: Yeah good, really good! Busy though.

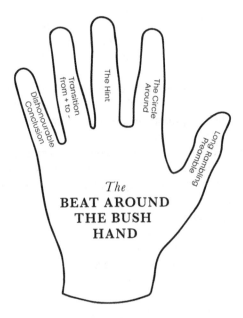

Figure 9.1 The Beat Around the Bush Hand.

Jeff: Great! I'm so pleased because you deserve a good break!

Deni: Thanks, I've certainly been busy lately.

Jeff: Yeah, we're all busy these days! [Circling around the complaint]

Deni: Sure feels that way! [Starting to get the feeling Jeff has a hidden agenda].

Jeff: Yeah, we're all so busy we really need to look out for each other, don't we? [The hint]

Deni: Looking out for each other is good. [Starting to get confused about what Jeff is wanting to say, but not saying]

Jeff: Yeah, when we're all busy, you've got to do the right thing, hey! [Transition from positive to negative underlying tone]

Deni: Of course. [Confused but feeling slightly blamed for something – not sure for what]

Jeff: Yeah, it is hard when you're expect something, but it doesn't happen!

Deni: Is there something you want to tell me? [Trying to clarify what is being hinted at]

Jeff: No, no!

Deni: Ok. [Not convinced, feeling yuk]

Jeff: Ok see you around. [Dishonourable conclusion; nothing is resolved, and the relationship is likely strained]

The Direct-Hit Hand goes something like this (Figure 9.2):

Jeff: Hey Deni! I've got a bone to pick with you! [Feedback given without any preamble]

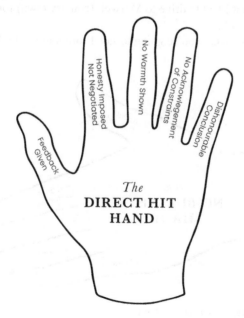

Figure 9.2 The Direct-Hit Hand.

Deni:	What? [Feeling attacked]
Jeff:	Yeah, you didn't fill up the company car and I was late for an appointment in the country. [No rationale for the confrontation; no signposting; no negotiation about honesty]
Deni:	I ... er, I'm sorry you feel that way. [Feeling defensive]
Jeff:	Yeah, we'll don't let it happen again. [Feedback given without warmth or acknowledgement of any constraints or context]
Deni:	Sure! [Options are attacking back or politely dismissing Jeff]
Jeff:	See you around. [Jeff maybe feeling relieved he's got it off his chest]
Deni:	Sure! [Angry, hurt, not feeling good]
Jeff:	Ok! [Dishonourable conclusion – nothing is resolved, and the relationship is definitely strained]

The NBT goes something like this (Figure 9.3):

Jeff:	Hi Deni! I've got something that's a little sensitive I'd like to talk to you about. Is now a good time? [Creating a good context and signposting]
Deni:	Yeah, now's a good time, I guess. [Cautious but prepared for a potentially confronting conversation]
Jeff:	Great! Look it's a bit difficult, but I wanted to say this directly to you because I didn't want it to get in the way of our friendship! [Providing a rationale]
Deni:	Goodo. Let me know what's on your mind.
Jeff:	I know you've been really busy, [Acknowledging a constraint with warmth] but I had to drive to Morwell (country town) for an appointment yesterday and ...
Deni:	Hey, I know what you're going to say. I forgot to fill up the car.

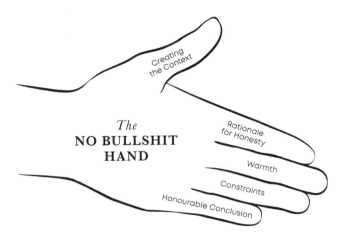

Figure 9.3 The No Bullshit Therapy Hand.

Jeff: Yeah, it's not a big deal, and I know you've been so busy but I wanted to raise it so I wouldn't stew over it – I was late for the appointment, so I was a bit upset. [Integrating acknowledging a constraint, warmth and restating the rationale]

Deni: Yeah, look I'm sorry and I'm glad you raised it directly with me. I got back late from my appointment, and I needed to get home for the kids, and I just forgot! [A bit hurt but appreciative of the directness, given the rationale]

Jeff: Yeah, it certainly feels hard to fit everything into one day, these days. I've forgotten to fill the car up more than once myself. [Warmth and acknowledging a constraint]

Deni: Yeah, it's not easy, but again, sorry I didn't get around to filling it up. [Apologising because not attacked]

Jeff: I knew there would be a reason, don't worry about it. I'm glad I said something because I didn't want it to come between us. [Reiterating the rationale]

Deni: Thanks. I'm glad you did too.

Jeff: Cheers, take care. [An honourable conclusion; the issue is resolved, and the relationship is likely to be ok, maybe after a while, and possibly even grow stronger]

I hope you find the NBT hand as helpful as I have in my own personal life. Ron Carucci (2021, p. 185), talking about workplaces, puts it nicely when he writes, "Giving others difficult feedback is a skill most of us don't relish using. We pull our punches. We ramble with long wind-ups to soothe our anxiety, only confusing the person we're trying to help. And commonly, under the ruse of being 'nice' we just don't say anything at all. … withholding feedback that could help someone improve is never nice or kind – it's cruel."

Maybe the NBT hand will inspire you to be tough *and* kind. The following chapter explores a core element that informs NBT, power.

Reference

Carucci, R.A. (2021). *To be honest: Lead with the power of truth, justice and purpose.* Kogan Page.

10   No Bullshit Therapy, power, and social identity

Clarity is the cornerstone of democracy. Confusion is the tool of the autocrat.
— James Ball (2017, p. 277)

Power

Therapy at its core is about change and hence, it is a political endeavour, especially for unmotivated customers who don't identify as clients. We need to be mindful of, and sensitive to, the ethics of using power and authority to influence change. More so if the person is not voluntarily seeking change, and especially if the person feels vulnerable, marginalised, shamed, powerless, or defeated. It is tempting, as Rooney (1992) pointed out many years ago, to try to socialise involuntary clients coercively into accepting the role of client and the identity of clienthood.

Clients with trauma backgrounds or with past experiences of service systems abuse are particularly at risk of feeling a lack of control when pressured to seek help. If issues of power and control are not addressed thoughtfully, directly, and transparently – whether the client identifies as a client or not – we are at risk of re-traumatising them.

During a particularly passionate early period in which family therapy was critiquing power in the therapeutic process, Virginia Goldner (1993) wrote a compelling article in *Family Process*, called "Power and Hierarchy: Let's Talk About It." In this article, she argued that psychotherapy is:

> a social practice shaped by, and embedded in, an elaborate professional culture that inevitably constrains what can be seen and named, and that, like any 'knowledge/power discourse', necessarily elevates those who produce and manage it over those for whom it is intended (pp. 159–160).

Exploring the role of social work in protective services as part of his master's degree, Mark Furlong (1991) encourages us to be clear about the distinction between coercive practices and legitimate use of authority. However, in practice, this distinction is not always obvious. Personal, professional, and institutional factors all need to be considered. Unacknowledged legitimate authority may be experienced

DOI: 10.4324/9781003354925-10

as coercion, and the overt use of legitimate authority by a worker without the people skills and personal confidence to use it wisely, may also be experienced as abusive.

The aspiration is to use personal and institutional power to influence clients in ways that encourage the use of their own power and responsibility (Hasenfield, 1987). Whilst in principle this may be simple, putting it into practice is again not so easy – especially in vexed situations and with clients, like therapy-haters, who may feel they have few options other than expressing their power by refusing to engage in the therapeutic work, sometimes angrily. To further quote Furlong (personal communication), *you cannot drive fast and straight down a winding road.* The following guidelines are presented, not as definitive knowledge, but to help navigate this windy path.

There is always a tension between authority and coercion, between influence and abuse of power, in all client-worker relations, even when the relationship seems to be working well. A simple guide I learnt from Julie Houniet, a colleague in my first job as a clinical psychologist at Mont Park Psychiatric hospital in 1984, is that power and responsibility should go hand in hand. Power without responsibility is likely to create a monster without restraint, and responsibility without power can lead to frustration, burden, and exhaustion. Power with equivalent responsibility in both the therapist and client creates a healthy relationship and a powerful context for change to occur. An NBT therapist needs sufficient legitimate power to be effective and respectful in helping the client get what they want and to ensure that the client takes responsibility for their part in the change process. This requires the therapist and client to be both explicitly aware of the extent and limitations of each other's roles, responsibilities, and power, particularly when bad faith exists. As the study of bullshit in Chapter 2 revealed, concealment about the enterprise at hand in any way, whether it be about role, responsibilities, power, even purpose, method, or rationale, is likely to exacerbate feelings of client powerlessness and distrust. When a client is pressured to attend therapy or feels pressured to accept the social identity of clienthood, the open clarification of each party's motivation is crucial, yet nuanced. O'Hanlon and O'Hanlon (1998) encourage therapists not to be the most motivated person in the room – meaning that it is important that the therapist creates a context in which the client feels actively in charge of the change they want, and where the therapist's role is to help the client achieve what they want. This means identifying what the client wants, being very active in creating a conducive context for the client to articulate the change they want, even if the therapist might argue for change, and even if it is by pointing out the consequence of not changing. This is nuanced work because therapy-haters may only begin to engage with the therapist due to the understanding that the alternative to *not changing* is even less desirable than *changing*.

Starting where the client is at and clarifying upfront the issues of power, authority, and influence, and the respective roles of the client and worker, go a long way to creating a productive context for change in vexed situations. There are usually logical and legitimate reasons why a prospective client is resistant, angry, or lacking in motivation. Clifton Mitchell (2007), author of *Effective Techniques for Dealing with Highly Resistant Clients*, defines resistance as the failure of the counsellor to co-operate with the client. It is the therapist's responsibility to find a way to discover what will motivate the prospective client. Therapy-lovers will usually work with the therapist to explore their motivation, if they don't present with a clear goal from the start; for therapy-haters, it is much harder, but more important. Unlike other approaches specifically designed to engage therapy-haters, such as motivational interviewing, NBT encourages the therapist to declare their heartfelt hopes and dreams for the client, once the client's goal is identified, while at the same time not being overly invested.

NBT cannot and does not strive to minimise power differentials between worker and client. It strives to make power and responsibility explicit, transparent, and specific around the task at hand. For example, a worker and client both have substantial power to make decisions, albeit about different things, and this is made overt, along with the consequences of each person's position. To put this theoretical stance into a real-world therapeutic example, NBT encourages the therapist to acknowledge and make overt that a client has the power to decide not to co-operate with the therapeutic process, or with the therapist. The consequences of not co-operating are made clear, in a non-blaming, non-judgemental, business-like, and specific manner. For a client pressured to attend therapy by his partner, but who wants to save his marriage, the client is acknowledged as having the power to walk out of the therapy at any time but is also informed that walking out of therapy is unlikely to save the marriage.

In essence, the NBT practitioner makes explicit the extent of the authority the client has and doesn't have, and what authority they have and don't have. The therapist also clarifies and makes transparent the advantages and disadvantages of therapy and the consequences of engaging and not engaging in the therapy. Clarifying these things can feel a little cumbersome, but if not clarified, the therapy-hater will assume the worst in each area. If the client feels a lack of power, they will be tempted to make a strong (angry, aggressive, or dismissive) stand in the areas where they do have power – i.e., by walking out, refusing treatment, or politely disengaging from the work. Reaching clarity about power, role, and responsibility in relation to the goals of the client, and to the consequences for the prospective client of not co-operating, and not achieving their goals, even if it is not what the prospective client wants to hear, will help move a therapy-hater towards real engagement.

In essence, the task for workers is to embrace their own legitimate power (personally, professionally, and organisationally) and at the same time give as much control to clients, especially if they feel powerless or are in fact powerless, without ignoring the realities of the situation and their responsibilities. As Rodney Rooney (1992) emphasises, it is important to simultaneously maximise the client's sense of choice and control while being clear about any non-negotiable matters such as those mandated by the court or other legislative powers.

In practice, clarifying roles and responsibilities, and providing as much legitimate power to clients whilst maintaining legitimate authority is complex and nuanced, as demonstrated by the simulation with Sarah, whom you met in Chapter 7 and who had been threatened to be made involuntary by her doctors if she was re-admitted to hospital without having attended counselling. In this 12-minute excerpt from the transcript that follows directly on from the section presented in Chapter 7, I try to be very explicit about the institutional power and control represented by the doctors, Sarah's own power, control, and responsibilities, and my own position.

Jeff:	So, what er, what did the doctors, um, if they er said you should come along.
Sarah:	Oh, fuck them!
Jeff:	Yeah.
Sarah:	Yeah. Um. Sorry.
Jeff:	That's alright. No, I said I'd …
Sarah:	They just, they spent two minutes with me at a time, there, and they told me, you know, I've got this diagnosis and yeah um, I mean how do you pick that up after meeting with me for two seconds and slapping me with heaps of medication. I mean yeah.
Jeff:	So, what, can I ask, and again, I'm not going to agree with them or take their side. But just so it can help me understand what you're, um struggling with. Because you sort of want to make sure you stay out of hospital. Um, what diagnosis did they say you had?
Sarah:	Um, they said that I've got psychosis actually and, so um and er, yeah and they said it pretty quickly too, they seem to think that the drugs mean that um, I get pretty sick, and I end up back there for yeah, and they didn't really ask a lot about everything else that's gone on in my life to make me need that so (drugs). Yeah, yeah. I was pretty pissed off about that.
Jeff:	Right, so, you felt that a major decision was made about you without really understanding a lot about the background?
Sarah:	Yeah, I sort of felt that they just wanted to knock me out with these drugs and yeah send me on my way.
Jeff:	Ok. Can I ask, they've sent you to counselling, and let's call it as it is. They sent you, you didn't want to come, um but …
Sarah:	(*laughing with some relief*) Yeah!
Jeff:	Um but that you know that if you didn't, if you sort of said, sort of bugger you, I'm not going there, there would be consequences.
Sarah:	Yeah, they said they'd probably keep me there for a bit little longer.
Jeff:	Ok!
Sarah:	And yeah. Sort of yeah, I said what I needed to say. I said I'd play along, I'll give it a go, um I'm but yeah.
Jeff:	Right. So, to summarise you were told if you don't go, you're going to get kept in hospital.
Sarah:	Yep.
Jeff:	So, you thought yeah, I'll go, but …
Sarah:	I'd rather have my own bed.
Jeff:	Yeah. I don't want to do any work, but I'll go along so I don't have to stay in hospital. Is that fair enough?

Sarah: Yeah, that's it.

Jeff: Ok great. So, um, err do you get a sense of what the doctors, and again I'm not agreeing with them, but what they thought you would need to do. Let's say you did want to do the work. What do they think you need to do in counselling, in order to, um make sure you don't go back to hospital.

Sarah: Um.

Jeff: What did they think?

Sarah: Well one of them was pretty blunt and said you've gotta stay away from the drugs and talk to someone about the stress that, you know, rather than using the drugs, basically. The drugs are basically a quick fix.

Jeff: Um, so, things have happened in your life. That, you know, sound difficult by the sound of it. Tell me if I've got it totally wrong?

Sarah: No that's right.

Jeff: For you, um drugs of your choice, can um, help you deal with it, but the doctors are saying that using the drugs makes it more likely you will finish up back in hospital.

Sarah: Yeah.

Jeff: What things do you see lead you to coming back into hospital. Not what anyone else thinks, but what do you think?

Sarah: I think, um, too much stress on my plate. So, actually it's my job. Not during this time in hospital but last time I lost my job. And I was having more fights with friends and um and yeah with Mum and Mary. And it just got a bit too much not having money and sitting around all day.

Jeff: Oh ok. Do you, so, tell me again if I've got it right, but what I heard was that because of the stress you've been through, like losing your job and conflict with friends and your family and, that's led you to be stressed out and finishing up in hospital.

Sarah: Yep, yeah.

Jeff: I'm really clear, again, tell me if I've got it wrong, but I'm really clear that you want to stay out of hospital.

Sarah: Yeah.

Jeff: Yeah?

Sarah: Yeah 100%!

Jeff: Are you serious about that?

Sarah: Yep!

Jeff: Ok. So, if I was able to talk to you, and I know that you don't like talking and I know that you don't want to be here, but if we could talk about things that, your stresses, that lead you to get stressed out and end up in hospital, would you be more interested in talking with me? Or not?

Sarah: I suppose. Can I have some conditions?

Jeff: Yeah Sure.

Sarah: Um …

Jeff: And just before you do that, I'll be clear about what my own conditions are too. Because, um there are certain things I can't do both ethically, or, if I'm going to help you. There are certain things I would need in order to help you and I'll be just very clear and upfront about that. So, I don't bullshit you.

Sarah: Well, if I am going to talk. Which again, like I don't know about it. But if I do talk. I don't want to end up in the same situation as before where if I say something, that I'm going to end up back in hospital, I, I just felt like I was totally blindsided. Yeah, and totally lost trust. You know. When I've been in mental health services, and I've said stuff. I want to know that you're not going to put me back in. And ...

Jeff: Can I respond to that, first and this is sort of my condition. Um, if you say something that is worrying. For example, essentially, it's like if you are going to hurt yourself or somebody else. Um, then I will talk with you about how we could make sure that doesn't happen and talk to you about it. But we'd have to problem solve it. And make sure that I was comfortable that you weren't going to do that. And I know that might feel like I'm pulling the authority on you, but it is sort of the reality, and I would only push that you had to go back into hospital if there was no other alternative. So, and I would be talking to you about what we could do and what you could do.

Sarah: So that means you're not just going to put me in.

Jeff: No!

Sarah: You would actually talk to me first?

Jeff: Yep. Yeah. You would know it. So, I wouldn't go behind your back.

Sarah: So that's what's happened in the past.

Jeff: But I would expect, um I would talk to you about it, but you would have to reassure me that you were safe.

Sarah: Ok.

Jeff: Yeah?

Sarah: As long as we can talk about it.

Jeff: Yeah.

Sarah: And you're not just going to put me in.

Jeff: Yeah.

Sarah: That was harmful.

Jeff: I can imagine. I'm happy with your condition, are you happy with mine?

Sarah: Yep.

Jeff: Ok. What's your other condition?

Sarah: As long as we can talk about it. Yeah, and I want to stay out at all costs. Yeah, and I suppose the other thing is that you are not just going to go talking to my Mum about things that we've talked about. Where, yeah, I've said stuff and then Mum has somehow known about it and she's sort of pulled me over hot coals for it. Yeah, I sort of feel like, I guess she cares for me but I'm 35, I just want to do my own thing. Yeah.

Jeff: Ok. Do you want to hear my condition? I'm a family therapist. So, I sort of think about families. But what I could assure you, again unless you were going to do damage to yourself or your family, that I would ask you what I can share and what I couldn't share. Because sometimes in my experience, if you can share information about people around you, it can actually help improve the situation.

Sarah: Ok.

Jeff: You've already implied that you want your mum to sort of back off a bit.

Sarah: Yeah.

Jeff: Without engaging your mum in some sort of discussion or some information, it's very hard for her to back off, because she is so worried about you, she's just going to push more and more and more.

Sarah: Yeah, its suffocating.

Jeff: And yeah, then in some ways to be honest, the less you give her, the more she is going to um er suffocate you. So that is my condition. I'll say what I think might be helpful. Because I think it will be helpful probably for what you want. But it's up to you, you would be in control of what information is shared or what isn't.

Sarah: So, I would get to tell you if there is stuff that I want to say but I don't want her to know about?

Jeff: Yeah. Yeah. And I would give you my opinion of what would be helpful to share. But if you said I didn't want to, that, that, I would abide by that, but I won't hold back on my opinion.

Sarah: Ok, no I appreciate, I just want to know what you think. Um, I hate it when I don't know what the person's thinking, and then it sort of feels like they've gone behind my back.

Jeff: As I've said before, the way I like to work is very upfront and direct. You will know, you might not like it, but you will know what I'm thinking.

Sarah: No, no, I appreciate that. That's what I want.

Jeff: (*empathically*) Um, so, what are some of the pressures that, where are the pressures coming from leading you to need to, you know, sort of take drugs to manage it and worry that it is going to overwhelm you so much that you finish up doing stuff that leads you to end up in hospital.

Having agreed on a way to work, earlier in the session, I now feel that I am able, with permission, to ask more personal questions that allow me to move towards getting an agreement (mandate) about what to work on. I feel that I have engaged Sarah enough to be able to ask more personal questions.

[I inquire if there is a cultural element to Sarah's situation. Sarah tells me she grew up in Australia, but her family is from the south of India, Christian, and so she has a foot in both the Australian and traditional Indian culture. There is an expectation that Sarah should be married by now. Mary is married, has kids and is working, and Sarah feels she is constantly compared to her sister.]

We will re-join Sarah at the end of this chapter.

Social identity

Conversations can connect but can also disconnect us, professors of social work Joshua Miller, Susan Donner, and Edith Fraser (2004) point out in their excellent article, "Talking When Talking Is Tough: Taking on Conversations About Race, Sexual Orientation, Gender, Class, and Other Aspects of Social Identity." The authors help us understand that conversations about difference that confront issues of social identity are difficult to have, especially if the participants in those conversations cross social identities themselves.

Why do we find difficult conversations ... well, so difficult? Miller and his colleagues provide three broad reasons. Firstly, many of us simply "lack experience in talking across and about differences" (Miller et al., 2004, p. 384). Secondly, we partly avoid sensitive issues to protect ourselves or others from feelings of vulnerability, and thirdly, we tend to avoid topics that highlight inequities and social injustice, all of which are often accompanied by strong emotions such as fear, embarrassment, shame, guilt, and anger.

There are no easy ways to address sensitive issues across cultural boundaries, especially where there has been a history of invasion, conflict, mistrust, or all three, and especially when there are major differentials of power and privilege. That's why I so admire cross-cultural bridge makers, from both sides.

I was anxious when first asked to present a one-day workshop on NBT to the graduates of La Trobe University's Graduate Certificate in Family Therapy: First Nations, which is delivered by The Bouverie Centre. It must have gone down well because it has become a much-anticipated part of this course over the past eight years. The lecturers, Alison Elliott and Banu Moloney, reflected that a straight conversation with someone in authority is refreshing for a colonised community, used to services that are not designed by or for them.

Since 2008, The Bouverie Centre, La Trobe University has delivered the Graduate Certificate in Community to over 170 First Nations students across Victoria and Queensland, with a graduation rate of 87%, which outstrips mainstream rates. In the most recent NBT workshop, conducted online due to COVID restrictions, I enjoyed a particularly open and robust discussion about the approach. Whilst the NBT Clinical Guidelines and the principles underlying them were warmly received, and maybe *because* they were warmly received, I was treated to a lesson in *Black Language*, as one participant called it via the Zoom chat.

Pre-invasion, there were over 300 distinct languages spoken in Australia, along with many dialects. According to Simpson and Wigglesworth (2019, p. 67), "At that time, many Indigenous people were multilingual, speaking at least four languages. Today many of those languages have been lost." The Bouverie Centre and La Trobe University are on the unceded lands of the Wurundjeri People of the Greater Kulin Nation. Their language is Woi Wurrung. The First Nations students advised changing the wording of NBT Clinical Guideline One, from *Establish a mandate* to *Establish a clear agreement* because the term *mandate* has many oppressive associations with colonisation, where Aboriginal and Torres Strait Islander people were subjected to forced internment and labour, as well as prohibition against practising their traditional language and culture. I was also advised to change NBT Clinical Guideline 2 from *Marry honesty and directness with warmth and care,* to *Marry-up honesty and directness with warmth and care,* because it too is a term reminiscent of when Aboriginal and Torres Strait Islander people had to apply for permission to receive basic rights, including the right to get married.

Miller and his colleagues (2004) point out that people who are less privileged are more likely to be aware of the institutionalised sources of oppression, than people who are privileged. Structural oppression is notoriously difficult to articulate, especially to someone of privilege. Therapy hating is likely to be borne out of a sense that the therapy-hater fears, expects, or experiences a lack of power, either generally or in the therapeutic context. Addressing this lack of power, if it is getting in the way of a productive working relationship, is likely to rest with the therapist. This creates a dilemma for the therapist: the therapist is required to address the in-equity, whilst aware of their own privilege in relation to the client and possibly un-der attack by the *powerless* client. Hence, at these sensitive times, there is a natural tendency for therapists to revert to the safety of political correctness, professional jargon, or outright counter blaming behaviours. The irony is that therapists must be sensitive to this dilemma, aware of the power analysis of working with therapy-haters, and not necessarily respond in overly sensitive or soft emotional ways. It takes a special courage for us to respect and acknowledge the different social iden-tities and any accompanying power differences between us and our clients and yet also, not to be constrained by them.

I am not an expert on cultural studies, but I know enough to realise that honesty and directness are understood and practised in very different ways in different cul-tures. Hence, NBT needs to be practised with a sensitivity to cultural differences when enacting the clinical guidelines. Kali Paxinos, an elderly Greek mother of an adult son with long-term mental health difficulties reminds us in a DVD series on Family Sensitive Mental Health Practice (FaST videos, 2007) that culture is more than national costumes and cuisine. Culture mediates, informs, and regulates our attitudes, beliefs, rituals, expectations, and priorities. Culture determines what we celebrate and how. Its influence is both profound and profuse. So profuse that for people in the dominant culture it can be invisible and may only become evident when in contrast or in opposition to another culture. Practice does not exist in a socio-cultural vacuum. In fact, the sensitivities and vulnerabilities that bring clients and practitioners together are likely to shine a light on the cultural context and the need to manage the cross cultural.

In the book, they edited from a successful cross-cultural conference at the London Institute of Family Therapy, *Exploring the Unsaid: Creativity, Risks and Working Cross-Culturally,* Barry Mason and Alice Sawyerr (2002) encourage prac-titioners to take greater risks in working cross-culturally. In a follow-up chapter, "The personal and the professional: core beliefs and the construction of bridges across difference," in *Culture and Reflexivity in Systemic Psychotherapy (2012),* *Mason* describes several case studies in which he attempts to build bridges across cultures without marginalising his own or his client's beliefs.

Mason generated a range of questions to negotiate taking risks working cross-culturally as a white Anglo-Saxon man. Rather than playing it safe, Mason's questions allowed him to create a context for robust discussions about sensitive issues. The questions, easily adapted to negotiate the degree of honesty and directness required to be effective in difficult or complex working situations, include:

If I was to work in a way that was comfortable, but not very helpful, what would that look like?

If I were to play it safe but not be very helpful, what would I do?

If I was to take risks, and create a space that was uncomfortable but useful, what advice would you give me?

If I wanted to talk honestly, without holding back, but in a sensitive way that worked for you, what would that look like?

Whilst very helpful for complex situations, especially if introduced thoughtfully, caution is required in order not to appear more clever than authentic.

My colleague Julie Warren observed that NBT was particularly pertinent in rural communities where colleagues often work and live in close proximity to each other and hence need to maintain positive working relationships, whilst at the same time, address difficult conversations professionally or personally. In my work attempting to engage with rural drought counsellors who were working with people affected by drought, there were active debates over whether insiders or outsiders needed to work with farmers and rural businesspeople. This debate raged even though some *insiders* and *outsiders* both appeared to be successful. I eventually expanded the dichotomy of *insiders* and *outsiders* to four categories: *distant outsiders, close outsiders, distant insiders,* and *close insiders.* Farmers found both *close outsiders* and *distant insiders* especially helpful. *Distant insiders* may be a farmer (*insider*) who understands farming, but from a different district (*distant*) and hence someone who can be told embarrassing personal material without it impacting on the client's proximal social network. *Close outsider* maybe a counsellor (*outsider*) who has made efforts to educate themselves about local issues, including farming practices (*close*), and hence is someone who can be trusted because they understand that they need to, and have attempted to, bridge a cultural divide.

The interpretation and implementation of the NBT Clinical Guidelines is influenced and mediated by work context, especially organisational culture, vision, and purpose. They are also influenced and mediated by our role and status within the organisation, by the assumptions we make about our own social identities, as well as the social identities of the people with whom we are working. I recall how I struggled to hold a young family member accountable for his violence. He and his family had recently escaped from a religious cult where they had all experienced abuse. Ted, the family member using violence was also physically affected by muscular dystrophy. I had to work hard to integrate my sympathy for Ted's disability whilst holding him accountable for his violence.

Our task is to check out our assumptions and *to neither ignore or to be captured by* sensitive social identity differences. Appreciating inequity by naming it (without rubbing a client's nose in it) called the *declaration of difference* by my colleague Mark Furlong, can, according to Miller and his colleagues (2004), help avoid recreating these inequities in the therapeutic space. This may translate into making overt both the power inequity and your dilemma, along the lines of, *I want to be respectful, but more so I want to be helpful.*

As mentioned earlier, NBT acknowledges and clarifies difference rather than obfuscating or avoiding discussion about difference. NBT attempts to build connection by acknowledging that these constraints exist. Openly acknowledging the cultural gap between the therapist and a therapy-hater reduces the need for the client to point to these gaps. Acknowledgement of difference is a key part of bridge-making.

Building a bridge with therapy-haters

I feel being able to build a bridge with Sarah, helping her to move from detached suspiciousness to cautious engagement, resulting in a robust, respectful, real two-way conversation, is immensely rewarding. I continue to acknowledge, in a direct and specific way, the constraints to her trusting me and remain within my mandate of how to work and what to work on. I ask questions and explicitly link my questions to her goals, whilst ensuring I have sufficient, legitimate authority to help her achieve her goals. With these ongoing sensitivities in place, I begin to feel that I can start to work in a more collaborative and straightforward way with Sarah.

Four minutes of the session have not been transcribed. During this part of the session, I find out that Sarah feels like the black sheep in the family, constantly compared to her sister Mary, who is married, has a family and a job. Sarah describes falling into relationships that are intense, but that quickly descend into awful fights, drug use, and finally break-ups.

Historically, Sarah's family has responded to problems by yelling at each other and then quickly moving on, but this strategy is no longer working, because the family gets stuck focusing on the drug use. When I seek Sarah's permission to ask about her drug use, she says she has tried different drugs but mostly dope and ice (methamphetamine). She also says she has not used ice since being discharged from hospital.

The final nine-minute segment of this 36-minute simulation demonstrates Sarah's gradual transition from therapy-hater to cautious, tentatively co-operative, client.

Jeff:	I know it is early days but is this starting to sound like something that could be helpful. This approach of being upfront and direct.
Sarah:	Yeah, I haven't had this before, and um yeah, I think it, I like it, but so long as you are not just going to put me in and that everything I say in here is not going to get spilled out there, like I said, I'm pretty private.
Jeff:	So, as I said, um, as I said, if you are not going to harm yourself or someone else, essentially, then I will keep things confidential, but even if you are considering hurting yourself, I'd talk to you about what we'd do

about that. Only if I felt we couldn't protect you or others, then I'd have to consider pushing for an involuntary stay.

Sarah: Ok. Yeah. I'll give it ago. I'll give it a go.

Jeff: Look, already, I imagine that by talking to someone about the pressures and trying to find out and understand them for yourself. And knowing that you could er, er, say anything, and I would be direct, and you'd know what I was thinking could be potentially helpful in staying out of hospital, potentially.

Sarah: I think so.

Jeff: Yeah.

Sarah: I mean you have to forgive me Jeff, but I have to see it to believe it. But you know, um yeah as I said, I've been through the ringer. But I like how you're telling me you'll be upfront. Yeah, I like that! Just so long as I'm not going to be taken for a ride again. Yeah.

Jeff: What does being taken for a ride mean?

Sarah: Um, I think, doing what I think is the right thing. Of coming in for appointments and um answering questions when I'm asked and then, yeah, as I said, being honest, and then, I've had like the case manager and the doctor walk out of the appointment and talk and then they come back in and they're like, you're going to hospital. And I didn't have anything packed and only had to wear what I was wearing and go. And I just thought I was doing what I had been asked.

Jeff: Can I ask, um what has been a little bit helpful in the past in talking to people. And I know that a lot hasn't been helpful. Even a little bit helpful.

Sarah: I've actually got on with some people I've worked with before. I think, just someone actually like taking my side, and feeling like they understand me. And yeah, just having that space has been helpful. Yeah.

Jeff: What do you think, if you were to be really upfront, what do you think causes you the, not causes you the most stress at the moment, but sort of where it sort of all started, if you like. If you were to say, like, what is it that has really knocked you about? What would you say? And feel free, it may be too sensitive, or it might be too early to say? But I just thought I'd cut to the chase.

Sarah: Ah, I might leave that if that's ok.

Jeff: Sure, sure.

Sarah: I feel that I'm not ready to go there.

Jeff: Sure, sure. Ok, that's fine. What's been the impact of having something like that, you can't talk about easily? Don't tell me what it is, but what is the impact of having something really hard to talk about with anyone, including like a professional counsellor like myself? What impact has it had on you and how you live your life?

Sarah: Just that constant burying, it's like carrying ten bricks in a bag on my shoulder. Like, yeah, just wondering when I'm going in and out of the system. I think that's sort of the biggest thing. It is just like I can't get on with my life just knowing that there's the possibility of going in. Um

	yeah. I just feel like people tell me, yeah like they mean well, but then it all happens again.
Jeff:	So, you're sort of walking about with ten bricks on your back wherever you go, it must be exhausting.
Sarah:	Yeah, yeah, I want to move on from things, I want to get out of the system. I don't want to be here.
Jeff:	It must make everything you do just harder work.
Sarah:	Yeah. I appreciate it's your job but yeah, I …
Jeff:	Yeah, it's my job, but um the way I like to work is that I want to help you get what you want. Like it's, it's not, you know, I go home at night, I've got my own life and job, there's other clients. Like, it's like, I'm not being rude, but its um, your change isn't necessary for me to feel like I'm ok, I'm going to work as hard as I can for you but at the end of the day it's what you would want. I can facilitate but I can't make you address these things.
Sarah:	Yep, yep, I appreciate it.
Jeff:	I hope that's not too bold.
Sarah:	No, I like it.
Jeff:	Ok.
Sarah:	Yeah, because it makes it mine, I want to be the one who decides, because I do want to get out of the system, I do want to get a job.
Jeff:	Yeah, it's sort of, in some ways to be even more upfront, if you want to walk around carrying those ten bricks, it's up to you. In some ways it makes you stronger, but it does make you a little less nimble, and it makes everything a bit harder.
Sarah:	(Laughing) I think I've overworked those muscles now. I'm ready to let go.
Jeff:	Um, if you do, if you ultimately want to get those bricks …
Sarah:	Yes, I do.
Jeff:	What would be one of those ten bricks that you could unpack and get off your back? Which would be the easiest. If we were to, and I guess I'm assuming that by talking about it and understanding it, sort of talking to me about it, thinking about it in a different way, or problem solving it, would actually, eventually dissolve it. Now that might not work for you and you might not believe that it could work for you, but that's, that's how, counselling works.
Sarah:	I want to, I miss the relationship I had with Mum and Mary. It was good before they started ganging up on me, and only wanting to talk about the mental health stuff. I miss that part of them. I want to talk to them like we used to, actually. I don't know if it is the easiest one, but I think it's an important one.
Jeff:	Ok. It might not be that easy, but it is important. And it would be one of the most important things.
Sarah:	Yeah, I miss them, in that way.
Jeff:	Do you think they miss the relationship they use to have with you too?

Sarah: I don't know.

Jeff: Right Ok. Well, being a family therapist, I could potentially help, because that's my stock and trade to try and help family members where they're not getting on to find ways to get on.

Sarah: Yep. I think that could be good.

Jeff: Alright, ok, well let's start looking at how we might, how you, not me, how you might do that.

Sarah: Yeah. I think that would be good.

Jeff: Ok.

In the following chapter, I make a case for the value of NBT practices to overcome the constraints caused by trauma, blame, and shame.

References

Ball, J. (2017). *Post-truth: How bullshit conquered the world.* Biteback publishing.

FaST Videos. (2007). *Family Sensitive Training video series (4)*, Produced by The Bouverie Centre, Melbourne, Australia.

Furlong, M. (1991). *The process of engagement for statutory cases referred to a public family therapy centre*, M.S.W. Thesis, University of Melbourne.

Goldner, V. (1993). Power and hierarchy: Let's talk about it, *Family Process, 32*(2), 157–162.

Hasenfeld, Y. (1987). Power in social work practice. *Social Service Review, 61*(3), 469–483.

Mason, B. (2012). The personal and the professional: Core beliefs and the construction of bridges across difference. In I-B. Krause (Ed.), *Culture and reflexivity in systemic psychotherapy: Mutual perspectives.* Routledge.

Mason, B., & Sawyerr, A. (Eds.). (2002). *Exploring the unsaid: Creativity, risks and dilemmas in working cross-culturally.* Karnac Books.

Miller, J., Donner, S., & Fraser, E. (2004). Talking when talking is tough: Taking on conversations about race, sexual orientation, gender, class and other aspects of social identity, *Smith College Studies in Social Work, 74*(2), 377–392. http://doi.org/10.1080/00377310409517722.

Mitchell, C.W. (2007). *Techniques for dealing with highly resistant clients: Innovative ideas and approaches to prevent, avoid, and resolve resistance* (2nd ed.). Clifton W. Mitchell Publishing.

O'Hanlon, B., & O'Hanlon, S. (1998). The dog ate it: When clients don't do their homework. *Family Therapy Networker, 22*(3), 21–22.

Rooney, R.H. (1992*). Strategies for work with involuntary clients.* Columbia University Press.

Simpson, J., & Wigglesworth, G. (2019). *Language diversity in Indigenous Australia in the 21st Century, in Current Issues in Language Planning. 20*(1), 67–80. DOI: 10.1080/14664208.2018.1503389

11   No Bullshit Therapy, trauma, blame, and shame

Complex, interpersonally generated trauma is severely disruptive of the capacity to manage internal states. It is particularly damaging if it occurs in childhood. Research establishes that if we cannot self-regulate (i.e., manage internal states and impulse control) we will seek alternative means of doing so in the form of defences and/or addictions.

— Pam Stavropoulos (2012, p. xxx)

I recall a 15-year-old male being referred to the (diversionary) program, who was noted to be quite angry, traumatised and dis-trusting of adults at the time of assessment. He didn't appear to appreciate the opportunity being offered to him and was quite self-destructive with some of his behaviours. Using the NBT approach, I was able to use a down-to-earth engagement approach with this young person. This significantly aided the rapport building process, and the young person became trusting enough of me, that he was willing to give the program a try. After 6 months … he graduated from the program without spending any additional time in custody … This outcome will have a significant impact on his future employment prospects, and highlighted to me the important role we play as practitioners … at times when they would be described as being "involuntary" and "resistant".

— Melanie Roche, 4/11/2019 email

Aspirations of honesty and directness are as common as the things that prevent us from putting such aspirations into practice. Unresolved trauma, in either client or worker, is one of many such constraints. The perceived or real vulnerability of a traumatised client, the experience of being blamed or feeling blamed, or the presence of shame typically make being honest and direct difficult and the allure of protecting the client or ourselves, greater. Cloaking sensitive details in generalities or avoiding them altogether are common strategies to protect ourselves or our clients; however, this is likely to elicit a search for hidden blame by clients suspicious of the therapist's motives.

According to psychiatrist Dr Colin Riess, honesty and directness without judgement is an underutilised antidote to the obfuscation that typically surrounds

DOI: 10.4324/9781003354925-11

shame – nice if you can do it. Certainly, curiosity and directness without judgement can be useful components of exploring, rather than avoiding, the topic of blame too. Why not be as curious about blame as we are about other sensitive issues: explore its impact, measure it, clarify it, describe it, and understand it (Furlong & Young, 1996). We helping professionals often try to prohibit it which only makes blame go underground.

This chapter aims to provide some examples of how No Bullshit Therapy (NBT) practices and ideas may be surprisingly suited to work in these sensitive areas of blame, shame, and trauma.

As Karen Rule (personal communication, 2022) of The Neuroleadership Institute points out, there is more brain real estate dedicated to searching for threat and danger than warmth and care. Historically, this neurophysiological emphasis on threat allowed humans to survive. It still does. When people feel they are in a dangerous environment, much of their brain space will be taken up with searching for potential threats, rather than focusing on collaboration and logical discussions about ways to solve the problems they are facing. This biological emphasis on threat will affect therapy-lovers and therapy-haters differently.

Therapy-lovers choose to seek out services and hence expect to have helpful positive experiences engaging with professionals. They are eager to trust and therefore will not be actively searching for threat, until maybe a sensitive issue is raised, by which time an established trusting working relationship can be used, with some gentle NBT ideas to ease the threat.

Therapy-haters, on the other hand, have usually been forced to attend services often approaching any contact with the service in an emotionally elevated state attuned to potential threat and with a highly sensitive internal bullshit meter. Despite our best intentions, the therapeutic context is likely to be experienced by them as an unfamiliar environment full of threats, directed by a person who cannot be trusted, and under the guise of being friendly and helpful, is out to manipulate, control, embarrass, blame, shame, or even attack.

A well-established set of evidence-based Trauma Informed Practice Principles (Kezelman & Stravropoulos, 2012, p. 12) documents five domains that services should satisfy, supported by service policies and screening. These guidelines, which are compatible with both Single Session Therapy (for therapy-lovers) and NBT (for therapy-haters), are:

DOMAIN 1A SAFETY: Ensure physical and emotional safety
DOMAIN 1B TRUSTWORTHINESS: Maximise trustworthiness through task clarity, consistency, and interpersonal boundaries
DOMAIN IC CHOICE: Maximise consumer choice and control
DOMAIN 1D: COLLABORATION: Maximise collaboration and sharing of power
DOMAIN 1E: EMPOWERMENT: Prioritise empowerment and skill-building

Clients with a trauma history who present as therapy-haters, unfamiliar and suspicious of the therapeutic context, are likely to be more interested in what is not said than what is said. Hence, creating a context for mutual honesty and directness, including a non-judgemental but clear and detailed acknowledgement and articulation of the referral process and a style of conversation that is transparent, simple, specific, and non-ambiguous, will calm the noise and threat-seeking activity in the brain, relaxing the amygdala, and allowing the client to more actively participate in the logic of the encounter. The more specific and direct you can be, especially about sensitive issues, the less the client will need to search for subtle or hidden threats. Making overt all the potential threats is surprisingly calming because it means that they are all out in the open and mutually acknowledged by all parties.

Signposting that you are about to ask a challenging question allows the therapy-hater with a high level of threat arousal to put up the necessary defences and prepare for what is about to come. Just knowing that something difficult is about to come creates a greater sense of control and safety. As Rooney (1992) points out, creating a context where the client has as much agency and choice as possible will help alleviate the client's sense of powerlessness. The more agency and choice a traumatised client have, the better. A suspicious, highly aroused person is going to be less threatened if they agree to hearing feedback and advice. Being asked if the therapist can even ask a particular question will help create a sense of control. The NBT practitioner who successfully creates a context where the client is agreeing to the work contract will also help settle the client's threat levels. This is not easy. Seeking motivational congruence by clarifying what the client really wants, and then in an unambiguous way, clearly articulating what the client needs to do to achieve their goal, and emphasising directly what they need to do differently to achieve their goal will also help relax the threat-seeking real estate in the brain.

Avoiding jargon and using clear, unambiguous, non-obfuscating, direct communication helps the brain to relax from searching for all possible hidden or inferred, unspoken criticisms or potential attacks. If the real challenges are identified in an open, direct, non-judgemental way, it allows the brain to focus on the visible, clearly articulated challenge. Creating the rationale of why this challenge must be tackled, for example, for the therapy-hater to achieve their ultimate goal, further reduces the threat.

The layering of challenge and the seeking of permission at each step to earn the right to challenge further give the therapy-hater some control over what will happen or not happen in the session. Small steps taken whilst understanding the "rules" of how therapy works – again – help calm the brain. Small steps help simplify the process and allows the therapy-hater to determine if each of the therapist's small promises can be trusted. Small steps allow the therapy-hater to make small choices and take manageable steps at each point – giving a sense of agency, control, and competency.

Honesty, transparency, and authenticity are essential elements of working effectively with people who have experienced trauma, service systems as abusive, or workers as blaming, shaming, or unhelpful. Ironically, clients facing complex situations like this are likely to be so emotionally volatile that they evoke an avoidance response in those around them, including professionals. If clients are critical, angry, or abusive, it is tempting for us all to attempt to pacify them by avoiding or obfuscating sensitive details of the working relationship. However, as George Orwell reportedly wrote, "In a time of universal deceit, telling the truth is a revolutionary act" (Whilst attributed to Orwell, it has not been traced to any of his writings).[1]

Complex and challenging situations requires an ongoing dance to link what the therapist thinks is possible with what the client wants. I gained considerable clinical insight doing role-plays with "ferocious" therapy-haters during NBT workshops. The advantage of role-plays and simulations are that they allow a more detailed debriefing from the person playing the client to learn what was helpful and what wasn't. In a memorable role-play exploring how to engage a therapy-hater, an articulate and reflective participant played Tiffany, a 24-year-old single mother of Geoffrey, who was two years of age. At the time of the role-play interview, Tiffany had not seen Geoffrey for five months. Geoffrey had been removed from Tiffany's care because a general medical practitioner had noticed bruising on Geoffrey's chest and upper arms. Protective services investigations found Geoffrey had been left alone for several hours and Tiffany had a history of methamphetamine use.

I began the role-play interview acknowledging that Tiffany was probably not keen to be involved in "mandated" counselling. The workshop participant was an exceptionally good actor and was, as Tiffany, very reluctant to engage in any meaningful work with me. With persistent exploration, I was able to ascertain that Tiffany did not see that she had any problems and was only interested in getting Geoffrey back in her care. She was not interested in addressing her drug use or her neglectful parenting that protective services wanted her to address in counselling. I repeatedly acknowledged that Tiffany's goal was to have Geoffrey back in her care, asking how serious she was about achieving this goal: Was she prepared to do whatever it took to achieve this goal? Was she up for it? Tiffany, who had a "horrible" relationship with her mother and no extended family support, increasingly argued that she was up for it. I was very clear, describing in practical detail, what Tiffany would have to do to have any chance of convincing protective services that she could provide sufficient parenting to warrant Geoffrey's return to her care and the steps she would need to take to show that she could provide a safe level of care. I pointed out that she would need to have (observed) access visits daily for several months, show she was responsive to Geoffrey's needs, etc. In line with Rooney's (2009) ideas of providing as much autonomy around negotiables and being very clear about non-negotiables, I was upfront about all the tasks Tiffany would have to undertake to convince protective services that she could look after Geoffrey, whilst pointing out that she was free to walk at any stage. I linked all these tasks to HER goal, whilst acknowledging how hard these tasks would be, how painful it must be for her to be estranged from son and tentatively acknowledged that I knew she wanted the best for Geoffrey and wanted to be the best mum she could be.

The most interesting feedback during the role-play debrief from the workshop participant playing Tiffany was that the "mantra" of me repeating Tiffany's goal (to get Geoffrey back in her care) and that it would not be easy but that I would be direct about every step required for her to achieve that goal helped "ground" Tiffany, who, because of her trauma background and current traumatising situation, was slipping in and out of conscious awareness of what was happening during the interview.

The following verbatim excerpts further highlight NBT with a traumatised client in a role-play interview I conducted with Jamie. Jamie is 36-years-old, in a relationship with Beth, and has been referred to counselling by his parole officer.

(The entire interview [21 minutes] can be seen as part of The Bouverie Centre's self-paced online learning suite www.bouverie.org.au/nbt)

This interview is accompanied by commentary from a neuropsychological perspective, by Robyn Elliott, Manager of The Bouverie Centre's academic program. (Used with permission of The Bouverie Centre, La Trobe University, Australia). Robyn has extensive experience in working with traumatised clients and their families. I start by asking Robyn what Jamie would be feeling approaching his session with me from a neurophysiological point of view and then work our way through part of the interview.

NBT session transcript with neuropsychological commentary

Robyn Elliott: Our whole neurophysiology is designed with a basic purpose in mind, physical survival in the world. In this regard we're not much different from the rest of the animal kingdom. Our whole physiology prioritises our survival in the moment, especially when under threat; we don't think about the future, we don't think about anybody else, we don't think about relationships. In new situations, everyone is a potential terrorist, from our nervous system's point of view. This is a new situation for Jamie, he doesn't know you, and he doesn't know what you're going to bring up, but he's probably got some past experiences of this sort of thing and it's probably not great. His nervous system is going to be particularly sensitised; he would be feeling anxious, not in a calm state of mind, but one that is likely to be inclined either toward an aggressive, running away or shutting down response, these are the three basic ways our nervous system responds to threat. And because he is on parole, we can also guess he has a whole history, including in the drug world, of bad experiences, but probably also in his early years, because we know drugs are one way of dealing with adverse experiences. So, he is going to have a whole range of stored up memories of difficult experiences in his life which is going to attune his system even more strongly toward looking out for threat and especially towards authority figures, people who have some sway over what is going to happen in his life. So, he is going to be particularly wired in his neurophysiology toward threat and he will have established strategies designed to protect himself from these threats. That's what you've got leading into this interview

Jeff: You've seen this video, but let's look through it again, stopping when you notice something significant.

Jeff: Gadday, it's Jamie, is it?
Jamie: Yeah

Jeff: I'm Jeff, Jeff Young, I'm the counsellor today. Um, so er, and I think you know that your parole officer um referred you here.

Jamie: Yep, yep.

Jeff: And were you keen to come? Maybe not?

Jamie: (*laughing dismissively*) Waste of time mate!

Jeff: Right, ok. Oh well good on you for being upfront, er that's the way I like to work. I actually prefer to work in a way I call No Bullshit Therapy.

> Robyn: Let's stop there. (Robyn comments on our respective postures) Jamie's lower body is a classic male bravado stance, but his upper body is very different, your upper and lower body matches, you're upright, not too smiley, but warmish, you present in a calm empowered state, which is in itself, potentially calming for Jamie. That sentence, "Were you keen to come? Maybe not?" gives him the message it's ok to be here in whatever state you are, and when you say, good on you for telling me, allows his nervous system to relax because it helps him feel he doesn't have to be any particular way.

Jamie: Yeah, funny name.

Jeff: Basically, that's where I try to not muck around, be upfront, be straight with you. Is that ok?

Jamie: (*not convinced*) Yeah, fair enough.

Jeff: Good on you for being upfront. You just didn't want to be here, is that right?

Jamie: Oh, just I don't put much value in all this sort of business.

Jeff: But your parole officer referred you, so you had to come otherwise …

Jamie: Yeah, between a rock and a hard place.

Jeff: Yeah. Um. So, er, do you know anything about counselling?

Jamie: Well, I've never been.

Jeff: It's asking lots of questions. So, I'll ask a lot of questions, tell me if they are too personal. But I just want to try and find out how I could be helpful. So that's the way I like to work. I just want to see how I can be helpful to you. Your parole officer has some ideas about why they wanted to send you here. From my point of view, I just want to find out how I can be helpful to you! Even if it is to get your parole officer, sort of, off your back.

> Robyn: Can we stop there. You declare that you want to have a pretty upfront direct interaction with him, and you congratulate him on being direct, but for all intent and purposes, you look like a bit of a do-gooder, already. You want to help him. But he's probably thinking, well let's wait and see. But I think the next little bit is really powerful in this interview.

Jamie: Oh, I don't think any of this is helpful. None of it. I hate the hoops and bloody things they make you to jump through. They're not helpful.

Jeff: Ok, ok. What would be helpful. Like, forget about all the hoops and whatever. Let's say if I was able to help you, really help you, for you. What would be the outcome of that?

Jamie: Oh. You tell the parole officer I'm good, that would help.

Jeff: Right. To be um clear about what I can and what I can't do. Um, I've got to respond to the parole officer. One, that you've come. And you've come, so, I can sort of tick the box and say yeah, he came. But if they said, what did you talk about. I've sort of got a couple of choices. And one thing, just to be upfront, I'll be honest, just professionally, I'll be honest with the parole officer. I could either say, well he came but we didn't talk about anything serious, or, and that probably wouldn't be that helpful to you. Or I can say, yeah, um you weren't that keen to come but we did talk about things that were important to him. And we can do what I call *real work*. That's sort of the two broad options.

Robyn: I think this part of the interview is powerful. Previously, you said you want to be helpful, which is not that different from a normal therapy session. What is convincing here, comes down to congruence. Our nervous system is very attuned to incongruence in our environment. For example, if you say, "I want to have a good relationship, I want to help you," but then your follow through is not congruent, it reads, you don't really mean it. Jamie is likely to think, you're going to establish a relationship and then use it against him. Jamie's world, for example, the drug world, is full of incongruence, deception, subterfuge. So, his nervous system is going to be highly attuned to incongruence and maybe from his childhood too. What you do here is, you say, "I want to help you," and he says, "Well I want you to put in a good word for me with the parole officer" and you say, basically, "Well I'm not going to give you what you want." Which seems incongruent, at a verbal level, you're not going to give him what he wants, but what his nervous system hears, is something completely congruent, I'm going to be upfront, I'm going to be honest with you, and I'm settled in myself, I don't need to use this relationship in any way. I think it is a lovely precursor to a whole lot of other stuff in the interview where you non-verbally give a message of congruence, to him, that is, I'm ok in myself, and you're ok to be you. I want to be helpful if I can, but I've got my limits, because I don't need you. And you're not afraid of him, some counsellors might be afraid to be that upfront, because they'd be afraid, he's thinking, I said what I wanted and you're not going to give it to me. But you're not afraid of that, which is another important meta-message to his nervous system, I'm not afraid of you. We can't drag the client, or force them, out of a particular nervous state, we can only relate from our regulated state to where they are and accept them in that state. And that's what's happening at this point, you're staying regulated, unafraid, unafraid to set boundaries, not really needing him, and then his nervous system gets this message. Because he doesn't baulk at your conditions and he doesn't object at all, he just says, ok let's move on. And opens himself up even more.

Jamie: Um.

Jeff: Like if, now you're here, if it was to be helpful, what is happening in your world that is not too good, not ideal for you? And again, you've been referred, but it is voluntary. You could say, I don't want to talk about anything. And I'd say, ok, that's fine. Um, and I'd just write back to your parole office and say, yeah, Jamie came but we didn't talk about anything. Now, that would waste your time. And you probably gathered one thing, I don't want to waste your time, but to be honest, I don't want to really waste my time either.

Robyn: Another message there, doesn't matter to me, it's totally for you.

Jamie: (*more serious*) Yeah. Um, er well my partner's pretty keen for me to get some help.

Jeff: (*warmer*) Oh, really. So, things aren't, haven't been so great?

Robyn: We can see as Jamie starts to talk about his relationship, his legs start to move. That's what we call an incomplete defensive response, it suggests he wants to run away. He doesn't want to sit there and talk with you, but he is. It's an indication of how vulnerable he is at this point and yet he is willing to go into this place with you. Which is an indicator of trust developing very quickly.

Jeff: And it has to be quick with someone who's so anxious, you don't get the luxury of time.

Robyn: No, he doesn't like therapy.

Jamie: Nah, yeah, she's worried about me. And, and threatening, that, saying she'll leave if I don't get some help.

Jeff: Oh really. And what's your wife's name? Can I ask?

Jamie: Beth.

Jeff: Beth. Ok. And you're worried about that? Like do you …

Jamie: Yeah, yeah, I want to …

Jeff: You want to make it work?

Jamie:	Yeah, I want to keep her around.
Jeff:	How long have you and Beth been together?
Jamie:	Oh, three and a half years.
Jeff:	Oh, ok, well that's a serious time.
Jamie:	Um.
Jeff:	And that would be one of the most important things for you, if you were able to make sure you saved your marriage. Are you married or partners?
Jamie:	Oh, no not married.
Jeff:	Save your partnership.
Jamie:	She'd like to, but we haven't had the money.
Jeff:	Ok. And that is something, that if I was to be able to help you, then that would be something really worth your while. Like, putting up with my pushy questions. Is that right, that would be something that would be worthwhile?
Jamie:	I'm not sure how you help that to be honest.
Jeff:	To be honest, in a way, and um you might not be a big fan of the talking therapies stuff, but that is something that's my area of expertise, trying to help people improve their relationships. I know you don't want to be here, but you're in the right place. If that's what you want.

Robyn: What you've done over the past few minutes, is to ask him about three to four times, "is this the area you want to work on"? And every time he says yes, out loud, it gives the brain a message, yes, I do want this, which reinforces the affirmative even more strongly. And you've reassured him that this is your area of expertise and that he's in the right place, so you've set it up nicely. And then you repeat, "if that's what you want." You're still feeding it out to him but you're giving him the space to move. There is a lot of permission for him to go either way. Which is going to be settling for his nervous system because we thrive on choice. That's about power.

Jeff:	How, can I ask, how serious you are about wanting to make sure you and Beth can work things out?
Jamie:	Yeah, I love her.
Jeff:	Yeah. Oh ok, right. So, you're serious.
Jamie:	Yeah.
Jeff:	So, um. Serious enough for me to ask some pushy questions?
Jamie:	(*amused*) Oh yeah, I guess. That's alright.
Jeff:	Maybe if we step back a step, what happened, what led you to getting into trouble?
Jamie:	Oh, the cops picked me up a couple of times and I had some drugs on me.
Jeff:	(*businesslike*) Oh, ok, what sort of drugs?
Jamie:	Oh, coke. Some ice.
Jeff:	And you went to court, and what was …

Jamie:	Yeah, kind of a community order or whatever and then the pushy bloody parole officer got involved.
Jeff:	Right. Ok, and there is some risk that if you don't …
Jamie:	If I don't jump through all these hoops, they'll chuck me in the slammer.
Jeff:	Yeah. Ok. So, and again, just to be really clear, the things that are going to help you get the parole officer backing off or supporting you more, actually lines up with what you want. If you were wanting things to work out with Beth and prepared to work with me, to look at what you might do to address that, and that's what I mean by *work*. Because it's a bit hard to know what counsellors mean by *work*, it's not picking up a shovel, but it is rolling up your sleeves and talking about something and addressing something that's important, and it's important that it's important to you, not to me. I sort of go home at night and things are fine. But there are some things that are not so good with Beth that you want addressed?

Robyn: Even the volume of your voice, at that point. You don't shy away from saying, "Yeah, I go home and sleep at night" and you say that in a normal tone of voice, but it's a very respectful way of saying, in a softer tone, that he doesn't. You're not in his space, but it's not unspeakable either. And there are lots of times in the session where you go to places that demonstrate to him that there's no off limits: "What are you in trouble for?" "What drugs to you use?" Later, you ask, "Is there any family violence?" There are no areas you won't go into which he tolerates very well. A lot of therapists wouldn't go there, worrying it would be too inflammatory, but you've established such a good rapport with him, and this habit of honesty, and from the respectful way you are dealing with it, that he knows you're not interested in blaming him. A bit later you ask him what he's doing when he's not on the drugs and he's working, rather than exploring what he does wrong. You ask what he does well, what gets in the way. Exploring strengths and constraints rather than what he's doing wrong.

Jamie:	Yeah, er she doesn't want, er she doesn't want me to get into trouble. But er, yeah, she wants me to stay away from the gear.
Jeff:	Right. Is that her biggest worry? And again, I'm just asking about her perspective in order to help you save your relationship.
Jamie:	Yeah, she'd talk about the using.
Jeff:	And um, so, er, and there's nothing else. You haven't got agro with her or … Again, I told you I'd be really upfront and direct with you and ask you some pushy questions.
Jamie:	Oh, um, there was once, when I'd came home, not kinda fully down yet, and I smashed up the place pretty good.
Jeff:	Right. Ok. Do you think she would have been frightened?
Jamie:	Yeah, she was probably shit scared.

Jeff: Ok. Right. Well at least good on you for being able to see it from her … step into her shoes. And presumably that's something that you wouldn't want to happen again. Is that right?

Robyn: That's really nice. You go there, with the intimate partner violence. But you focus on how she might have felt, which then touches him of course, but rather than focus on the bad, you immediately divert to good on you for seeing it from her shoes, so you reward stuff rather than blame him. His nervous system would be feeling in a good way at the moment, because you are accepting of who he is. In a determined way you are finding strengths and good things he does and who he is as a person. Later, you ask if anyone in his family or friends would be on his side, who would be supporters of him, and you say that Beth is the only person who sees the good in him. This would be a relief because you are referring to acceptance of him, which is something we all crave. Because as pack animals, we need to belong. Any sign of acceptance, forgiveness, grace, being upfront, but at the same time saying, I care about you, which is the message you're giving him. You are doing what his nervous system craves, we are always working towards that place where our nervous system can relax and find peace. And that's a sense of being acceptable so we can be accepted into the pack and be safe. He starts out at the beginning of this session with a real sense, "I'm not going to belong here, this guy is going to reject me in some way, blame me, shame me, and then I'll have to be ejected from the pack." But the messages you are giving him is that you are acceptable no matter how you are, you can not want to be here, and you can still be here, I don't need you for anything, but I care about you, and I care about what you care about. I'm going to set my limits, because I'm not scared of you, but you are a good person, you are acceptable, things have been hard for you, you've made an effort, and we can make something happen here.
Jeff: It's quite moving.
Robyn: It's quite moving. It's quite moving watching it. Even though Jamie won't recognise it because he's been toughened, but his nervous system will come out of this with a sense of hope. And it is very good evidence that in skilled hands, therapy can move quickly, very dramatically.

Jamie: No. She'd probably leave if it happened again.
Jeff: And that's not what you want.
Jamie: No.
Jeff: Ok. What er, and that's the only occasion? And she was ok, she wasn't hurt, she was just really frightened?
Jamie: Yeah. I've never hurt her.
Jeff: And how long have you been on the gear for?
Jamie: On and off since I was a teenager, I suppose.
Jeff: Ok.

Jamie:	I don't use every day, I don't use all the time. You know, just let off steam.
Jeff:	Ok. And now you are in a relationship with someone you really care about, with Beth. What do you think are the things that the drugs give you, that would be hard, if you did what Beth wanted and you stayed away from the drugs?
Jamie:	Oh, oh, I don't really know. I don't even know.
Jeff:	Is it just sort of now just become a bit of a habit?
Jamie:	It's not like I've put a whole lot of thought into it, um, sometimes you feel like you've gotta go out and let off steam or let loose a bit.
Jeff:	You've mentioned that a couple of times, like letting off steam. Are things a bit pressured. What do you do for, in terms …
Jamie:	What for work?
Jeff:	Yeah.
Jamie:	I bounce around a bit for work. I've done some labouring and other bits and pieces.
Jeff:	Right. So, finances must be pretty tight?
Jamie:	Oh, yeah.
Jeff:	And Beth, what does she do?
Jamie:	She's training to be a nurse.
Jeff:	So, um, it sounds like though, and I know you didn't want to be here, but have things changed a bit that you'd be happy to see what you could do and what maybe even what Beth could do to really strengthen the relationship so that you weren't at risk of losing it?
Jamie:	Oh, if you think you could help there, I'd give it a go.
Jeff:	I can ask the questions and give you some advice about what you could do. And as I said, I'll be really upfront and direct, so you'll know exactly what I'm thinking, um, but it would be up to you to do the things that would make a difference. Yeah?
Jamie:	Yeah.
Jeff:	Oh well, good on you, in a way I think we might get on pretty well, you're upfront and direct and I like that. And you'll give something a go.
Jamie:	Yeah, thanks Jeff.
Jeff:	What do you think, if Beth was here today and I asked her what is one thing that Jamie could do that would make your life much better, and hence you know, the relationship better. What would she say?
Jamie:	Make her life better?
Jeff:	Yeah, make her life better. And I'm only asking what would make her life better in trying to help you save your relationship, which is what you want. Because that's what I'm going to focus on, I'm going to focus on how you could make your relationship with Beth safer.
Jamie:	Oh, she'd probably say to not use.
Jeff:	And you've been using since you've been a teenager, so that would be. I was going to assume that it would be hard to stop, but is it?
Jamie:	Well, I've put it down for, you know at times.
Jeff:	Oh, for how long? Like, what is the longest?
Jamie:	Oh, a few months.

Jeff: Oh, ok. And how have you been able to do that, what have you learnt from that?

Jamie: Um, er, I think it is most of the times when I've had a job for a while.

Jeff: So, if you've got work, what is it about work that means you'd be less likely to be tempted by using. Or need to.

Jamie: Oh, you keep busy, and you've kinda got a reason to be clear headed and get up in the morning.

Jeff: Ok. So that's something that you've really learnt, um that's sort of helpful. That in some ways that would be another way to go about saving your marriage, er, your relationship, to think about what you could do to get work, which actually helps reduce your interest in using. Is that right or am I pushing, am I putting words into your mouth?

Jamie: Oh. I think I missed what you were saying then, um.

Jeff: Just thinking, er, you were saying, well, you want to save your relationship with Beth, what would make it more likely to save the relationship from Beth's point of view is you not using, and then I asked like have you been able to put it down and you said yeah, for a few months, and that was when you were working. So that's something that …

Jamie: Oh, I think she'd be stoked, you know, if I had a job and not using, it would be her dreams come true really. If it was that easy.

Jeff: Well, I suppose you've done it for a few months. What do you think, um when you think about it now actually doing that, what would be the thing that would get in the way, and I just really encourage you to be upfront, as I've been. What do you think, would …

Jamie: Oh, oh, well, um, just getting the opportunity, I think. You know, when I've had jobs before, you know, it's not because I haven't been a decent worker, er I've lost the job because the company's downsizing or running out of work.

Jeff: So, you're a good worker. It's only been circumstance, that …

Jamie: Yeah.

Jeff: Tell me, just changing tracks a bit. Who do you think is your biggest supporter, who in your family or network that would sort of think, yeah …

Jamie: What you mean outside of Beth?

Jeff: Yeah, Jamie, he's a good worker, he's a decent guy. I want the best for him.

Jamie: I don't have heaps of family around. (*pause*) Um, yeah, not heaps of them.

Jeff: And would they have been supportive, family? Would they have sort of …

Jamie: No not really, not much support there.

Jeff: So, you've sort of had to fight your own way in this world?

Jamie: Yeah, I left school early, out of home since I was a teenager.

Jeff: So, Beth is the key person at the moment who can see the good in you and …

Jamie: Yeah.

Jeff:	And she is also the person most upset with um …
Jamie:	Yeah, because it affects her the most.
Jeff:	Right. Ok. But it sounds like um it's something that you really want to address. Is this the first time you've sort of really thought about talking to someone about a way to make things better between you and Beth?
Jamie:	There's been a couple of other times where, er, I've had a counselling, or er, a drug service. It didn't go very far.
Jeff:	Right. What didn't work out then, because there's no point in me doing the same thing if it wasn't helpful, I don't want to do the same thing that wasn't helpful for you.
Jamie:	Oh, I don't know, they got a bit preachy. (*pause*) And er, I was in a different place I suppose.
Jeff:	Ok, so you were in a different place, but they were a bit preachy? And, um some ways hopefully I've come across, in some ways I don't care really what you do, but the main thing, as a counsellor, I just want to be helpful to you and it does seem like you're pretty keen to try and make things better, or make sure you don't lose Beth.
Jamie:	Yep.
Jeff:	Ok.

The work is yet to be done, but at this stage, after 21 minutes, Jamie is starting to engage in real work that will be helpful to him; work I'm able and willing to do with him. I asked my colleague, Nick Barrington, who played Jamie, to review the session and respond to three questions, as Jamie, but in the third person, to provide us with a further perspective of the session.

NBT client commentary

Jeff:	How did Jamie feel approaching the session?
Nick:	Jamie approached the session with resignation; feeling powerless because the parole officer had forced him to attend. This sense of powerlessness fuelled his dismissive attitude and his belief that therapy would not be helpful to him. As an attempt to gain some degree of power, Jamie was looking for a confrontation with the therapist. While not conscious, for Jamie, confrontation, particularly with another male, was somewhat comfortable and familiar. Focusing on a confrontation also helped him avoid sensitive and emotional topics.
Jeff:	What did the therapist do to avoid a confrontation and engage Jamie in meaningful work?
Nick:	Naming the parole officer and immediately acknowledging Jamie's reluctance, helped establish a context for plain speaking from the outset. It was significant for Jamie that his comment, "Waste of time, mate," was responded to in a non-reactive manner. Jeff's response, "That's the way I like to work," also created a sense that we had one point of connection. The repeated comments, "I want to know what will help you" grabbed Jamie's curiosity and began to open a possibility that the session could be

helpful. This built on the therapist having already acknowledged that Jamie didn't want to be there and that he didn't think it would be helpful. All this avoided the confrontation Jamie was expecting and instead, felt like small steps toward creating a genuine interaction.

When the therapist asked, "If I were to help you," Jamie wanted to respond more positively, but his defensive wall quickly came up, resulting in the dismissive "You can tell the parole officer I'm good." The therapist's business-like response, including what he wouldn't do, made Jamie confront his own choice of what he wanted, which gave Jamie a degree of control.

Having laid out the options for Jamie, about how he could and couldn't use the space, the therapist's question, "Now you're here," created a sense for Jamie, "I'm not going to get beaten over the head with this stuff, we're moving on, I'm being given real choices, and Jeff wants to know what I really want."

When he started talking about Beth and the importance of his relationship with her, Jamie is a little surprised he is being this uncomfortable, this honest, this vulnerable. The therapist returning to 'that would really be worth your while' slowed down the conversation for Jamie which reinforced that he had choices, and that the choices laid out by the therapist were real, and that the therapist was genuine in wanting to know what he wanted. He began to feel that the choices were real and not just a gimmick to get him to talk.

The therapist providing a rationale of why he was asking "pushy questions," linking this to what Jamie wanted, helped create a safe collaborative space. This safe(r) place allowed Jamie to accept the compliment, "Good on you for being able to step into her shoes."

The continual talking about the talking such as, 'I think we might get on pretty well, you're upfront and direct and I like that. And you'll give something a go' created a containing environment for Jamie; it titrated the intensity of the discussion and the emotion.

Jeff: What would be a likely outcome of this (21 minute) session?

Nick: Jamie ended the session much clearer in himself, about what he wanted, and about his motivations. Jamie was left with a positive sense of himself, greater awareness of his behaviour, and more empowered within his life. Jamie felt respected throughout the session and safe enough to be vulnerable in a way that he did not anticipate. He left the session believing that work with Jeff could be helpful. Jeff would need to maintain the sense of safety and belief in the work ahead.

The following chapter outlines some of the additional challenges and opportunities of working with more than one person.

Note

1 https://quoteinvestigator.com/2013/02/24/truth-revolutionary/

References

Furlong, M., & Young, J. (1996). Talking about blame. *Australian and New Zealand Journal of Family Therapy*, *17*(4), 191200.

Kezelman, C., & Stavropoulos, P. (2012). *The last frontier: Practice guidelines for treatment of complex trauma and trauma informed care and service delivery*. Blue Knot Foundation.

Rooney, R.H. (1992*). Strategies for work with involuntary clients*. Columbia University Press.

Rooney, R.H. (2009). *Strategies for work with involuntary clients* (2nd ed.). Columbia University Press.

Stavropoulos, P. (2012). Introduction. In C. Kezelman & P. Stavropoulos (Eds.), *The last frontier: Practice guidelines for treatment of complex trauma and trauma informed care and service delivery* (pp. xxx–xxxi). Blue Knot Foundation.

12 No Bullshit Therapy with couples, families, and at work

I am afraid that if I do not speak to you and tell you how I am, I will slowly withdraw and leave you; however, if I do speak to you, I am afraid that you will slowly withdraw and leave me.

— Peggy Penn (2001, p. 39)

Couples

Poet, family therapist, director of the Language and Writing Project, and Training Director at the Ackermann Institute for the family in New York between 1986 and 1992, Peggy Penn had an interest in the relationships surrounding chronic conditions. When I first read the quote above, I felt Penn had captured an essential dilemma facing many couples and raised the important question, *What is the consequence of couples not speaking about the important stuff?*

Kerry called to make an appointment for herself and her husband Dominic. Prior to the first appointment, Kerry rang to defer the appointment because Dominic had started to see an individual therapist and wasn't keen to also participate in couple therapy. We agreed to postpone the appointment for several months. Prior to the deferred scheduled appointment, Kerry rang to confirm the appointment but asked if we could have a 60-minute rather than the usual 90-minute consultation, because her husband had a business commitment later in the day. Suspecting that Dominic may not be as enthusiastic about attending the session as Kerry, we agreed to a 60-minute session and assured Kerry that Dominic could be as upfront as he liked about what would be helpful and what wouldn't be. In keeping with a single-session thinking approach, I reassured her that my co-therapist Sally, and I, would try and make the most of the 60 minutes.

The intake indicated that Kerry's and Dominic's daughter, Rosa, had a severe eating disorder, which, although significantly improved, had really knocked the family around. When Dominic and Kerry arrived for their appointment, Dominic was reticent, but not as much of a therapy-hater as I had suspected. Sally, building on my conversation with Kerry, shared that being open and direct was our preferred way of working, which seemed to engage Dominic and set the scene, later in the session, for Sally to engage in the following exchange:

DOI: 10.4324/9781003354925-12

Dominic: Two years ago, I was bullied at work and so I saw a therapist. He recommended that I had to confront the bully and it was helpful. So, when Kerry wanted me to see someone, I recontacted this therapist.

Sally: Was it helpful?

Dominic: I was feeling a bit down and suicidal. I guess it was helpful to talk about how things with our daughter had impacted our relationship. But I did think to myself, as I was talking to the therapist, why are we talking about these trivialities?

Sally: I said we'd be pretty direct, so can I ask what we'd be talking about right now if we didn't talk about trivialities?

Dominic: (*pause*) I think Kerry thinks I'm going to leave her!

Kerry: For both of us, leaving would be a good idea. We were out recently, and he looked at me as if he didn't want to be with me.

Dominic: I don't know what to say other than I can absolutely guarantee that I am not going to leave Kerry!

Having created a warm culture of openness, and non-blaming directness in the pre-session phone call and at commencement of the session, Sally and I felt we could be both compassionate and direct. Conveying that we genuinely wanted the best for Kerry and Dominic and their relationship, Sally and I began to feel confident about exploring their relationship difficulties in greater detail. Building on Sally's opening, I continued.

Jeff: But there is a difference between guaranteeing to stay and wanting to stay!

This led to a productive discussion about the state of the couple's relationship, in which we explored the impact of the losses and crises that they had experienced over the past three years dealing with Rosa's eating disorder and the wear and tear of 18 years on their marriage.

Sometimes in couple work, the task of the No Bullshit Therapy (NBT) practitioner is to mediate between two very different approaches to honesty and directness. For example, one member of the couple might be direct but brutal and the other member, warm but fuzzy. The brutally direct member of the partnership often wears their honesty as a badge of honour and their lack of warmth can further discourage their partner from expressing what they really think. The warm fuzzy member of the couple is often extremely sensitive about hurting or provoking others, although their lack of clarity can lead to frustration which provokes greater brutal honesty. This cyclic pattern of attack and avoidance can reinforce itself and become entrenched over time. It is a pattern of communication that may point towards violence and if violence is occurring, this must take precedence in the work. If, however, it is simply an unproductive communication pattern between the two people, the following questions inspired by Barry Mason (2012) can be useful. Brutally direct Joe and warm fuzzy Judy are struggling to communicate effectively.

> Joe, suppose you talked straight, without holding back, but in a way that was sensitive to Judy, what would that look like?
> How could you take a no bullshit approach, Joe, and at the same time fit in with Judy's sensitivity?
> Joe, how could you reassure Judy, that despite your straight talking, you are keen to hear what she really thinks?
> Judy, if Joe was to be direct, but not hurtful, how should he proceed?
> What is your greatest fear Judy, about sharing what's on your mind?
> If Joe was keen to know what you really think, Judy – and this can be checked out with Joe – what would he need to do for you to feel comfortable sharing it with him?

The following NBT steps may also be helpful.

Step 1: Ask the couple, *What needs to be talked about in order to sort things out as a family/couple?* List in general terms, like an agenda – being careful to avoid going into detail at this point.

Step 2: Choose or negotiate an issue (from the agenda) which is not too controversial, as a practice item or first step.

Step 3: Ask each member of the couple, *How could you raise and discuss this issue directly, showing warmth and care, and acknowledging the difficulties involved?*

Step 4: Provide suggestions and coaching for honesty and directness, warmth and care, or appreciation of the constraints/difficulties, whichever is needed. If appropriate, each partner can be invited to coach each other. For example, in our earlier example, Joe could be asked to coach Judy on how to be more direct with him, and Judy could be asked to coach Joe on how to deliver his message with warmth and care.

Step 5: Reflect on what has been learnt, celebrate successes, or learning, and address the next most appropriate issue from the agenda, using steps 2–5.

Families

> Happiness is having a large, loving, caring, close-knit family in another city
> — George Burns (Comedian)

The full range of views about therapy can often be found in one family. For example, a therapy-lover may instigate bringing the family to therapy whilst other family members' views about attending therapy may range from indifference to hostility. Unlike individual therapy, professionals working with families are often confronted with the challenge of engaging the *problem person* (therapy-hater) alongside the person who is hopeful that the family intervention will help (therapy-lover). The following ideas may be helpful to work with combinations of therapy-lovers, therapy-haters, and those in between.

Therapy-haters attend family therapy for several reasons: They are dragged in by other family members, come for the benefit of others rather than for themselves, agree to attend out of loyalty to another family member, attend simply to avoid conflict or because it is the line of least resistance. The NBT approach of creating a context for mutual honesty and directness for the therapy-hater(s) in the family can be facilitated by acting quickly, acknowledging in a non-blaming, non-invested way that the person may not want to be in the session. When made overt in a non-critical, non-judgemental way, acknowledging that therapy is simply *not their thing* can help therapy-haters to be more open to exploring the possibilities of family work. An open exploration of their reasons for attending, despite their cynicism, can also be helpful.

Making overt the reluctance of therapy-haters can help avoid their need to communicate their reluctance by slouching, grunting, looking angry or sullen, being silent, and adopting a distant politeness or some other display of dissatisfaction or protest. This creates an opportunity to briefly acknowledge the benefits and/or their reason for attending despite their reluctance (judicious warmth and care). When a first session is approached in this way, many family members who don't want to be in therapy are open to exploring the possibilities that the work might help other family members or the family as a whole, even if it may not help them personally.

Acknowledging the therapy-hater's reasons for attending, despite their reluctance, whilst at the same time ensuring that other family members get what they want, is a balancing act that family therapists get good at, and if this balance can be maintained, a goal palatable to all often seems to emerge.

One of the challenges specific to family work is to create a context for mutual honesty and directness for the therapy-hater(s) whilst not intimidating, upsetting, or silencing the therapy-lover(s) within the family. Luckily, therapy-lovers are more tolerant of delays than therapy-haters and so if therapy-lovers see the therapist engaging with the therapy-haters, they are usually happy to be ignored for a period. Therapy-lovers often bring therapy-haters to family therapy to change them individually under the guise of attending as a family.

The Thompson family, dad Jason (44), mum Patricia (48), daughter Lisa (18), and son Tyler, (15), is referred for family therapy by Lisa's individual therapist Rachel, who feels that if things improved between Lisa and her mum, Lisa's depression would be easier to treat. Lisa was referred to Rachel because she'd talked about suicide and had taken some of her mother's Panadol (medication to treat fever and pain) but is not actively suicidal when I see the family. There has been tension in the marriage since Patricia's mum, Stacey, passed away 18 months ago. Patricia and Jason are both concerned about their daughter but have very different approaches to helping her; Patricia takes a tougher line, Jason, a softer one.

Jason, Lisa, and Tyler are all quite keen to attend family therapy, but Patricia is a very reluctant attendee and only comes to support Lisa and her husband, although she does not easily admit to this. Using an NBT approach, I engage Patricia and discover she would like things to be better between her and her daughter. Lisa would also like things to be better between herself and her mum.

I say hello to everyone, find out that Tyler likes football, Lisa wants to be a vet, Jamie is an accountant, and Patricia a senior financial analyst in a large prominent firm. I acknowledge and confirm that Lisa's individual counsellor had referred the family to me. I start checking out if everyone had been keen to attend.

Jamie:	Pretty much, pretty much everybody was ok. Hard to take time off from work.
Patricia:	I won't be able to do this a lot in the future. So, I hope we can get this sorted out today. I can't keep taking time off from work, not this time of year. Sorry.
Jeff:	Good on you for being upfront.
Patricia:	Thank you.
Jeff:	And I got the sense, being upfront myself, that you weren't so keen to come along.
Patricia:	Not really. I can't see how this is going to help matters. She (Lisa) is already seeing a counsellor and I don't think we've got any problems. Does anyone else here think we have any problems? (*silence*) I mean my mother died, and that disrupted things, but that's a family's standard situation. And they (Lisa and Stacey) were very close. Um.
Jeff:	Can I ask how long ago that your mum died?
Patricia:	18 months.
Jeff:	Ok, so that's not very long ago. I'm sorry to hear that.
Patricia:	Thank you.
Jeff:	So, but you weren't keen to come. Is that right? Or …
Patricia:	Well not particularly, I'm sorry.
Jeff:	No, don't be sorry.
Patricia:	I'm sure you're very nice and all, and it's great to talk about things and all, but I'm not really seeing what the point is, we are already engaged in services. She's (Lisa) already seeing a counsellor.
Jeff:	Alright. Well, good on you for being upfront. But you (Jason) were, so Jason was keener to come (*looking at Patricia*).
Patricia:	Yes, he was. He's all about this stuff.
Jason:	I was.
Jeff:	So, it fits more, and you came along because you're really keen to help Lisa? What were you hoping? What do you think Lisa's counsellor was hoping you'd get out of making this appointment?
Jason:	I think she was feeling like if Lisa and Patricia could get on a bit better, then it would make it easier for Lisa in her progress.
Jeff:	Oh. Ok. Were you keen to come along Lisa?
Lisa:	Yeah. Yes.
Jeff:	What about you, Tyler, were you keen to come?
Tyler:	Yeah, I was happy to help Lisa.
Jeff:	Ok, so you and Lisa are close?

Tyler:	(*nods*) Yeah.
Jeff:	Ok That's good. That makes a bit of an explanation in my head why you weren't so keen to come (*looking at Patricia*)... [*I was going to say the individual counsellor's view, helps make sense of why Patricia would feel blamed and hence less keen to come, but Patricia somewhat defensively interrupted.*]
Patricia:	Definitely, I'd do anything for my kids. I'm here, aren't I.
Jeff:	Right and that's why you came. Even though you're not someone who likes this sort of counselling business and Lisa is already seeing a counsellor. The reason you came along, is because you'd do anything for your kids.
Patricia:	Definitely, I'm really worried about Lisa right now. That's why we've had her engaged with the other counsellor.
Jeff:	Ok. And it is also why you came along.
Patricia:	Yes. Of course.
Jeff:	Are you someone who likes to be upfront and not muck about and really sort of say it as it is? I get that sense. Would I be correct?
Patricia:	Yes, you'd be correct.
Jeff:	Ok. And that can be very helpful. Because if I can be upfront, and you can be upfront, and I know that you want to be here for Lisa, and you'd be prepared to do anything. Yeah?
Patricia:	Yeah.
Jeff:	So, can I just get a bit of background?

[I find out that Lisa's counsellor felt that family therapy would help Lisa and her mum to get closer. I find that things have become tense between them after the death of Stacey. I find out that Patricia is very different from her mum, Stacey, but her mum was similar, loving, and very supportive, to Lisa. And that Lisa has struggled at school, and with life in general, following the loss of her grandmother. I acknowledge that Lisa's mum and dad must have been really worried about her, especially when she took the Panadol. I acknowledge and normalise that Stacey's death has had a huge impact on everyone in the family, and that everyone has reacted differently to the profound grief. I share that it is common for everyone in a family to react differently to such a significant loss and for those differences to cause further tension. During the session, we all discover that Lisa is starting to feel better, that her and her mum were closer before Stacey's death, and they both want things to be better. Patricia becomes aware that the current fights between herself and her daughter particularly affect Tyler, making him feel sad. It emerges that the loss of Stacey has had a practical impact on the family as well as an emotional impact. Prior to the loss, Patricia was able to focus on her work, guilt-free, knowing that her mum was providing the support Tyler and especially Lisa, needed. I continue (24 minutes into the session) to use NBT approaches to engage Patricia, knowing that, whilst all family members will need to change, Patricia is more likely to feel blamed and hence struggle to change.]

Jeff:	So, I'm getting a sense of what you've been through as a family. If I was to be helpful to you today, what would you walk away with by the end of today? And I might start with you, Patricia. And I know you were not so keen to come along, but do you think the way we've been talking, do you think it could be helpful?
Patricia:	Yes, I do, actually. I'd rather get it out in the open and deal with it, rather than let it fester.
Jeff:	So, you're ok, if we get things out in the open. Let's talk about it and let's address it directly. Would you be open, even if it was something that might be a bit challenging, or if it meant you doing something differently, would you be up for that, if it was for your kids and your family?
Patricia:	For the kids, definitely!
Jeff:	Ok, alright. I thought we'd get on well. So, can I sort of ask anything? You know, I'm happy if you don't want to answer. And the kids can say whatever would be helpful too, yeah, especially Lisa? Because I get the sense that what you want most, and tell me if this is right or not, that you're all here to help you (pointing to Patricia) and you (pointing to Lisa), mother and daughter to get on better. Yeah, is that right? (Turning to Tyler) Have I got that right? You're my co-therapist.
Tyler:	(*laughing*) Yeah, that's right.
Jeff:	Jason, is that right?
Jason:	Yeah, yeah.
Jeff:	And the two key people I need to check with. Is that right Lisa, is that what you really want?
Lisa:	Yeah, and that mum would be kinda a bit more supportive of what I want to do after I leave school.
Jeff:	Ok, ok. So, two things. Part of getting on better would be … and I said that I'd be straight, and you (Patricia) said you could hear anything, yeah? Is that right?
Patricia:	(*a little wearily*) Yep.
Jeff:	That, if your mum somehow, or at least, if you felt that your mum was more supportive of what you're wanting to do, career-wise. Yeah?
Lisa:	Yeah.
Jeff:	And I get the sense that career is important to you, Patricia?
Patricia:	Yeah.
Jeff:	Ok. And is that what you want to walk away with today, Patricia? To have some ways of thinking how you and your daughter could get on better.
Patricia:	Yes, definitely!
Jeff:	Is there anything else? Or is that the main thing I could be helpful with? (*brief silence*)
Jason:	That's probably it.

[Lisa wants to do more things with her mother, and Patricia is keen. She also wants her mother's support for her dream of being a vet. Patricia is keen to provide support and says she thinks Lisa is smart enough to be a vet, and that her heart is in the right place. Patricia clarifies why she has not been so effusive in her encouragement: she is worried that Lisa is too soft and would find it hard to make hard decisions about her animal clients. Lisa feels that the motivation to work hard is coming back and that with her mum's support she would be able to get the marks to do veterinary science. Patricia says she just wants her children to be happy, which is reassuring for Lisa (and Tyler) to hear. I want to know what support Lisa wants from her mum, but to soften it, I ask what support she needs from her family.]

Jeff: Maybe it would be helpful to know now, if you're up for it, not 18 months ago, but now, to hear what could your mum and dad and Tyler could do to help you do the hard work you'd need to do to become a vet, given that you're a bit behind in your schoolwork, because of all that's happened?

Lisa: Well, Tyler has always been really supportive; we get along great. And Dad's like pretty chilled. Yeah. He makes it a lot easier to study because it doesn't seem like a chore, he makes it like something I want to do. Um, er, maybe if it wasn't, I don't know, basically, if it wasn't such a big pressure, um er, that would help.

Jeff: (*matter-of-factly*) So, we're talking about your mum and your mum has an agreement here today that you can be as upfront as you can, so, and I think what's come out of today that's really helpful is that she's supportive of you becoming a vet, and you didn't know that, but she is.

Lisa: No.

Jeff: (*turning to Patricia*) And again, I can understand that you might have come along today expecting to get hit over the head with a lot of criticism and blame, but good on you for being so open. Because to be honest, it seems like Tyler and your husband are doing things that are helpful, now. (Turning to Lisa) What could your mum do that would help, because she wants to be helpful, she wants to be supportive, she is supportive of the idea of you becoming a vet. What could she do to help? And, you know her personality, she's your mum, she's not your dad, she's not your grandma she's got lots of skills.

Lisa: Yeah, I know that Mum wants me to do well, obviously.

Jeff: Ok. I didn't know that, or I didn't know that you (*looking at Patricia*) knew that.

Lisa: Ok. Well, I know that she wants me to do well.

Jeff: So, what could she do that would help or what could she stop doing that would help? I'm pushing here because this will be helpful. You actually want to know, don't you? (*looking at Patricia*)

Patricia:	Yes, I do.
Jeff:	So, your mum wants to know.
Patricia:	I don't want to be making you miserable.
Jeff:	She's an upfront character, she's different to you and maybe your dad.
Lisa:	I don't know, maybe not making such a big deal of me not studying one night …

[Lisa is now talking openly and specifically, and Patricia is listening. The family session starts problem solving.]

Work meetings

When we listen and celebrate what is both common and different, we become a wiser, more inclusive, and better organisation
— Pat Wadors (Chief People Officer, *Ultimate Kronos Group)*

A colleague emailed me about her success in using NBT concepts to create a context for respectful open discussions in a multi-disciplinary, multi-agency meeting. The meeting had several people with strong personalities and differing professional perspectives. Some members felt their views were not being heard or valued. She and a colleague set the context for the meeting by role-playing a published (Findlay, 2007) interview about NBT Ron Findlay had conducted with me.

She reported that all participants in the meeting responded to the concept of marrying directness with warmth and care, in order to help them be upfront about the difficulties and constraints they were experiencing. Some participants had associated *directness* with *conflict* and role-playing the interview had helped create a *communication framework* for raising sensitive issues without others taking offence or becoming "patch protective." For example, a disability worker who had been working with the family being discussed raised her concern in the following way, *I know you are working hard with this family and want the best for the children* (warmth/care). *Unfortunately, the family are fearful that you* [Child Protection] *will remove the children, and they don't fully understand the things you say to them about court and how they system works* (directness). *Perhaps we could explain this together to them in a simpler way.*

My colleague commented that the NBT concepts helped create an environment for the meeting where it was ok to disagree, have different views about what was/ was not working, and to get to the nuts and bolts quicker without having to dance around the issues.

Saying the unsayable in the workplace

Early in my role as Director at The Bouverie Centre, Robyn Elliott, manager of our academic programs, introduced a process that was conducted once a year in an all-staff planning meeting called *saying the unsayable.*

The aim of *saying the unsayable* is to create an opportunity for staff to raise issues that can't easily be talked about in public. Staff vote on the most important two issues that require addressing, and the executive leadership team commit to following up these two top issues. It is made clear from the start that only the two top issues will be addressed, but having raised the other issues publicly, they usually can be talked about more easily and staff are encouraged to use the usual management structures and processes to address issues outside of the top two.

Step 1

Staff, minus the executive leadership team, are randomly allocated to small groups (3–5), with instructions to *identify things that are difficult to raise in the organisation but need attention*. Group members are encouraged to listen carefully to all issues raised (because it can be difficult to talk coherently and fluently about issues that can't be talked about openly in an organisation).

Step 2

Each small group is asked to prioritise if multiple issues are raised and only share the top two with the larger group in step 3.

Step 3

A member of each small group is invited to write up the group's top two issues on a whiteboard. In some years, the face of the whiteboard was in view of the larger group, in other years, the whiteboard was turned away from the larger group. It is important to provide some sense of anonymity without arguing that it is completely anonymous.

Step4

Similar concerns are collapsed. For example, if one group lists workload and another too much work, they are likely to be combined.

Step 5

Everyone votes (once) on which issue is the most important that needs addressing.

Step 6

The top two issues are designated as critical for the leadership team to address. The other issues are recorded (a useful resource for the leadership team) and staff are encouraged to follow up these issues using the usual management processes.

Step 7

The large group then brainstorms potential solutions or identifies which team or person is best suited to follow up (only) the top two issues. The executive leadership team undertakes to ensure that the top two issues are addressed in a timely manner and to report progress to staff.

Step 8

Finally, an opportunity is provided to reflect on this process and to consider any adaptations.

Saying the unsayable has led to productive outcomes and important discussions. Staff have raised the obvious that it is not possible to say the unsayable. True, but the process conveys a strong message that the leadership team values feedback about sensitive issues as part of a culture of honesty and transparency. Even encouraging critiques of the saying the unsayable process contributes to this culture. Saying the unsayable has also identified the most significant issues for staff that, with some encouragement, can be talked about. It has allowed the leadership team to address these issues, which further provides confidence in staff that raising concerns is valued by the leadership team.

Now it is time to wrap things up – it's been a pleasure!

References

Findlay, R. (2007). A mandate for honesty: Jeff Young's No Bullshit Therapy. *Australian and New Zealand Journal of Family Therapy, 28*(3), 165–170.
Mason, B. (2012). The personal and the professional: Core beliefs and the construction of bridges across difference. In I-B. Krause (Ed.), *Culture and reflexivity in systemic psychotherapy: Mutual perspectives*. Routledge.
Penn, P. (2001). Chronic illness: Trauma, language, and writing: Breaking the silence. *Family Process, 40*(1) 33–52.

13 Concluding comments

If insincerity is "the great enemy of clear language," as postulated by George Orwell (1946, p. 137), then jargon-free, honesty, and directness must be the close friends of sincerity.

I hope you engage with No Bullshit Therapy (NBT) in a reflective, critical, and creative way, making it part of your work context. I also hope this book encourages our field to make therapy fit our clients and not to expect all our clients to fit mainstream ways of providing help. I will be chuffed if therapy-haters influence the field as much as therapy-lovers. Demystifying therapy can only be a good thing.

Reflecting on my own experience of embracing NBT over a couple of decades; it has been gradual and profound. The NBT Clinical Guidelines, as simple as they are, inform an ever-increasing range of elements in my life. The most obvious is that I've become more aware of when I am obfuscating, not quite telling the truth, or simply fudging to avoid a difficult situation or to protect myself or someone else. It is as if my *internal bullshit* meter has become even more sensitive and has turned itself on me, in my relationships with work colleagues, friends, and family. Being more aware when I'm not being exactly truthful doesn't mean I always act on this knowledge, but it does allow me to more consciously decide if, and how, to respond.

The principles underlying NBT, maybe more than the practices themselves, are likely to have an enduring impact on the way you approach difficult conversations and difficult situations. Rather than succumbing to the temptation to avoid these vexed, risky situations, or respond in an unfiltered reactive way, NBT provides guidance on how to lean into these conversations and situations with authenticity and transparency, armed with the integrated practices of honesty, directness, warmth, and care. Something spiritual-like happens when a functional bridge can be constructed between people in conflict, especially people from communities who have historically not trusted each other, such as therapists and therapy-haters, when this conflict is addressed directly and honourably, driven by wanting the best for the relationship, and appreciating and articulating the inherent and historical difficulties of the situation. NBT can move us from thinking of difficult people to people facing difficulties, to people I find difficult, as my colleague Brendan O'Hanlon describes it, and this position is frighteningly challenging and immensely empowering at the same time. This is why I have written about ways to change our

DOI: 10.4324/9781003354925-13

approaches to suit *difficult-to-engage clients* rather than providing strategies to *engage difficult clients*, throughout this book.

In simple terms, I'm encouraging you to never give up on people, to consider having that authentic, real, engaged conversation, no matter how difficult, in order to facilitate an honourable outcome.

Cynthia, a youth-worker student receiving additional support by her university, is scheduled to attend her mid-placement review. Cynthia has a trauma history and has fallen into criminal activities. Her criminal record makes getting a *Working With Children (WWC)* card, a requirement in Australia for professionals working in any capacity with children, difficult. Despite her criminal record, I know she is a decent person.

The placement had begun well. Cynthia presented as warm, charming, and capable. Then Cynthia and her partner split, she had a car accident, and she began missing placement days. I started to worry and started feeling a bit frustrated given I had advocated for her to be able to complete her placement.

Cynthia is 30 minutes late for the review. I ring; she is on her way. When she arrives, Cynthia begins providing reasons justifying her lateness, without apologising. I suggest we focus on the work and understand how her difficult family situation has impacted her rather than starting with her excuses. The placement co-ordinator, Dr Suzanne Walton is lovely. She takes notes, I take notes, Cynthia does not. Cynthia has not completed her learning goals. Suzanne, the placement co-ordinator, is supportively providing Cynthia with potential learning goals. Cynthia is saying the right things but isn't convincing, having not started her assignments.

I begin to realise we were all bullshitting; Suzanne is aware that Cynthia is falling behind and is trying to help by doing Cynthia's work for her. I am being pleasant but starting to notice that I'm feeling uncomfortable about Cynthia's lack of progress and especially her fast talking excuses. Cynthia appears to notice the disappointment I'm trying to hide.

I decide to speak honestly in an NBT way. I preface my comments to Cynthia:

Jeff:	I'm being direct out of respect for you and your abilities. When you are here you are fantastic, you are warm and "can do," you put your hand up for everything and you have been a great asset to us. But what I suspect, is that you are not so comfortable with documenting and assignments. Is that right? Suzanne and I are writing things down, but you're not.
Cynthia:	Yeah, *(tearful)* I just don't know what to write. I'll often write stuff down and then look at what someone else's written and think what they've written is much better.
Jeff:	It's good you can talk so openly about that – it makes it so much easier to do something about it. I think having confidence in yourself makes such a difference, but I know saying *be confident* isn't helpful.
Cynthia:	Mmm.
Jeff:	I think it is important to build your skills in this area which is part of being a professional. You have made a huge transition, I don't think

you would have thought you'd be able to work in a place like this six months ago, and now here you are. This Centre is a perfect place to learn this stuff, we have a no-blame culture; I just expect staff to learn from any mistake. You can talk to me about stuff you write up.

Suzanne: You can send me a draft of your learning goals and I can provide some feedback.

Cynthia: I just worry about all these small things. Should I say Dear or Hi in an email?

Jeff: This is a perfect place to check out things like that.

Cynthia: Yeah, I just try to forget about them.

Jeff: Part of learning to be a professional is to follow certain protocols, like letting people know when you can't make a meeting, or if you're running late for a meeting like you were today. For me, I've learnt it's good for the other person and a relief for me – to ring ahead. I'm just being direct out of respect, because I know how competent you've been when you're here, and I also know what you are capable of.

Cynthia: Can I borrow a pen?

Jeff: Sure.

Suzanne: Maybe a good learning goal would be to develop your professional protocols.

Cynthia: Yeah.

Jeff: Imagine when you reflect on getting through this difficult phase and down the track supporting someone else to move into being a professional, how much knowledge and wisdom you'll have to share.

[Cynthia started taking notes and appeared less detached, looked less guilty, and wasn't focussing on making excuses for her lack of work. Interestingly, Suzanne started being more direct about what was required and asked Cynthia to name what would help her complete the assignments.]

Suzanne: Do you find deadlines help?

Cynthia: Yeah.

Suzanne: OK, well what about you have a draft of your learning goals done by the time you leave the Centre today. You can have my notes.

Jeff: What is the required structure?

Suzanne: The format is in your student guide, Cynthia.

[The rest of the meeting is more business-like. It is much more productive. We calculate the hours of placement completed, of the required 200. The 146 hours completed is more than we all thought, deadlines are decided for three assignments, all in a relatively short period of time. Suzanne and I had spent 30 minutes waiting for Cynthia, 60 minutes avoiding the obvious, trying to be nice, during which time I looked disappointed, Cynthia looked guilty, and Suzanne and Cynthia became even more polite and then, 30 minutes in which we achieved a lot.]

Jeff: Good productive meeting. I'll take your cup Suzanne; would you show Suzanne out please Cynthia?

The NBT Clinical Guidelines are simple, but not simplistic, and may take a lifetime to master. They tackle difficult conversations and situations which are not easily addressed. They are both frightening, full of risk, and can potentially cause relationship injury, but at the same time, they are full of opportunities for growth, healing, and intimacy. Having an ethical framework in which to approach these difficulties really helps. Hopefully, the NBT Clinical Guidelines and the examples I've provided will help you build greater confidence to manage the risk and make the most of these hidden, nuanced, and exciting opportunities. I hope the mix of philosophy, theory, and practice in this book stimulates your own reflections on how to make therapy fit your clients, rather than the other way around. If you decide to integrate NBT ideas into your practice, I hope your journey will never end, and you will steadily and progressively find and refine your own individual NBT voice, in your work, in your organisation, and in your everyday life.

Exploring NBT will also no doubt begin to influence your own personal life. It certainly has mine. I have learnt to wait for a good time to raise difficult issues, to signpost my intention, to make overt my rationale, and to integrate warmth and care before providing unwanted critical feedback to my much-loved children. I've also realised how hard it is to follow all these steps when you are so desperate to help but caught up in the complexities of close and important relationships, or when working in an organisation that does not encourage and support honest and direct conversations.

Translating NBT ideas into both your workplace and one's everyday life requires self-honesty, as a starting point. Hence, the potential for personal development is immense. I can say from experience that as your NBT reputation grows, so will the number of people who will expect you to be honest and upfront, including yourself.

Reference

Orwell, G. (1946). Politics and the English language. In S. Orwell & I. Angos (Eds.), *The Collected essays, journalism and letters of George Orwell. 4*(1), (pp. 127–140). Harcourt, Brace, Jovanovich.

Index